Complete Filipino (Tagalog)

Corazon Salvacion Castle
and
Laurence McGonnell

The publisher has used its best endeavours to ensure that the URLs for external websites referred to in this book are correct and active at the time of going to press. However, the publisher has no responsibility for the websites and can give no guarantee that a site will remain live or that the content is or will remain appropriate.

For UK order enquiries: please contact Bookpoint Ltd, 130 Milton Park, Abingdon, Oxon OX14 4SB. Telephone: +44 (0) 1235 827720, Fax: +44 (0) 1235 400454. Lines are open 9.00–18.00, Monday to Saturday, with a 24-hour message answering service. Details about our titles and how to order are available at www.teachyourself.com

For USA order enquiries: please contact McGraw-Hill Customer Services, P.O. Box 545, Blacklick, OH 43004-0545, USA. Telephone: 1-800-722-4726. Fax: 1-614-755-5645.

For Canada order enquiries: please contact McGraw-Hill Ryerson Ltd, 300 Water St, Whitby, Ontario L1N 9B6, Canada. Telephone: 905 430 5000. Fax: 905 430 5020.

Long renowned as the authoritative source for self-guided learning – with more than 30 million copies sold worldwide – the Teach Yourself series includes over 300 titles in the fields of languages, crafts, hobbies, business, computing and education.

British Library Cataloguing in Publication Data: a catalogue entry for this title is available from The British Library.

Library of Congress Catalog Card Number: on file

First published in UK 2000 as *Teach Yourself Filipino (Tagalog)* by Hodder Headline Ltd, 338 Euston Road, London, NW1 3BH.

First published in US 2000 by Contemporary Books, a Division of the McGraw-Hill Companies, 1 Prudential Plaza, 130 East Randolph Street, Chicago, IL 60601 USA.

This edition published 2010.

The **Teach Yourself** name is a registered trade mark of Hodder & Stoughton Ltd.

Typeset by MPS Limited, a Macmillan Company.

Printed in Great Britain for Hodder Education, an Hachette UK Company, 338 Euston Road, London NW1 3BH by CPI Group (UK) Ltd, Croydon, CR0 4YY.

Impression number 10 9 8 7 6 5 4 3
Year 2014 2013 2012 2011

Contents

Meet the authors

Corazon Salvacion Castle grew up in Pinamalayan, Oriental Mindoro, Philippines. She received a Master's degree in TESL (Applied Linguistics) at the University of the Philippines. Before that she trained to teach Tagalog as a Second Language to non-Filipinos at a language school in Quezon City using their unique method, and later was herself a teacher there. She left the Philippines and arrived in the UK in the early 1970s. She continued teaching Tagalog to Filipino children and their parents at the Philippine Resource Centre in London. Nowadays she is commissioned to teach Tagalog to British diplomats at the Foreign and Commonwealth Office, and to students at the School of Oriental and African Studies (SOAS). She has been a contributing editor, writer and columnist to several Filipino newspapers and magazines and has written a number of Tagalog teaching and reference publications. Her first book was entitled *How to Speak, Read and Write Tagalog* (Vols I & II) followed by *Fluency in Tagalog*. She is an assessor and examiner of Tagalog for a linguistic governing body and also teaches ESOL and Life in the UK. She is married to Roy Castle, the illustrator of the current volume.

Laurence McGonnell was born and raised in the North-East of England. He holds Masters' Degrees in Theology, Pastoral Psychology and Psychotherapy. He is an educator with a specialist interest in psychology, language and culture and has lived and worked in East Africa and South East Asia. In 1989 he moved to the Philippines where, over a period of seven years, he took up the challenge to learn no fewer than three Filipino languages: Tagalog, Hiligaynon and Kinaraya. Laurence's enthusiasm for all things Filipino led him to spend weeks, months and even years in remote villages and on far-flung islands, honing and practising his language skills as well as immersing himself in the rich tapestry of rural Filipino life. A keen amateur photographer, he enjoyed visually documenting the everyday customs and traditions of village life, many of which are slowly disappearing. For several years he worked closely with Filipino colleagues on community education and development projects based on local needs. He also taught undergraduate students at Saint Anthony's College in the Western Visayas Province of Antique. Currently based in his native UK, Laurence retains strong links with South East Asia. He enjoys developing and delivering educational programmes and still regards himself as a student of Tagalog.

Carazon Salvacion Castle
and Laurence McGonnell

Only got a minute?

The Philippines is undoubtedly one of the most culturally and linguistically diverse countries on our planet. Across 171 languages spoken over the 7,107 islands that make up this archipelago nation, we encounter a curious parallel: a fascinating pride in their difference, standing side by side with a strong sense of unity, harmony and togetherness.

Historically, these factors lie at the root of the Filipino language. Imbued with a vision for a 'new society', the Marcos government of the 1960s and 70s tasked Filipino scholars to forge a new national language, building on the dominance of Tagalog but drawing from other prominent Filipino languages. While this arguably resulted in a new hybrid language, few would admit to speaking Filipino at home. Perhaps the mark of success is not that Filipino is widely spoken, but that the national sense of unity and identity has been strengthened. In its pure form, Filipino continues to find a place in education and government.

The similarity between Filipino and Tagalog is so striking that many Filipinos and non-Filipinos have ceased to distinguish them as separate languages. When asked what language they are speaking, many Filipinos will loosely reply, 'Filipino', when in fact they are speaking Tagalog. An internet search for a 'Filipino' language course will invariably bring results for a Tagalog language course. Some writers have referred to Filipino as a *de facto* version of Tagalog. Others have simply referred to Filipino as Tagalog *plus*. Tagalog, even when referred to as Filipino, is the living language of this programme. For Filipinos living abroad, Tagalog has become the language of choice. Filipinos moving around in their own homeland use Tagalog as the preferred means of communication.

Whether you are confused, bemused or excited by the variety of Filipino languages or were simply drawn to learn Filipino (Tagalog) in the hope of building new language skills, you have come to the right place! With a solid foundation in Tagalog, access to the riches of Filipino culture, life and relationships will be opened up to you as never before.

5 Only got five minutes?

One of the most common assumptions made about the Philippines is that it is a Spanish-speaking country. To a degree this is understandable, given that the Philippines came under Spanish rule for over three hundred years. Evidence of Spanish rule is seen everywhere in ornate and highly decorative churches, municipal offices or other public buildings. But the Spanish legacy is also present in Filipino culture and language. The traditional *rondalla* music bands reveal an unmistakably Iberian flavour, while the *Cariñosa* dance with fan and handkerchief clearly discloses its Spanish origin. Note that both are Spanish words!

Any native speaker of English or Spanish approaching Tagalog for the first time will have an advantage. The linguistic stamp of both former colonial rulers (Spain 1521–1898; United States 1898-1946) is evident in modern Tagalog. While Tagalog springs from the Malayo-Polynesian language family (itself a branch of the Austronesian language family), learners will encounter many words which have made the transition from Spanish or English into Tagalog. Indeed, some researchers assert that as much as 20% of Tagalog vocabulary is of Spanish origin. A cursory glance through the pages of this book will reveal that Filipinos are fond of **afritada** (*fried food*) and that they will cook in a **caldereta**. Ask a Filipino what year it is, and the response will either be in English or Spanish!

A careful study of modern Tagalog reveals that many (if not most) technical words and terms originate in English. '**May problema ang sasakyan ko sa drive shaft!**' (*My vehicle has a problem with the drive shaft!*). '**Kailangan ko ng top-up card para sa aking cell phone**' (*I need a top-up card for my cell phone*). Other words in common usage may have been blended, compounded or re-shaped before finding their way from English into the modern Tagalog lexicon. A few examples will illustrate the point: **telepono** (*telephone*), **gets mo?** (*do you get it?*), **makaideal** (*idealistic*), **teknikal na inpormasyon** (*technical information*).

The cross-over between Tagalog and English is equally revealing. Filipinos have even coined a word to describe this link: *Taglish*. It is far from unusual to hear cross-over conversations in everyday life: '**Pupunta ba kayo sa Shopping Mall tomorrow?**' (*Are you going to the shopping mall tomorrow?*) Both the presence of Spanish and English vocabulary in Tagalog as well as the popular use of *Taglish* can help to build confidence in language progress and proficiency for the student. Naturally, we would always recommend that students aim to progress beyond *Taglish*. A solid grounding in Tagalog grammar is essential for building real insight into the language, as well as holding conversations at a more advanced or idiomatic level. Many Filipinos who use *Taglish* do so because they have had the advantage of completing a high school or college/university education. Those who have had fewer educational opportunities may struggle with *Taglish*, leaving them feeling **nahihiya** (*ashamed*).

Filipino communities have emerged in even the remotest parts of the world. With almost 1.5 million speakers, Tagalog was recognized by the US Census Bureau in 2010 as the fourth most spoken language in the United States. Filipino migrant workers have travelled the world in search of work and a better standard of living for themselves and their loved ones back home. Across the globe, local Filipino organizations have become commonplace where people can meet, talk, offer support or just relax together. Most such organizations are welcoming to outsiders, particularly when they want to learn more about the Philippines or practise their Tagalog!

While it is normal to feel anxious about learning a new language, particularly in adulthood, the close links with English and Spanish will hopefully indicate that Tagalog is a very learnable language. Even for the complete beginner, elements of the 'familiar' are already present. The greatest hurdle is always *to begin*. Learning any new language is a journey, and the fact that you are reading this page indicates that you have already begun or are seriously considering making this journey. Naturally the temptation is to focus on the scale of the task, or perhaps more negatively, on what we do *not* know. Flicking through the pages that follow will confirm that there are indeed many things you do 'not' know about Tagalog . . . at least not yet. There may be a temptation to write off any possibility of success by saying, 'I'm no good with languages.' Consider this.

The most complex journey any human being makes into the world of language is learning their *mother tongue*. If you can read and understand these words, you have already succeeded in language learning! Learning a new language is always possible; learning it well will depend on your willingness to try; even when the task seems daunting or unfamiliar.

This book is designed to be a companion on your journey. Carefully divided into twenty chapters, you will be guided through the unfamiliar until it begins to feel more like home. Where there are smoother paths along the way, we will try to show you. A common question often asked of us is, 'How long does it take to learn Tagalog?' Even though one of us is a native Tagalog speaker, we are both in agreement on this; 'we are still learning!' This is not to dodge the question, but rather to recall the living and changing nature of language. The Tagalog spoken today has its differences from the Tagalog spoken two or three decades ago or the Tagalog that will be spoken thirty years from now.

A clear advantage for modern language learners is the enormous increase in resources in recent years. The arrival of the internet has brought the option of stepping into the world of the Philippines from the comfort of our own homes. We may be thousands of miles away from Manila and yet we can access Filipino newspapers, tune in to Filipino radio stations, and visit websites or blogs. The internet has provided us with the opportunity to 'chat' with others online or to connect with far away friends or family through social networking sites such as Facebook or MySpace. Access to Tagalog movies has never been easier, with video clips on YouTube or modern Tagalog songs. It is possible to carry some of these resources with us away from home, listening to podcasts or learning the words to popular Tagalog songs via the convenience of our mp3 players. In short, learning a new language no longer needs to be an isolating or purely 'academic' experience. It is possible to connect with other learners in a 'virtual classroom' or learning community experience. Resources have become versatile, flexible and mobile. The process of learning a new language is back where it belongs; in the context of 'connecting' with other people; in the context of building relationships.

Tagalog is a living, thriving modern language. It provides a rich point of access to the culture, history and psyche of the Filipino people. Like all modern languages, Tagalog is in a constant process of growth and change. By setting out on the exciting road to learning Tagalog, you become a contributor to shaping its future. In the words of Nelson Mandela, 'If you talk to a man in a language he understands, that goes to his head. If you talk to him in his language; that goes to his heart.'

Acknowledgements

Cora and Laurence would like to express their sincere thanks to all who have contributed to the development of this project. Particular thanks go to Roy Castle for the illustrations.

Credits

Front cover: © D. Hurst/Alamy

Back cover and pack: © Jakub Semeniuk/iStockphoto.com, © Royalty-Free/Corbis, © agencyby/iStockphoto.com, © Andy Cook/iStockphoto.com, © Christopher Ewing/iStockphoto.com, © zebicho–Fotolia.com, © Geoffrey Holman/iStockphoto.com, © Photodisc/Getty Images, © James C. Pruitt/iStockphoto.com, © Mohamed Saber – Fotolia.com

Pack: © Stockbyte/Getty Images

Introduction

Welcome to *Complete Filipino* (*Tagalog*)! First a word about the title of this course.

Over the years, there has been little strict differentiation between Filipino and Tagalog. Many would argue that they are essentially one in the same language. While it is true to say that Filipino is based on Tagalog, it also contains elements of other languages spoken in the Philippines. Some have even described Filipino as *Tagalog Plus*! While the title of this course reflects and acknowledges the close connection between the two languages, we wish it to be clear from the outset that our sole purpose is to teach Tagalog. From here on, the text of this course will refer exclusively to *Tagalog*.

This *Complete Filipino* (*Tagalog*) course is intended to supply the beginner with a simple and well-selected stock of words in easy-to-understand lessons.

This course is a fascinating introduction to not only the Tagalog language but also the Filipino way of life. Here, we will follow the day-to-day 'adventures' of the Cook family: Bill, Louise and Roy. Follow them from the minute they touch down at Ninoy Aquino International Airport, as they check in to their hotel, visit places of interest and attend local festivities while travelling around the country by bus, jeepney and boat. By following them, we will learn much about the ways and customs of the Filipino people, and of course plenty of Tagalog!

The units are graded in complexity and each includes a dialogue, a Quick vocab list, a comprehensive grammar explanation, drills and practice tests. Author insights provide you with useful cultural information. Prepare to be informed and entertained: Learn how to haggle at a market and discover your ability to mix with the locals while enjoying the pleasures of Tagalog learning. *Complete Filipino* (*Tagalog*) is a veritable treasure trove of information, activities – and learning.

To simplify the learning process, we have opted to use a phonetic pronunciation system. These phonetics are specifically designed for native English speakers and follow standard English pronunciation. They offer the nearest possible approximation of Tagalog sounds available to the native English speaker. For a highly polished Tagalog pronunciation, listen carefully to native Tagalog speakers.

◀) This symbol indicates material included on the recording.

A list of common words can be found as an appendix for your convenience and interest.

The authors want you to be able to learn Tagalog as painlessly as possible and to develop self-confidence in speaking and writing your new language. So relax and teach yourself Tagalog!

Pronunciation guide

The Tagalog language is relatively easy to pronounce for the English speaker. It is in fact read or pronounced as written or printed, making it almost phonetic. We can safely say that the pronunciation of Tagalog more or less rests on the five vowels:

a *ah*　e *eh*　i *ee*　o *aw*　u *oo*

The consonants are as follows:

b *bah*　k *kah*　d *dah*　g *gah*　h *hah*　l *lah*　m *mah*　n *nah*
ng *ngah*　p *pah*　r *rah*　s *sah*　t *tah*　w *wah*　y *yah*

The letters C, F, J, Q, V, X and Z are not strictly part of the Tagalog alphabet though they do appear in the names of people, e.g. Corazon, Josefa, Victoria; places, e.g. Quezon, Luzon, Virac, Zamboanga; and names of things, e.g. Xerox, Kleenex.

The letters **b**, **p** and **t** are not aspirated in Tagalog. An easy way to test whether your **b**'s, **p**'s and **t**'s are aspirated is to hold a piece of paper in front of your mouth while pronouncing each letter. The paper should not move whenever these letters are pronounced. Why not try it out? If the paper didn't move then congratulations, you have pronounced them the Tagalog way.

Every syllable in Tagalog is pronounced. Even if a word has two successive vowels, then each vowel is treated as a separate syllable and pronounced. For example, the Tagalog word **Oo** (meaning: yes) is not pronounced as 'ooh' but rather as *aw-aw*. This rule does not however apply to foreign words that have been assimilated into the Tagalog language, for example, Quezon (a personal noun of Spanish origin).

Examples:

Aa	(ah-ah)	dirt; filth (*used only when speaking to small children about anything dirty. Also used by children themselves.*)
Saan	(sah-ahn)	where
Leeg	(leh-ehg)	neck
Iniiwan	(ee-nee-ee-wahn)	being left (*passive voice*)
Uuwi	(oo-oo-wee)	will go home (*active voice*)
Biik	(bee-eek)	piglet
Tsaa	(tsah-ah)	tea
Maasim	(mah-ah-seem)	sour

The more you study and listen to Tagalog, the more foreign words (mainly Spanish and English) you will begin to notice in the vocabulary.

Examples:

Garahe	(gah-rah-heh)	garage	(origin: Spanish)
Recibo	(reh-see-baw)	receipt	(origin: Spanish)
Kalye	(kahl-ye)	street	(origin: Spanish)
Tseke	(tseh-keh)	cheque	(origin: English)
Notbuk	(nawt-book)	notebook	(origin: English)

In Tagalog, **ch** is pronounced like the '*ch*' in 'cheque' or 'cha cha'. There is no **sh** combination in Tagalog, hence the English word 'shoes' is likely to be pronounced '*syoos*' and the word 'shame' becomes '*syaym*'. The soft **th** as in 'thing' does not exist and so is pronounced as '*teeng*'. The hard **th** as in 'that' is also absent from Tagalog and so the word is pronounced as '*daht*'.

The final **s** is never pronounced as a **z** in Tagalog. Any word ending in **s** is therefore pronounced as an **s**.

The letters **f**, **ph** and **v** are replaced in Tagalog by **p** and **b** respectively.

Examples:

Father	*pronounced 'pah-dehr'*	=	pader
Philip	*pronounced 'Pee-leep'*	=	Pilip
Vanilla	*pronounced 'bah-neel-yah'*	=	banilya
Victory	*pronounced 'beek-taw-ree'*	=	biktori

b, **d** and **g** tend to be voiceless and heard as **p**, **t** and **k**.

When a group of consonants (non-vowels) appear at the beginning of a word, they tend to invite the softening touch of a vowel. These vowels are known as *intrusive vowels*. For example:

School	*becomes*	eskul	*(es-kool)*
Start	*becomes*	istart	*(is-tart)*
Scheme	*becomes*	iskim	*(is-keem)*

The endings of words can sometimes be dropped or changed, and this is most apparent in the pronunciation of words ending in **d** or **t**.

Examples:

Stand	*becomes*	stan	*(stahn)*
Trends	*becomes*	trens	*(trehns)*
Wants	*becomes*	wans	*(wahns)*
Canned	*becomes*	can	*(kahn)*

There are no **wh** sounds in Tagalog pronunciation. The straightforward **w** sound replaces it.

Examples:

What	*becomes*	wat	*(waht)*
When	*becomes*	wen	*(wehn)*
Which	*becomes*	wits	*(weets)*
Why	*becomes*	wahy	*(wigh)*

Tagalog makes no regular distinction between the **i** in 'hit' and the **i** in 'heat', between the **u** in 'tool' and the **u** in 'pull'.

Examples:

Kit	*becomes*	keet	*(keeht)*
Keats	*becomes*	keets	*(keehts)*
Sit	*becomes*	seet	*(seeht)*
Seat	*becomes*	seet	*(seeht)*
Rule	*becomes*	rool	*(roohl)*

Accents have been provided on all words in the Tagalog–English glossary at the back of the book to assist with a more accurate pronunciation.

Sa paliparan
At the airport

In this unit you will learn how to:

- Introduce yourself and address others
- Greet people at different times of the day
- Form simple sentences

Introducing yourself and addressing others

Dialogue 1

🔊 **CD 1, TR 1, 00:54**

The Cook family has arrived at Ninoy Aquino International Airport (NAIA) in Manila. It is 7.30 in the evening. A friendly customs official approaches them.

Opisyal	Magand**ang** ga**bi** *po* sa in**yo**. Kumu**sta** ka**yo**? Si Gino**ong Sa**ntos ak**o**. An**ong** pangalan nin**yo**?
Bill	Ma**bu**ti nam**an**, sal**am**at. Bill Cook ang pangalan ko.
Louise	Ma**bu**ti rin nam**an**. Mar**am**ing sal**am**at. Louise Cook ang pang**a**lan ko.

| Roy | Ma**bu**ti *po* nam**an**. Sal**a**mat *po*. Roy Cook *po* ang pang**a**lan ko. |
| Opi**syal** | Ikinaga**ga**l**a**k ko kay**ong** makil**a**la. |

To help build your confidence, we have included two simple pronunciation aids in the Unit Dialogues throughout this book. The **bold** typeface syllables in each word indicate where to add stress, while the *italicized* words indicate a glottal stop.

QUICK VOCAB

magandang gabi po	*good evening* (polite)
sa inyo	*to you* (plural)
kumusta kayo	*how are you* (polite)
anong pangalan ninyo?	*what's your name?* (formal)
ang pangalan ko	*my name is* _____
mabuti naman	*fine also* (lit.)
maraming salamat	*Thank you very much*
ikinagagalak ko kayong makilala	*I'm pleased to meet you*
mabuti rin naman	*I'm fine too*
mabuti po naman	*I'm fine too* (formal)

Translation

Officer	Good evening to you. How are you? I'm Mr. Santos.
Bill	(I'm) fine. Thank you. My name is Bill Cook.
Louise	I'm fine too. Thank you very much. My name is Louise Cook.
Roy	I'm fine too. My name is Roy Cook. Thank you.
Officer	I'm pleased to meet you.

Notice the different ways in which the official and the Cook family introduced themselves. Bill Cook simply said: 'Bill Cook ang pangalan ko', whereas Roy Cook said: 'Roy Cook po ang pangalan ko.' Filipinos traditionally place a high value on respect and politeness. They often insert the word '**po**' or '**opo**' into a sentence as an indicator of respect, especially when addressing older people or persons in authority. It is good practice for the visitor to the Philippines to show sensitivity to this cultural value from the outset. By using the more formal '**po**' or '**opo**', you are assured of making a good first impression. Now try using the two different ways of introducing yourself (formal and informal). Write the sentences down, this time using your own name. Why not try recording the new sentences and listening to your own voice and pronunciation. Listen once again to Dialogue 1 and compare your Tagalog pronunciation with that of Bill Cook.

Anong pangalan mo?   *What is your name?*

Notice how the official asked Bill Cook for his name. There are different ways in which people may ask your name.

◀) **CD 1, TR 1, 01:37**

Listen and try to repeat what you hear as closely as you can.

Magandang umaga po.	*Good morning.*
Anong pangalan mo?	*What's your name?*
Joe Bulman.	*(I'm) Joe Bulman*
Sino ka?	*Who are you?*
Si Phil ako.	*I am Phil.*
Sino po kayo?	*Who are you? (polite)*
Si Ginoong John Smith ako.	*I am Mr John Smith*
Sino po kayo?	*Who are you?*
Si Margaret Hough ako.	*I am Margaret Hough.*

Addressing others   *I, you, he/she etc.*

anong pangalan mo	*what's your name?*
pangalan mo	*your name*
sino	*who*

In our day-to-day conversations, we do not always use people's names. Sometimes we drop the names in favour of words such as **I, he, she,** etc. These are known as personal pronouns.

The following table shows both singular (only one person) and plural (more than one) personal pronouns.

Tagalog sometimes uses the plural form (normally reserved for addressing more than one person) to address a single individual. For the Tagalog speaker, this has the same effect as using 'po' or 'opo', in that it conveys politeness and respect to the listener. For example, we would normally understand 'kumusta kayo?' to mean, 'how are you (all)?' However, when addressed to a single individual, it can be understood as a very polite way of asking how someone is.

	Singular	Plural
1st person (speaker)	**ako** I	**kami** we (excluding listener) **tayo** we (including listener)
2nd person (spoken to)	**ka/ikaw** you (informal) **kayo** you (formal)	**kayo** you (plural)
3rd person (spoken about)	**siya** he/she	**sila** they

Notice that 'you' (singular) has two forms: **ka** and **ikaw**. The simple difference is that **ka** is *always* used as part of a sentence, 'kumusta **ka**?' (how are you?), whereas **ikaw** can stand alone (without being used in a sentence).

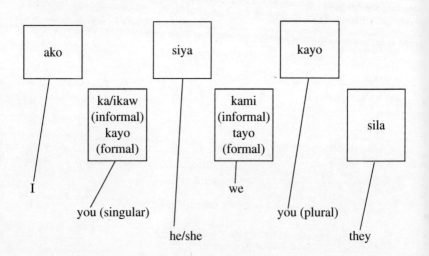

Insight

A simple rule to help you remember when to use **po**: **po** always expresses **po**liteness!

Oo = *yes*

Oo + po = opo (*Yes*, polite form)

Remember: to express politeness in Tagalog is not just about good manners. It is about the public recognition of another person's dignity.

Exercise 1

Listen to the following Tagalog sentences on the CD. Practise reading each sentence aloud. Follow the pronunciation closely until you can repeat each word and sound with confidence.

◀) **CD 1, TR 1, 02:38**

Tagalog	Literal translation	Translation
Si Mary Smith **ako**	Mary Smith I	*I am Mary Smith*
Si Letty Zapanta **ako**	Letty Zapanta I	*I am Letty Zapanta*
Si Doktor Rivera **kayo**	Doctor Rivera you	*You are Dr Rivera* (formal)
Si Ramon Tenoso **siya**	Ramon Tenoso he/she	*He is Ramon Tenoso*
Pilipino **kami**	Filipinos we	*We are Filipinos*
Estudyante **tayo**	Students we	*We are students*
Amerikano **sila**	Americans they	*They are Americans*

Exercise 2

Underline the correct word.

1. He/she is a nurse.   Nars (ka, ako, siya).
2. We are Americans.   Amerikano (kami, kayo, sila).
3. I am a tourist.   Turista (tayo, ako, kami).
4. You are a teacher.   Guro (ka, siya, ako).
5. They are priests.   Pari (kayo, tayo, sila).
6. You (plural) are doctors.   Doktor (kami, ka, kayo).
7. We are students.   Estudyante (tayo, ako, sila).
8. You (polite) are British.   British (ka, ikaw, kayo).
9. They are engineers.   Inhinyero (siya, sila, kayo).
10. He/she is a lawyer.   Abogado (kayo, siya, ka).

Greeting people at different times of the day

1.

2.

3.

4.

Exercise 3
Match up the correct sentence with the correct drawing.

1. Magandang umaga   *Good morning*
2. Magandang tanghali   *Good noon* (midday)
3. Magandang hapon   *Good afternoon*
4. Magandang gabi   *Good evening*

Exercise 4
What greeting would you use at the following times of day?

1. 6:00 a.m.   Magandang _____
2. 6:30 p.m.   Magandang _____
3. 12:00 a.m.   Magandang _____
4. 3:00 p.m.   Magandang _____

Saying hello and goodbye

How you say 'hello' in Tagalog depends very much on who you are talking to. Four possible ways of saying hello follow, ranging from the informal '**kumusta**', commonly used with friends and family, to the very formal and polite '**Kumusta po kayo**'. Try practising each of the examples given and think of someone you would use each example with. Saying goodbye in Tagalog is much less complicated than saying hello. Any of the three examples given are acceptable in most circumstances.

Look at the different ways of saying hello and goodbye. All are commonly used. Listen carefully to the pronunciation on the accompanying **CD**. Try to copy what you hear by repeating each sentence.

◀) **CD 1, TR 1, 03:00**

Hello, goodbye

1. Kumusta? *Hello/how are you?*
   Mabuti naman *Fine, thank you*
   Paalam na! *Goodbye for now*

2. Kumusta ka? *Hello, how are you?*
   Mabuti naman *Fine, thank you*
   Hanggang sa muli *Till next time*

3. Kumusta kayo? *Hello, how are you?*
   Mabuti po naman *Fine, thank you* (formal)
   O, sige ha? *Until next time*

4. Kumusta po kayo? *Hello, how are you?* (formal)
   Mabuti po naman *Fine, thank you*

Dialogue 2

◀) **CD 1, TR 1, 03:46**

Using what you have learned so far, translate the following dialogue into English. Use the **Quick vocab** to help you with words you have not yet met. See how much you have learned in only a few pages!

Jobert meets the Cook family at the airport.

Bill	Jobert, kum**us**ta kay**o**?
Jobert	Ma**bu**ti po nam**an**, at kay**o**?
Bill	Ma**bu**ti nam**an**.
Jobert	Kum**us**ta kay**o**, **Gi**nang Cook?
Louise	Ma**bu**ti nam**an**.
Jobert	Kum**us**ta ka, Roy?
Roy	Ma**bu**ti rin nam**an**.

QV

at kayo	*and you*
Ginang	*Mrs*
rin	*too, also, as well*

Exercise 5

How would you say hello to the following people? Align the correct answer with the right person.

a. your mother	**1.** Kumusta ka
b. close friend	**2.** Kumusta kayo
c. doctor	**3.** Kumusta po kayo
d. young shop assistant	**4.** Kumusta kayo
e. the local mayor	**5.** Kumusta po kayo
f. taxi driver	**6.** Kumusta

Language Skills

1 *Si, Sina*

In Tagalog, when using a person's name (including your own) always place the word 'si' before the name, i.e. **si** Cora, **si** Harry (Cora, Harry). When Cora or Harry are with their friends (i.e., more than one person) then '**sina**' is used which is the plural of **si**, i.e., **sina** Cora, **sina** Harry (Cora and her friends, Harry and his friends). In grammar, **si** and **sina** are known as markers.

2 Simple sentence construction

Broadly speaking, a simple English sentence consists of two main elements:

a *subject* (that is, 'who' or 'what' is being talked about) and a *comment* or a word which tells us something about the subject. For example, Bernie (subject) eats (comment), Tina (subject) sings (comment). Of course, there are different types of words and exceptions involved, but we will address each of these as we come to them. Look at the following table and compare the English sentence construction with that of Tagalog.

English				Tagalog	
Manny *subject*	is	an	engineer *comment*	Inhinyero *comment*	si Manny *subject*
You *subject*	are		beautiful *comment*	Maganda *comment*	ka *subject*
This *subject*	is	a	table *comment*	Mesa *comment*	ito *subject*
Bernie *subject*	is		eating *comment*	Kumakain *comment*	si Bernie *subject*

You will notice that the Tagalog is much simpler than its English equivalent.

Insight

Filipinos commonly have a more relaxed approach to time. Don't worry if a Filipino arrives later than expected. Locally, this is known as 'Filipino time'.

3 Formal or informal? *Ka, kayo* You

The emphasis on politeness in Filipino culture comes through clearly in the language of the people. In the Philippines, the English word '*you*' is represented in two forms: One form is informal: **ka**, the second is the formal, polite form: **kayo**. At work, Filipinos address their superiors with **kayo** (you, polite singular) and use **ka** (you, familiar singular) with their colleagues and friends. Here is a table showing the differences in use:

Situation	Polite formal	Informal familiar	Plural
Child to parent	kayo		kayo
Parent to child		ka/ikaw	kayo
Friend to friend		ka/ikaw	kayo
Worker to superior	kayo		kayo
Superior to worker		ka/ikaw	kayo
Person to stranger	kayo		kayo
To older people	kayo		kayo
To people in authority	kayo		kayo
Colleague to colleague		ka/ikaw	kayo

Insight

Begin conversations *formally* with people you do not know or are meeting for the first time. It communicates respect from the outset. It is easier to move from formal to informal, than from informal to formal.

Exercise 6

Look at the pictures. Can you decide which is the correct word to use? Is it **ka** or **kayo**?

a. A little boy kissing his grandmother's hand

b. A father to a son

c. A husband to wife

d. A child to another child

One-minute phrases

> **Segunda mano** (*seh-goon-daw mah-naw*) Of Spanish origin, meaning *second hand*
>
> **Bilugin ang ulo** (*bee-loo-geen ahng oo-law*) Literally, *to make the head round*. A common colloquial phrase meaning *to fool someone*
>
> **Aywan ko sa iyo** (*eh-one-ko-sah-ee-yo*) Literally, *I don't know with you*. A common Tagalog phrase, used to mean *it's up to you*
>
> **Huwag naman** (*hoo-wag-nah-man*) This phrase is used as a polite way of saying: *please don't*
>
> **Hindi na bale** (*hin-dee-nah-bah-lee*) Can be used to mean *not to worry* or *it's not worth worrying about*

Summary

1. **Maraming salamat** always elicits a polite response.
2. Remember: **Po kayo** is the polite form used for both singular and plural. **Opo** is used for '*yes sir'*/'*yes ma'am*'.
3. **Kumusta ka** is very informal and therefore **not polite**.
4. **Kumusta kayo** or **Kumusta po kayo** is **polite**.
5. Do not interchange the use of **Kami** and **Tayo**. Kami is *we* **exclusive** of speaker while Tayo is *we* **inclusive** of speaker.
6. **Never** use **Ka** on its own. Use **Ikaw**.
7. **Kayo** *you* can be used to mean **(i)** singular polite and **(ii)** plural informal.
8. Always use **Si** before a person's name including your own. *Si Cora* ako. *I am Cora.*
9. Always use **sina** before names of persons meaning plural. **Sina Patricia ang mga narses.** *The nurses are Patricia and her friends.*
10. In Tagalog, the word **hindi** means *No, negative.*

2

Anong oras ang almusal?
What time is breakfast?

In this unit you will learn how to:

- Check into your hotel
- Ask simple questions
- Use the verb 'to be'

Checking into your hotel

Dialogue 1

◀) CD 1, TR 2

Bill Cook and family arrive at their hotel. They will be staying here for five days, before moving on to the Abiva home in White Plains. Try to notice the different sounds of the Tagalog words.

Bill	May kuwarto ba kayo?
Manedyer	Mayroon *po*. Ibig po ba ninyo ng pang-isahan o pandalawahan?
Bill	Ibig namin ng pandalawahan at pang-isahan para sa anak kong si Roy. Magkakano ba ang mga kuwarto?
Manedyer	Ang pandalawahan *po* ay ₱900 isang gabi at ang pang-isahan ay ₱750 isang gabi. Puwede na po ba para sa inyo?
Bill	Oo, mabuti, salamat. Saan ako pipirma?
Manedyer	Dito lang *po* sa *ibaba*, sir.

may kuwarto ba kayo	*have/has*
mayroon	*there is/there are*
ibig po ba ninyo ng	*do you want/like a*
pandalawahan	*double*
at	*and*
pang-isahan	*single*
ibig namin	*we want/like*
para sa anak kong	*for my son*
magkakano	*how much each*
ang mga kuwarto	*the rooms*
isang gabi	*per night*
puede na po ba	*is it alright sir/ma'am?*
para sa inyo	*for you*
oo, mabuti	*yes, good*
salamat	*thank you*
saan ako pipirma	*where do I sign?*
dito lang po sa ibaba	*just below here*

Translation

Bill	Do you have a room?
Manager	Yes sir, we have. Do you want a single or a double room?
Bill	I need a double room and also a single room for my son, Roy. How much are the rooms?
Manager	The double is ₱900 per night and the single is ₱750. Is that all right, sir?
Bill	Yes, that's fine. Thank you. Where do I sign?
Manager	Just below here, sir.

Asking for a room . . . or anything else

Notice how Bill enquired about the rooms. He asked: 'May kuwarto ba kayo?' It's very easy to make an enquiry in Tagalog. Whether you want to ask about rooms, tee-shirts, suntan lotion or banana splits, just remember to use the word 'may' (**pronounced MEH**) before the subject (thing) you want to ask about. Notice the word 'ba'. This is a simple word which follows the subject and lets the other person know that you are asking a question. Let's look at a few examples:

Tagalog	Literal translation	English
May tsinelas ba kayo?	Have sandals you?	*Do you have any sandals?*
May kuwarto ba kayo?	Have room you?	*Do you have a room?*
May mangga ba kayo?	Have mango you?	*Do you have a mango?*
May panahon ba kayo?	Have time you?	*Do you have time?*

Exercise 1

Here are pictures of some everyday items you might need to ask for in your hotel. Practise asking for them using the formula: 'May (name of item) ba kayo?'

Tuwalya
Towel

Sabon
Soap

Telepono
Telephone

Menu
Menu

Telebisyon
Television

Language skills

1 Verb 'to be'

Remember the 'comment' we met in Unit 1? A comment tells us something about the subject. When the comment is a verb, then we know that an action is involved. Verbs are 'doing' words which describe an action. For example, Bob (subject) is reading (verb/action word). The dog (subject) is barking (verb/action word). The verb 'to be' is used as a helping verb to form parts of other verbs. For example, we say 'I am working', not 'I working'. The verb 'to be' has eight different forms. They are: be, am, is, are, was, were, being, been.

There is no direct translation of the verb 'to be' in Tagalog. It is usually implied in the construction of the sentence. For example:

Tagalog	Literal translation	English
Guro ako	Teacher I	*I am a teacher*
Doktor kayo	Doctor you	*You are a doctor*
Nars siya dati	Nurse she formerly	*Formerly she was a nurse*
Nanggaling si Anna sa palengke	Came from Anna the market	*Anna has been to the market*

16

Look at the Tagalog equivalent of the verb 'to be':

Singular	Tagalog	Plural	Tagalog
I am/was	Ako	*We are/were*	Kami, tayo
You are/were	Ka, ikaw	*You are/were*	Kayo
He/she is/was	Siya	*They are/were*	Sila

(There are more ways in which the verb 'to be' may be used in a sentence. We will look at these in later units.)

Exercise 2
Listen to the following sentences.

◀) **CD 1, TR 2, 00:56**

Tagalog	Literal translation	English
Turista ako	Tourist I	*I am a tourist*
Amerikano siya	He/she American	*He/she is American*
Pilipino kami	We Filipinos	*We are Filipinos*
Matangkad ka	Tall you	*You are tall*
Doktor tayo	Doctors we	*We are doctors*
Maganda sila	Beautiful they	*They are beautiful*

You will notice that each sentence is spoken slowly. Try to repeat what you hear during the pause after each sentence. Carry on until you become familiar with the words in each sentence.

Exercise 3
Now let's see how well you've mastered what you heard on the CD. Write down a Tagalog sentence to translate the English. The first one has been done for you.

They are doctors.
Doktor sila.

I am a tourist.

_____

They are tall.

_____

She is beautiful.

_____

You are an American.

_____

Insight

The day often begins early in the Philippines. It is very common for people to take a nap or 'siesta' after lunch. Try to avoid making unannounced social calls during siesta time. Custom may vary locally, so if you are unsure, ask your Filipino friends for advice.

_____

Enquiring about meals

Dialogue 2

We join Bill Cook at the reception desk of the hotel. He is asking the receptionist about mealtimes.

◀) **CD 1, TR 2, 01:23**

Bill	Maganda**ng** umaga ma'am. A**no** ang mga **o**ras ng pag**ka**in **di**to sa hotel?
Receptionist	Aba **o**po. Ang almus**al** ay **bu**hat sa **a**las **s**ais y **me**dya hang**gang** a**las** nu**we**be y **med**ya. Ang tangha**li**an ay **bu**hat sa **a**las **do**se hang**gang** a**las** dos nang **ha**pon. Ang ha**pu**nan ay **bu**hat sa **a**las **s**ais hang**gang** a**las** nu**we**be nang ga**bi**. May room service *po* sa lah**at** ng **o**ras.
Bill	May ma**ka**ka**i**nan bang mal**a**pit **di**to?
Receptionist	A**ba**, **o**po. Ang 'Lola's Litson' ay may pag**ka**in hang**gang ha**tinggabi.
Bill	Ma**bu**ti kung gano**on**. Hin**di** ba ma**hal**?
Receptionist	Hin**di** *po*. Masa**rap** ang pag**ka**in at **mu**ra ang hala**ga**.
Bill	Ma**ra**ming sa**la**mat.

magandang umaga   *good morning*
ano ang mga oras ng   *what are the times of . . .*

18

pagkain dito	*food here*
aba opo	*certainly sir*
almusal	*breakfast*
buhat sa	*from*
alas sais y medya	*6.30*
hanggang	*until*
alas nuwebe y medya	*9.30*
tanghalian	*lunch*
alas dose	*12.00 midday*
alas dos nang hapon	*2.00 p.m.*
hapunan	*supper*
alas sais	*6 o'clock*
alas nuwebe nang gabi	*9.00 p.m.*
sa lahat nang oras	*at any time*
may makakainan bang	*is there any place to eat*
malapit dito	*near here*
may pagkain	*there is food*
hatinggabi	*midnight*
mabuti kung ganoon	*that's good*
hindi ba mahal?	*not expensive (I hope)?*
hindi po	*no sir*
masarap ang pagkain	*the food is delicious/great*
mura ang halaga	*the price is cheap/right*

QUICK VOCAB

Translation

Bill	Good morning, Madame. What time are the meals in the hotel?
Receptionist	Of course, sir. Breakfast is from 6.30 until 9.30. Lunch is from 12.00 until 2.00 pm. Supper is from 6.00 until 9.00 pm. Room service is available at any time sir.
Bill	Are there any nice places to eat nearby?
Receptionist	Certainly sir. 'Lola's Litson' serves delicious food until midnight.
Bill	That's good. Is it very expensive?
Receptionist	No sir. The food is good and the price is cheap.
Bill	Thank you.

Language skills

2 *May, mayroon* Has/have, there/there are *Wala* None (no)

Remember the word 'may' we met in **Asking for a room or anything else?** **May** always expresses possession of some specific but previously unidentified object or objects. **May** is always followed by the word or phrase expressing the object possessed. Take a look at these examples:

May problema sila.	*They have a problem*
May sukli ba kayo?	*Do you have change?* (formal)
May taksi na po.	*There is a taxi now* (formal)
May tao pa sa banyo.	*There is still someone in the bathroom* (lit.)
	or *Someone is still in the bathroom*
May lapis ka ba?	*Do you have a pencil?*

Mayroon (also meaning has/have, there is/there are) is very similar to the word **may**, differing only in that it is used as a form of reply which stands alone. Whereas **may** must always be used in conjunction with a sentence, **mayroon** can be used as a one word reply. Don't be surprised if you often hear people say **meron** instead of **mayroon**. Both words have exactly the same meaning!

Q: May aklat ba si John?	*Has John got a book?*
A: Oo. Mayroon	*Yes, he has* (a book)
Q: May problema ba kayo?	*Do you have a problem?*
A: Mayroon	*We have*

Exercise 4 Listening and understanding

Listen to the following example sentences:

◀) **CD 1, TR 2, 02:27**

1. Q: May guro ka ba?   *Do you have a teacher?*
   A: Oo. Mayroon   *Yes I have* (a teacher)
2. Q. May barya ka ba?   *Do you have change?*
   A: Oo. Mayroon   *Yes I have* (change)

3. Q: May lapis ba kayo?   *Do you have a pencil?* (formal)
   A: Oo. Mayroon   *Yes. I have* (a pencil)

4. Q: May asawa ba kayo?   *Do you have a husband/wife?*
                                (formal)
   A: Oo. Mayroon   *Yes. I have* (a husband/wife)

5. Q: May anak ba kayo?   *Do you have any children?*
                                  (formal)
   A: Oo. Mayroon   *Yes. I have* (children)

Repeat each sentence as you hear it, following the sound of the words as closely as possible. Why not try repeating the same exercise, this time without the help of the CD?

Insight

Filipinos may greet you through a combination of eye-contact and moving their eyebrows. A friendly smile completes the greeting, all of which says *hello, how are you?* (**kumusta ka?**), without uttering a single word! The same actions mirrored in response say **mabuti naman!** *(I'm fine!)*

Exercise 5

Try constructing five sentences of your own, using the vocabulary provided. Answer all sentences by using **Oo, Mayroon** ('Yes. There is/there are').

sasakyan	*vehicle*
payong	*umbrella*
kutsilyo	*knife*
pinggan	*plate*
baso	*drinking glass*
ka	*you* (singular)
kayo	*you* (formal)

QUICK VOCAB

1. _____

2. _____

3. _____

4. _____

5. _____

This time practise answering in the negative. The opposite to **may**, **mayroon** (there is, there are, has, have) is **wala** (no, none). This time, answer using **wala** or **wala akong** (I do not have).

Examples:

1. Q: May asawa ba kayo?   _Do you have a wife/_
                                         husband?

   A: Wala (Wala akong asawa)   _No (I don't have a wife/_
                                         husband)

2. Q: May problema po ba kayo?   _Do you have a problem?_
                                         (formal)

   A: Wala (Wala akong   _No (I don't have a problem)_
       problema)

3. Q: May anak ba kayo?   _Do you have children?_
   A: Wala (Wala akong anak)   _No (I don't have any_
                                         children)

Exercise 6

Use the pictures to help you fill in the space with the correct answer (using **may** and **wala**). The first one has already been done for you. The **Quick vocab** will help you, too.

barko	_ship_
dagat	_sea/ocean_
mesa	_table_
kuwarto	_room_
walang pera	_no money_
pitaka	_wallet_
basura	_rubbish_
daan	_road_
sombrero	_hat_
lalaki	_man_
walang pasahero	_no passenger_
taksi	_taxi_
sanggol	_baby_
babae	_woman_

QUICK VOCAB

1. May libro si Anna.

2. _____ sa dagat.

3. _____ sa kuwarto.

4. _____ ang pitaka.

5. _____ sa daan.

6. _____ ang lalaki.

7. _____ ang taksi.

8. _____ ang babae.

3 Question words: *Sino? ano?,* Who? what?

When we want to ask a question we start with words such as who, what, why, when, whose, where, how, etc. Let's take a closer look at two of these words.

Sino

The Tagalog question word **sino** (meaning 'who' or 'whom') is used in three different ways:

1. with personal pronouns: ako, ka, siya, kami, tayo, kayo and sila (I, you, he/she, we, you (pl.), they)
2. with **si** plus a person's name (see Language skills, Unit 1)
3. with **ang** plus a word that tells us something about the subject.

Listen to the following examples on the CD and repeat them.

◄》 **CD 1, TR 2, 03:14**

Question	Translation	Reply	Translation
Sino po kayo?	*Who are you?* (formal)	**Si Larry** ako	*I am Larry*
Sino siya?	*Who is he?*	**Si Louie** siya	*He is Louie*
Sino ang guro?	*Who is the teacher?*	**Ako** ang guro	*I am the teacher*
Sino ang guro mo?	*Who is your teacher?*	**Si Cora** ang guro ko	*Cora is my teacher*
Sino ang bisita?	*Who is the visitor?*	Ang **babae** ang bisita	*The woman is the visitor*
Sino ang estudyante?	*Who is the student?*	**Ikaw** ang estudyante	*You are the student*

Notice how **sino** has been substituted with **si**, followed by the name of a person. Remember that every time you ask a question using **sino**

24

(who?), the reply you receive will either be a person's name, **ang** + a noun, or a personal pronoun. Look at these examples:

Question	Translation	Reply	Translation
Sino ang British dito?	*Who is the British (one) here?*	**Siya** ang British dito	*He is the British (one) here*
Sino ang guro?	*Who is the teacher?*	**Ako** ang guro	*I am the teacher*
Sino ang estudyante?	*Who is the student?*	**Ikaw** ang estudyante.	*You are the student*
Sino ang mga turista?	*Who are the tourists?*	**Kami** ang mga turista	*We are the tourists*

Ano

This is the most versatile of all Tagalog question words and is used to mean 'what?'. It may be used in connection with any of the following:

a noun (a name of a person, place or thing)
an adjective (a word that describes a noun, e.g. big, dirty, small)
a verb (a 'doing' word, e.g. drink, eat, sleep, sing).

Examples:

Question	Translation	Reply	Translation
Ano po kayo?	*What are you?** (very formal) (* = what do you do?)	**Guro** ako.	*I am a teacher*
Ano siya?	*What is she?*	**Nars** siya.	*She is a nurse*
Ano ang* pangalan mo?	*What is your name?*	John Joseph	*(My name is) John Joseph*
Ano ito?	*What is this?*	**Lapis** iyan	*That is a pencil*

* **Ano ang** is often contracted to **anong**.

Insight

When speaking English, many Filipinos will respond to something they did not quite catch or hear by saying *What?* This is not intended to be disrespectful, but is a direct translation of the Tagalog **Ano?** Notice that the pitch is raised at the end of the word. This raising of the pitch is intended to convey politeness.

Exercise 7

Try using the words **sino** and **ano**. Look at the pictures. Can you ask a simple question using either **sino** or **ano**? Use the examples and the vocabulary box provided to help you.

pagod	*tired*
oras	*time*
reyna	*queen*
bandera/bandila	*flag*
kulay	*colour*
ng	*of the*
na	*now/already*

English: Who is tired?
Tagalog: _____

English: Who is the Queen?
Tagalog: _____

English: What time is it now?
Tagalog: _____

English: What is the colour of the flag?
Tagalog: _____

One-minute phrases

Laman ng kalye (*lah-man-nang-kal-yeh*) Literally, *contents of the street*. This phrase is commonly used to refer to a person who seems to spend more time on the streets than at home.

Lutong Makaw (*loo-tong-mah-kao*) Literally, *cooked in the Portuguese colony of Macau*. This phrase is used to refer to something that has been manipulated or 'fixed' behind the scenes in order to ensure a particular outcome (i.e. the results of an election or a beauty contest, etc.).

Pantulak (*pahn-too-lahk*) Literally, *something to push with*. This popular and common Tagalog expression applies to any kind of drink consumed following food. The implication is that it will help the food slide down more easily to the stomach. For example: 'Ako ang bibili ng pansit at tinapay, ikaw ang bahala sa pantulak.' *I'll buy the noodles and bread and you take care of something to wash it down with [drink]*

Kape at gatas (*kah-peh-at-gah-tas*) Literally, *coffee and milk*. This phrase is similar in meaning to the English expression 'chalk and cheese'. It can be used to express notable differences between two people.

Kanang kamay (*kah-nang-kah-my*) Literally, *right hand*. This phrase is almost identical to the English expression 'my right hand'. It denotes a clear level of dependability.

Insight

Sometimes Filipinos are unsure how to interact with foreigners. Your facial expressions and body language may be scrutinized for signs of openness. A smile communicates friendliness and reassures that you are open to contact.

Summary

1. **May** Has/Have is always used with a noun.
2. **Mayroon** can be used on its own. **May** cannot.
3. **Mayroon** can be used with a noun but is changed to **mayroong**.
4. **Anong** is the contraction of **Ano ang**.
5. There is no direct translation of the verb *to be*.
6. **Anong oras** = *What time (is it)?*.
7. **Anong oras** can be answered in Tagalog, Spanish or English.
8. In Tagalog, the subject of the sentence comes second whereas in English the subject comes first.
9. **Sino** = *Who?*
10. **Ano** = *What?*

3

Para sa inyo ang regalong ito
This gift is for you

In this unit you will learn how to:

- Meet your friend's family
- Say 'thank you'
- Use the definite and indefinite article
- Make a statement negative

Meeting your friend's family

Dialogue 1

◄)) CD 1, TR 3

Roy Cook goes to the Abiva house to say hello to Jobert's family. He feels a little nervous, but Jobert is at hand to introduce him to everyone.

Jobert	Halikayo, ito ang kaibigan ko na taga England.
Roy	Magandang hapon sa inyong lahat. Si Roy ako, Roy Cook.
Jobert	Ang nanay ko ito, si Teresita.
Teresita	Kumusta ka, Roy?
Jobert	Ang tatay ko ito, si Juan.
Juan	Kumusta ang England?
Jobert	At si Pinky at Lovely, ang kapatid ko.
Pinky	Maligayang pagdating, Roy.
Jobert	At ang Lolo at Lola.
Roy	Ikinagagalak ko kayong makilala!

halikayo	*come on everyone*
ito	*this*
kaibigan	*friend*
ko	*my*
taga	*from*
magandang hapon	*good afternoon*
sa inyong lahat	*to you all*
nanay	*mother*
tatay	*father*
kapatid	*sister/brother*
lolo	*grandfather*
lola	*grandmother*

Translation

Jobert	Come on everyone, this is my friend from England.
Roy	Good afternoon to you all. I'm Roy, Roy Cook.
Jobert	This is my mother, Teresita.
Teresita	How are you, Roy?
Jobert	This is my father, Juan.
Juan	How is England?
Jobert	And Pinky and Lovely, my sisters.
Pinky	Pleased to meet you, Roy.
Jobert	And finally, grandfather and grandmother.
Roy	I'm pleased to meet you all!

Notice how Jobert introduced his family. Study the Tagalog dialogue for a few minutes, reading it aloud. Following Jobert's example, use the same formula for introducing other relatives or friends, too. Here are some more examples:

Kapatid ko ito, si Anne.	*This is my sister, Anne.*
Pamangkin ko ito, si Lina.	*This is my niece, Lina.*
Pinsan ko siya.	*He/she is my cousin.*
Bayaw ko si Bob.	*Bob is my brother-in-law.*
Hipag ko ito, si Elizabeth.	*This is my sister-in-law, Elizabeth.*
Pamangkin ko ito, si Paul.	*This is my nephew, Paul.*
Pamangkin ko ito, si Beth.	*This is my niece, Beth.*

Exercise 1

Using Jobert's words as a guide, try to introduce your own family to your Filipino friends. Use the examples just given and the **Quick vocab** to help you.

	English	Tagalog
a.	Good afternoon to you all.	_____
b.	This is my grandmother.	_____
c.	This is my father, _____.	_____
d.	And _____, my brother.	_____
e.	This is my grandfather.	_____
f.	This is _____, my sister.	_____
g.	And finally, my mother.	_____

Exercise 2

The plane journey to the Philippines is very long and tiring. Roy still has a bit of jet-lag and needs your help. Look at the picture gallery of different members of the Cook family. The names and pictures appear to have been mixed up. Can you help Roy place them in the correct order?

a) Nanay

b) Kuya at Ate

c) Pamangkin

d) Lola at Lolo

e) Hipag

g) Bayaw

f) Tatay

Insight

Never be afraid to try out the Tagalog you know. What you say may not be 'perfect', but it will be highly appreciated by your Filipino friends. You will be surprised just how far a little goes!

Language skills

1 The indefinite article, *a* and *an*

The English words 'a' and 'an' are known as indefinite articles. We use these words when referring to a person or thing about which we do not want to be specific. For example, a house, a car, a doctor, a tree. When the word begins with a vowel (a, e, i, o or u), then the indefinite article becomes 'an', for example, an apple, an aeroplane, an elephant. In Tagalog, there are two basic ways of representing the indefinite article. First, the indefinite article is implied (i.e. estudyante = a student, lapis = a pencil, aeroplano = an aeroplane). Second, both 'a' and 'an' are represented by the word **ng** pronounced (*nang*) when there is an action word (verb) in the sentence followed by an object. For example, 'Domingo has bought a book.' Bumili **ng aklat** si Domingo. 'Mario ate an apple.' Kumain **ng mansanas** si Mario.

Look at these sample sentences:

Tagalog	Literal translation	English
Kumakain si Manny ng mansanas	Eating Manny an apple	*Manny is eating an apple*
Arkitekto si Roy	Architect Roy	*Roy is an architect*
Doktor si Jonathan	Doctor Jonathan	*Jonathan is a doctor*
Nagbabasa si Joe ng aklat	Reading Joe a book	*Joe is reading a book*
Bumili kami ng mapa	Bought we a map	*We bought a map*

Exercise 3

When you arrive in Manila, you may need to buy a few things before travelling around the country. Complete the sentences below using the sample sentences and the **Quick vocab** to guide you:

kailangan ko	*I need/want*
gusto kong bumili	*I'd like to buy*
payong	*umbrella*
posporo	*a box of matches*
nagtitinda ba kayo	*do you sell*
shampoo	*shampoo*
tee-shirt	*tee-shirt*
street guide	*street guide*
tinapay	*bread*
mapa	*map*

Tagalog	English
1. Kailangan ko ng _____.	I need a map.
2. Gusto kong bumili ng _____.	I want to buy an umbrella.
3. May _____ ba kayo?	Do you have a box of matches?
4. Nagtitinda ba kayo ng _____?	Do you sell shampoo?

Exercise 4

Translate into Tagalog.

English	Tagalog
1. I need a tee-shirt. (use **ng**)	_____
2. I want to buy a ticket (use **ng**)	_____

32

3. Do you have a street guide? _____

4. Do you sell bread? (use **ng**) _____

Insight

If you don't know the Tagalog word, use the English one. Mixing Tagalog and English is known as *Taglish* and is quite acceptable. It is much more acceptable than just speaking English. If you have a keen ear, you may also have noticed many Spanish words in the Tagalog vocabulary. This is hardly surprising, given that the Spanish occupied the Philippines for more than 300 years. Spanish, however, has not been used as an official language in the Philippines for over 100 years.

---

2 *Ang* the definite article, *the*

In English, when we want to be specific about a person or a thing, we use the word 'the'. This word is known as the definite article. In Tagalog, the word 'the' is translated as '**ang**'. For example: masarap **ang** pagkain = the food is delicious; matangkad **ang** estudyante = the student is tall; maganda **ang** dalaga = the girl is beautiful.

Exercise 5

Bill Cook had a little too much to drink last night and is now having trouble with his Tagalog. His sentences are a bit jumbled. Can you help him sort them out? Use the vocabulary box to help you. Don't forget, the correct Tagalog sentence structure should be comment – definite article – subject. The correct English sentence is on the left:

English	Jumbled words	Tagalog
1. The weather is hot.	panahon mainit ang	_____
2. The street is dirty.	ang kalye marumi	_____
3. The car is clean.	kotse ang malinis	_____
4. The house is beautiful.	bahay maganda ang	_____
5. The man is a doctor.	ang lalaki doktor	_____

Bill has now sobered up a little, and some of his sentences are correct. However, he is still making a few mistakes. Can you tell which sentences are correct and which ones are not?

	English	Tagalog
1.	The room is small.	Maliit ang kuwarto.
2.	The Jeepney is colourful.	Jeepney ang makulay.
3.	The flower smells fragrant.	Mabango ang bulaklak.
4.	The family is happy.	Masaya ang pamilya.
5.	The fish is fresh.	Isda ang sariwa.

panahon	*weather*
mainit	*hot*
kalsada	*street*
marumi	*dirty*
kotse	*car*
malinis	*clean*
bahay	*house*
maganda	*beautiful*
isda	*fish*
sariwa	*fresh*
pamilya	*family*
masaya	*happy*
bulaklak	*flower*
mabango	*fragrant*
makulay	*colourful*
maliit	*small*

Saying 'thank you'

Dialogue 2

◀) CD 1, TR 3, 00:50

Roy gives a **pasalubong** (*gift*) to Jobert's parents.

Roy	**Pa**ra sa iny**o** ang re**ga**long i**to**. Magustu**han sa**na nin**yo**.
Mrs Abiva	I**sang** ka**hon** ng tsoko**la**te! Muk**hang** masa**rap**! Mar**a**ming sa**la**mat, Roy.
Roy	*Wala* pong anuman. **Pa**ra sa in**yo** nam**an** ito.
Mr Abiva	Ang pabo**ri**to kong ta**ba**ko **bu**hat sa Inglaterra! Mar**a**ming-mar**a**ming sa**la**mat na *muli*.
Roy	*Wala* pong anuman.

para sa inyo	*for you*
regalong ito	*this gift*
magustuhan sana ninyo	*I hope you'll like it*
rin	*also*
isang kahon	*one box*
mukhang	*looks/appears*
ang paborito kong	*my favourite*
buhat sa	*from*
muli	*again/once more*

Translation

Roy	This gift is for you. I hope you'll like it.
Mrs Abiva	A box of chocolates! They look delicious! Thank you very much, Roy.
Roy	You're welcome (polite). And this is for you.
Mr Abiva	My favourite cigars from England. Thank you very much again, Roy.
Roy	You're welcome (polite).

Expressing gratitude

Filipinos have many different ways of expressing their gratitude. This is part of the cultural stress on politeness. It is a good idea to learn as many different ways of saying 'thank you' as possible.

Here are some commonly used examples:

Salamat	*Thanks/Thank you*
Salamat sa iyo	*Thank you* (used with friends, informal, and family members)
Salamat sa inyo	*Thank you* (formal)
Salamat sa inyong lahat	*Thank you all* (informal)
Salamat po sa inyo	*Thank you* (very formal)
Maraming salamat po sa inyo	*Thank you very much* (very formal)
Maraming salamat	*Thank you very much*
Maraming salamat sa iyo	*Thank you very much* (informal)
Maraming-maraming-salamat	*Thank you so very much*
Maraming-maraming salamat sa iyo	*Thank you so very much* (informal)

Maraming-maraming salamat sa inyo	*Thank you so very much (very formal)*
Naku, nag-abala ka pa, salamat	*Oh, you should not have bothered! Thank you*
Naku, nag-abala pa kayo, salamat	*Oh, you should not have bothered! Thank you (very formal)*
Salamat na lang	*I can only say thank you*

Insight

Have you ever noticed how much luggage overseas Filipinos carry when returning home? A strong cultural expectation is the **pasalubong** or *gift*. Filipinos will ensure that they carry plenty of **pasalubong** for family members and friends in order to renew and strengthen relationships. Nobody must be left out; hence the heavy bags!

Exercise 6

Which of the forms of 'thank you' would you use with the following people? Can you see more than one answer for some of them?

a. Guest to waiter   _____
b. Waiter to guest   _____
c. Guest to guest (of same age)   _____
d. Young guest to an older guest   _____
e. Older guest to a young guest   _____

When someone says 'thank you' to you in any of these ways, a simple and polite response is **walang anuman**. Cover up the list of common expressions. How many different ways of saying 'thank you' can you remember? Try to recall five of them and use them on your Filipino friends. They will be impressed not only by your knowledge of Tagalog, but also by your good manners!

Language skills

3 *Hindi* No/not

Hindi is the most common and versatile way of saying *no* in Tagalog. **Hindi** transforms a positive statement into a negative statement.

The word **hindi** comes before the comment (what is said about the subject) and the subject. For example, **hindi** masarap ang pagkain = the food is not tasty; **hindi** mainit ang kape = the coffee is not hot; **hindi** malayo ang palengke = the market is not far.

	Tagalog	**Literal translation**	**English**
Hindi + noun	Hindi doktor si Fred.	Not doctor Fred	*Fred is not a doctor.*
Hindi + adjective	Hindi malinis ang kotse.	Not clean the car	*The car is not clean.*
Hindi + ba	Hindi ba nars si Letty?	Not nurse Letty?	*Isn't Letty a nurse?*
Hindi + pa	Hindi pa hinog ang mangga.	Not yet ripe the mango	*The mango is not yet ripe.*
Hindi + verb	Hindi umiinom ang bisita.	Not drink(ing) the visitor	*The visitor isn't drinking.*
Hindi + personal pronoun	Hindi siya Pranses.	Not he/she French	*He/she is not French.*
Hindi + pronoun	Hindi ito sariwa.	Not this fresh	*This is not fresh.*

Exercise 7

Look at the pictures. Each picture is followed by a statement. Using the word **hindi**, turn each of these sentences into a negative statement.

1. Barko ito. Neg. _____
(*This is a ship.*) (*This is not a ship.*)

2. Malinis ang mesa. Neg. _____
(*The table is clean.*) (*The table is not clean.*)

3. Estudyante si Amy.
(*Amy is a student.*)

Neg. _____
(*Amy is not a student.*)

4. Tumatakbo ang Jeepney
(*The Jeepney is moving.*)

Neg. _____
(*The Jeepney is not moving.*)

4 *Wala* None

The word **wala** expresses absence of something. **Wala** is a reply to a **may** or **mayroon** question. Unlike **hindi, wala** is followed by a ligatured pronoun. Example: Wala akong lapis, *I don't have a pencil.* Wala kaming guro, *We don't have a teacher.* Wala itong takip, *This has no cover.* However, when followed by a noun, **wala** takes a ligature. Example: Walang kotse si Shirley, *Shirley doesn't have a car.* Walang pera si Maria, *Maria doesn't have money.* Walang panahon si Julie, *Julie doesn't have time.* Look at the sample sentences:

Question	Reply:
May pera ba si Ginoong Cruz?	Wala. Walang pera si Ginoong Cruz.
Has Mr Cruz got money?	*No. Mr Cruz hasn't got money.*
May asawa ba kayo? (formal)	Wala. Wala akong asawa.
Do you have a husband/wife?	*No. I don't have a husband/wife.*
May problema ka ba? (informal)	Wala. Wala akong problema.
Do you have a problem?	*No. I don't have a problem.*
May bus na ba?	Wala. Wala pa.
Is there a bus now?	*No. There's no (bus) yet.*

38

May pagkain ba dito?	Wala. Walang pagkain dito.
Is there food here?	*No. There's no food here.*
May Coke o Pepsi ba kayo?	Wala. 7-Up lang.
Do you have Coke or Pepsi?	*No. Just 7-Up.*

Exercise 8

Using the formula already given in the sample sentences, give the reply to the following questions:

1. May sasakyan ba sa bus stop? Neg._____
Is there a vehicle at the bus stop? *No. There is no vehicle at the bus stop.*

2. May yelo ba kayo? Neg._____
Do you have any ice? *No. We have no ice.*

3. May katulong ba si Ginoong Reyes? Neg. _____
Has Mr Reyes got a helper? *No. Mr Reyes has no helper.*

More on *Hindi* No/not
Wala No/none

It is common for English speakers to experience some confusion between the use of **hindi** and **wala**. When we use the word 'none' in English, the Tagalog translation of this is 'wala'. The problem arises when we realize that in English, the word 'no' can also be used to mean 'none'. For example, the response to the question, 'do you have a ticket?' can be 'no'. In this situation, the word 'no' expresses an absence of something. That's why non-Tagalog speakers sometimes make the mistake of saying **hindi** instead of **wala** when they mean 'none'; for **hindi** also means 'no'! Study the sample sentences:

Sentence	Negative	Question	Reply
Amerikano si Jim.	Hindi British si Jim.	British ba si Jim?	Hindi.
Jim is American.	*Jim is not British.*	*Is Jim British?*	*No. Jim is American.*

Tagalog si Elvie.	Hindi Bisaya si Elvie.	Bisaya ba si Elvie?	Hindi.
Elvie is Tagalog.	*Elvie is not Visayan.*	*Is Elvie Visayan?*	*No. Elvie is Tagalog.*
Malaki ang Australia.	Hindi maliit ang Australia?	Maliit ba ang Australia?	Hindi.
Australia is big.	*Australia is not small.*	*Is Australia small?*	*No. It is big.*

Remember: If you want to express the absence of something or someone, then the correct word to use is **wala**.

Finally, **hinding-hindi** means *never*.

Insight

Words such as **wala** can prove a challenge to native English speakers. The final **a** ends abruptly; a pronunciation feature known as a *glottal stop*. Imagine switching off a tape-recording of your voice just as you reach the final **a** of **wala**. The resulting sound may be unusual to English ears, but is at home to Tagalog ears.

One-minute phrases

Walang wala (*wah-lang-wah-lah*) Literally, *no nothing*. This commonly used Tagalog phrase means: *I have no money* or *I'm broke*.

May sama ng loob (*my-sa-mah-nang-law-awb*) Literally, *having a bad feeling inside*. If Filipinos feel hurt or offended, they will typically not express their feelings in a direct manner. This phrase suggests a common Filipino way of expressing feelings in more general terms. 'May sama ako ng loob sa kaniya.' *I have a bad feeling towards her/him.*

Magmahabang dulang (*mag-ma-hah-bang-doo-lang*) Literally, *a long dining table*. This expression indicates a forthcoming marriage. 'Magmamahabang dulang ang anak ni Ginoong Cruz.' *The son of Mr Cruz is getting married.* The long dining table is typical of buffet-style meals used during Filipino festivals.

May sinasabi (*my-see-nah-sa-bee*) Literally, *to have something to say*. This Tagalog expression denotes wealth. 'May sinasabi ang pamilya Santos.' *The Santos family are well-heeled/wealthy.*

Maraming kuskos-balungos (*mah-rah-ming-kus-kus-bah-loo-ngoos*) Literally, *a lot of scrubbing and fussing.* This expression is used in connection with a person who has difficulty in making his or her point. 'Maraming kuskos-balungos si Pedro.' *Pedro beats around the bush a lot.*

Insight

You may have noticed some Filipinos kissing the hand of a senior member of the family or people of social standing. This custom, known as **mano**, is seen as a mark of respect. Do not be surprised if Filipino children do this to you! It is also a way of showing respect to the visitor.

Summary

1. The indefinite article *a/an* = **ng** in Tagalog. **Kumain ako ng mansanas.** *I ate an apple.*
2. The definite article *the* is **ang** in Tagalog. **Binili ko ang kotse.** *I bought the car.*
3. Kailangan = *need, necessary.*
4. Gusto = *like, want.*
5. In Tagalog, the word **hindi** means **No** (negative).
6. **Hindi** follows the word it negates. *Hindi doctor.*
7. **Hinding-hindi** = *never.*
8. **Wala** = *none* or *nothing* (absence of something).
9. **Wala** becomes **walang** when used with a noun.
10. **Walang-wala** = *broke* (lack of money).

4

....

Naasan ang post office?
Where's the post office?

In this unit you will learn how to:

- Ask 'where?'
- Buy stamps and send a parcel
- Use adjectives

Asking 'where?'

Dialogue 1

🔊 **CD 1, TR 4**

Louise Cook wants to go to the post office. Let's join her as she asks the hotel receptionist how to get there. Listen carefully to the sound of the words. You will notice that when a question is asked, the tone of the final word goes up. All question words in Tagalog have this feature.

Louise	**Na**saan ang pinakama**la**pit na post office **di**to?
Receptionist	**Na**sa Kalye Maningning po.
Louise	Pu**we**de bang la**ka**rin?
Receptionist	A**ba, o**po.
Louise	Ma**a**ari bang big**yan** mo a**ko** ng direksi**yon**?
Receptionist	Ganito *po*. Pagla**bas** ni**nyo** sa hotel, tuma**wid** ka**yo** at kuma**na**n. Dumi**ret**so ka**yo**. Pagka**ta**pos kuma**li**wa ka**yo** sa Kalye Rondolo. Ikali**mang** gu**sa**li **bu**hat sa **kan**to ang post office.
Louise	Ma**ra**ming sa**la**mat.
Receptionist	*Wala* pong anu**man**.

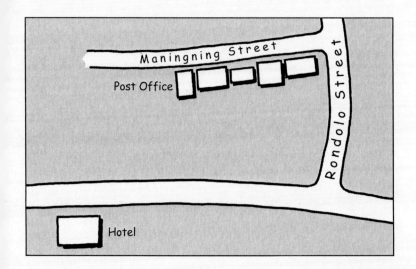

nasaan	*where*
pinakamalapit	*nearest*
nasa	*at/on/in/at the/on the/in the*
puwede bang	*is it possible*
lakarin	*to walk (it)*
aba	*of course/hey/my*
opo	*yes* (formal)
maaari bang	*is it possible* (see also **puwede bang**)
bigyan mo ako	*give me*
direksiyon	*direction*
ganito po	*like this*
paglabas ninyo	*once you've come out*
tumawid kayo	*you cross (the street)*
dumiretso kayo	*walk straight ahead*
kumanan	*turn right*
pagkatapos	*then*
kumaliwa	*turn left*
ikalimang gusali	*fifth building*
kanto	*corner*
wala pong anuman	*you're welcome* (formal)

Translation

Louise	Where's the nearest post office here?
Receptionist	It's located at Maningning Street ma'am.
Louise	Can I walk it?
Receptionist	Yes, ma'am.
Louise	Could you give me directions? [Could you tell me where it is?]
Receptionist	It's like this ma'am. When you leave the hotel, cross [the street] and turn right. [You] Walk straight ahead. Then turn left onto Rondolo Street. The post office is the fifth building from the corner.
Louise	Thank you very much.
Receptionist	You're welcome.

Exercise 1

Listen carefully to the 'direction' words on your CD. The pictures should help you.

🔊 **CD 1, TR 4, 00:51**

Kaliwa
(Left)

Kanan
(Right)

Diretso

Tumawid

44

Match the Tagalog with the correct English:

English	Tagalog
1. Turn left	kumanan
2. Turn right	diretso
3. Straight ahead	tumawid kayo
4. Right	kaliwa
5. Cross (the street)	kumaliwa
6. Left	kanan

Language skills

1 *Nasaan? Where?*

In Dialogue 1, Louise Cook introduced you to a new question word: 'nasaan' or 'where'? She asked: 'Nasaan ang Post Office?' (*Where is the post office?*). **Nasaan** is a commonly used question word which asks where a thing or a place is located. e.g. **nasaan** ang aklat ko? (where is my book?), **nasaan** ang immigration office? (where is the immigration office?). Notice that the hotel receptionist began her reply with **nasa**. This has nothing to do with American astronauts but is the way to answer a **nasaan** question in Tagalog. The reply to **nasaan** should always begin with the word **nasa** followed by the location of the subject of the sentence. For example, '**nasaan** ang bahay mo?' (*where is your house?*), '**nasa** Kalye Cruz ang bahay ko (*my house is in Cruz Street*).

Exercise 2

Listen to the following **nasaan** questions and answers on your CD. Repeat what you hear until you feel confident. Why not try to make up a few **nasaan** questions for yourself? Ask your Filipino friends to help you. First try asking the **nasaan** question, then change places and try giving the **nasa** answers.

◄)) **CD 1, TR 4, 01:12**

Question	Reply
Nasaan ang Maynila?	**Nasa Pilipinas** ang Maynila.
Where is Manila?	*Manila is in the Philippines.*

Nasaan ang Mayon Volcano?	**Nasa Albay** ang Mayon Volcano.
Where is the Mayon Volcano?	*The Mayon Volcano is in Albay.*
Nasaan ang barko?	**Nasa dagat** ang barko.
Where is the ship?	*The ship is on the ocean.*
Nasaan ang mga bata?	**Nasa bahay** ang mga bata.
Where are the children?	*The children are at home.*
Nasaan ang sombrero?	**Nasa silya** ang sombrero.
Where is the hat?	*The hat is on the chair.*

> **Note:** In English, two vowels may occur commonly together (a, e, i, o, u) and be pronounced as one sound. For example, hoop, keep, people, tea, beach. These double vowel sounds are known as diphthongs. In Tagalog, each vowel is pronounced separately and so there are no diphthongs. For example, the word **nasaan** is not pronounced *nasan* but rather *nah-sah-an*. Both a's are pronounced separately. **Remember:** This applies to all Tagalog words where two vowels occur together.

Exercise 3

Look at the pictures. Roy Cook is confused and doesn't know where these places are. He needs to ask a passer-by for help. What question would Roy ask and what reply would the passer-by give? For example: 'Nasaan ang Robinson's Shopping Mall?' 'Nasa Edsa ang Robinson's Shopping Mall.' Use the clue words accompanying each picture to help you formulate your answers.

1.

Clues:
Simbahan
Sto.
Domingo

2.

Clues:
Jeepney stop
Guzman
Street

3.

Clues:
Palengke
Cubao

4.

Clues:
Bangko
Makati

Read out your answers and practise them with your Filipino friends. You will be surprised how quickly you can ask where something or somewhere is!

Buying stamps and sending a parcel

Dialogue 2

◀) CD 1, TR 4, 02:05

Louise Cook has arrived at the post office and is talking to a clerk.

Louise	Gusto kong bumili ng selyo para sa mga postcards ko.
Clerk	Saan *po* ang punta ng mga postcards?
Louise	Sa Inglatera at sa Amerika.
Clerk	3.80 *po* ang isang selyo. Ilang selyo *po* ang kailangan ninyo?
Louise	Labinlima. May pakete rin ako papunta sa Inglaterra, airmail.
Clerk	57.00 pesos *po* ang selyo. Pakilagay *po* sa timbangan ang pakete. Ano *po* ang laman ng pakete?
Louise	Isang aklat. Magkano naman ito?
Clerk	240.00 pesos ang pakete. Paki-abot *po* sa akin ang pakete.
Louise	Salamat. Eto ang bayad ko.
Clerk	*Wala* pong anuman.

gusto ko	*I like/I want*
bumili ng selyo	*buy some stamps*
para sa mga	*for* (plural)
saan	*where* (direction)
ang punta	*the destination/going to*
isang selyo	*one stamp*
ng mga	*of the* (plural)
ilang selyo	*how many stamps*
ang kailangan ninyo	*what you need*
labinlima	*fifteen*
papunta sa	*going to*
pakilagay	*please put/place*
sa timbangan	*on the scales*
ang pakete	*the parcel*
ang laman	*the contents*

QUICK VOCAB

isang aklat	*one book/a book*
paki-abot sa akin	*please pass to me/hand to me*
magkano naman	*how much is it?*
eto	*here is*
bayad ko	*my payment*

Translation

Louise	I want to buy some stamps for my postcards.
Clerk	Where are they going to?
Louise	To England and to America.
Clerk	One stamp costs 3.80. How many stamps do you want?
Louise	Fifteen (stamps). I also have a parcel going to England by airmail.
Clerk	The stamps cost 57 pesos. Please put the parcel on the weighing machine. What is the content of the parcel?
Louise	A book. How much is it?
Clerk	The parcel will be 240 pesos. Could you please hand me the parcel?
Louise	Thank you. Here's my payment (money).
Clerk	You're most welcome.

Exercise 4

Read through Dialogue 2 again. Imagine that you too are making a trip to the post office. Using the dialogue and the **Quick vocab** provided to help you, how would you say the following in Tagalog?

1. I want to buy stamps for my parcel.
2. I want to buy stamps for a letter to America.
3. How much are the air letters each?
4. Where are the scales?
5. Kindly weigh the parcel for me.

Listen to Dialogue 2 again. The clerk at the post office asks you: 'Ano pong maipaglilingkod ko sa inyo?' or 'How may I help you?' You may respond by using the answers you have already provided in this exercise.

🔊 CD 1, TR 4, 02:05

papunta sa	*going to*
sulat	*letter*
magkakano	*how much (each)*
para sa akin	*for me*

Exercise 5

🔊 CD 1, TR 4, 03:07

Listen to the following words on the CD and then try repeating them. Cover the list up and try to see how many you can recall without looking at the book. Why not ask your Filipino friends to help you?

Listen and repeat

stamp	selyo
envelope	sobre
parcel	pakete
scales	timbangan
to post	ihulog
letter	sulat
pen	bolpen
string	tali
box	kahon
wrapping paper	pambalot

Exercise 6

Look at the drawings. Listen to the list of items read out on the CD and tick or circle the ones you can see:

◄)) **CD 1, 03:41**

Language skills

2 *Adjectives, words that 'describe'*

Pretty, tall, good, large, far, terrific, amusing, runny, fat, tired, etc. All of these words are describing words. They create a picture of a person or a thing. These words are known in English as adjectives: words that describe a noun (the name of person or thing). Remember pronouns, which we first met in Unit 1? Adjectives also describe pronouns. For example, he is tall, they are old, we are wealthy. Sometimes we use both adjectives and nouns together. When we do this, then the adjective always comes before the noun it describes. Look at these examples: clean (adjective) table (noun) = clean table. Good (adjective) news (noun) = good news. Short (adjective) story (noun) = short story. The good news is that this is written the same way in Tagalog (adjective followed by noun). In Tagalog, there is only one simple addition to remember: if the adjective ends with a vowel (a, e, i, o, u), then 'ng' is added to the end of the adjective. If the adjective ends with a consonant (any letter other than a vowel), then 'na' comes in between the adjective and the noun. Let's take a look at some examples.

Adjective + **ng**	+ noun	= phrase
maganda + ng	bahay	= magandang bahay (*beautiful house*)
mahaba + ng	pila	= mahabang pila (*long queue*)
mabuti + ng	guro	= mabuting guro (*good teacher*)
maligaya + ng	Pasko	= maligayang Pasko (*happy Christmas*)
matalino + ng	estudyante	= matalinong estudyante (*intelligent student*)
Adjective + **na**	+ noun	= phrase
masarap + na	pagkain	= masarap na pagkain (*delicious food*)
maliit + na	kotse	= maliit na kotse (*small car*)
mahirap + na	buhay	= mahirap na buhay (*hard life*)
madilim + na	kuwarto	= madilim na kuwarto (*dark room*)
pagod + na	kabayo	= pagod na kabayo (*tired horse*)

Exercise 7

Look at the four cartoon drawings. Each one is numbered. Now listen carefully to a description of three of the women. Can you identify which ones are being described? Use the examples and vocabulary just given to help you. Can you write down a description of the woman who is not mentioned on the CD?

1   2   3   4

Insight

A good knowledge of Tagalog becomes even more effective when combined with an understanding of subtle Filipino habits and behaviours. When expressing disagreement or disapproval, Filipinos can do so with a smile and a calm voice. A harsh tone or raised voice is viewed as disrupting harmony.

Exercise 8

Look carefully at the following pictures. Using the **Quick vocab** below, describe what you see in as many different ways as possible, using as many adjectives as you can. For example, 'Magandang, maliit na bahay' (*beautiful, small house*).

1.

2.

3.

4.

Well done! Whether you are in the house, taking a break at the office or sitting outside, look around you for a moment. Try to describe some of the things you see using the vocabulary you have learned so far in this book. Why not try it out with your Filipino friends, too?

mabango	*fragrant*
maganda	*beautiful/pretty*
malaki	*big*
masaya	*happy*
mabilis	*fast*
makulay	*colourful*
mabaho	*bad smelling*
mabait	*kind*
mahaba	*long*
siksikan	*crowded*
mabagal	*slow*
maikli	*short*
malinis	*clean*
marumi	*dirty*
kaakit-akit	*attractive*

One-minute phrases

Balat-sibuyas (*bah-laht see-boo-yahs*) Literally, 'onion-skinned' or 'thin-skinned'. This phrase is used when referring to a *very sensitive person*.

Pabigla-bigla (*pah-beeg-lah beeg-lah*) – lacking in self-control, hasty, abrupt, impulsive. For example **Kung magsalita siya'y pabigla-bigla.** *He/she has an abrupt way of speaking.*

Suwerte sa buhay (*soo-wer-teh sah boo-high*) Literally, *lucky in life*. A common Tagalog phrase meaning someone has been bringing *good luck* to the family. The opposite is:

Malas sa buhay (*mah-lahs sah boo-high*) Literally, *bad luck in life*. A common Tagalog phrase meaning someone has been bringing *bad luck to the family*.

> **Malinis sa katawan** (*mah-le-nees sah kah-tah-wahn*) Literally, *clean in the body*. This expression refers to a person who likes being physically clean and tidy.

Insight

Filipinos will rarely use their hands or fingers to point when giving directions. Instead, they may purse their lips or even nod their heads to indicate the general direction you need to go in. This is normal, so don't be surprised if it happens.

Summary

1. To show where something is use **Nasa. Nasa mesa, nasa garahe, nasa akin.**
2. For a person, use **Nakay** + person's name. e.g., **Nakay Lyn.**
3. For people, use **Nakina** + persons' names. e.g., **Nakina Yoly.**
4. **Nasaan** is used to find where *something* is.
5. **Nakanino** is used to find *with whom* something is.
6. A word that describes a noun is called an **adjective**.
7. In Tagalog, the adjective usually begins with **ma**.
8. Add **ng** to an adjective ending with a vowel when describing a noun. e.g., **maganda+ng = magandang. Magandang bestida** (*beautiful clothes*).
9. **na** follows an adjective ending with a consonant. e.g., **malinis+na = malinis na. Malinis na bahay** (*clean house*).
10. To say '*very*', repeat the adjective using **ng** or **na**, e.g., **magandang-maganda** = '*very beautiful*'.

5

Pera
Money

In this unit you will learn how to:

* Ask the price of goods and haggle
* Ask 'how much?' and 'how much each?'
* Change currency/travellers' cheques at the bank
* Tell the time

Asking the price of goods

Dialogue 1

◆) CD 1, TR 5

All over the Philippines you will find small stores selling basic items such as food and school supplies. These small businesses sell various and 'assorted' items. The Tagalog word for assorted is **sarisari**. These small shops are known in the Philippines as 'sarisari stores'. In this dialogue, we join Bill Cook at a local sarisari store.

Bill	Tao po!
Owner	Maganda**ng ha**pon *po*.
Bill	Maganda**ng ha**pon *po* nam**an**. May **s**obre ba ka**yo**?
Owner	Ma**yroon** *po*, mali**it** *po* ba o mala**ki**?
Bill	Iy**ong** mali**it** lang. Mag**kano** na**man**?
Owner	Lim**ang pi**so *po* i**sang** dosena.
Bill	O si**ge**, is**ang** dosena *nga*. At ang **bol**pen?
Owner	Tig-tat**long pi**so *po*. A**nong** ku**lay** *po*?
Bill	I**tim**. Big**yan** mo *nga* ak**o** ng i**sa**.

may	*has/have*
mayroon	*has/have* (used in replies)
bigyan	*give*
itim	*black*
limang piso	*five pesos*
isang dosena	*one dozen*
sige	*all right/okay*
nga	*please/indeed/really*
iyan lang	*that's all (just those)*
tig-tatlong piso	*three pesos each*
anong kulay	*what colour*
tao po?	*anyone at home?*
naman	*to you too/on the other hand*
heto	*here you are*
disi-otso pesos	*eighteen pesos*
lahat-lahat	*all in all/altogether*
ano pa?	*anything else/what else?*
bayad ko	*my payment*

QUICK VOCAB

Translation

Bill	Anyone at home?
Owner	Good afternoon.
Bill	Good afternoon to you, too . . . do you have any envelopes?
Owner	Yes we have sir, small or large (ones)?
Bill	Just the small ones. And how much are they?
Owner	Five pesos a dozen sir.
Bill	All right, a dozen please. And the ballpens?
Owner	Three pesos each sir. What colour?
Bill	Black. I would like to buy one.
Owner	Here you are sir. Eighteen pesos altogether. Do you want anything else?
Bill	That's all. Here you are. (*lit., here's my payment*)
Owner	Thank you sir.

Language skills

1 *Isa, dalawa, tatlo,* etc. *One, two, three, etc.*

Filipinos tend to use both Tagalog, Spanish *and* English when counting. This is hardly surprising when we look at the history of the country. The Philippines was under Spanish rule for over 300 years and American rule for 50 years. Both countries have left their mark on the Philippines in both its culture and language. Note, however, that the Spanish spelling and pronunciation used in the Philippines is not the same as the standard Spanish spelling and pronunciation. Look at this table:

Listen to the correct pronunciation on your CD and repeat the words.

◀) CD 1, TR 5, 00:58

English	Tagalog	Filipino Spanish spelling
one	isa	uno
two	dalawa	dos
three	tatlo	tres
four	apat	kuwatro
five	lima	singko
six	anim	sais
seven	pito	siyete

eight	walo	otso
nine	siyam	nuwebe
ten	sampu	diyes

Memorizing tip

Cover up both the Tagalog and Filipino Spanish columns. Try repeating first the Spanish numbers, then the Tagalog numbers. How many can you remember? Do not move on to the next set of numbers until you feel confident with numbers one–ten. If you want to memorize the numbers effectively, then try not to swallow too much at once. You will be surprised to see how much more quickly and effectively you are learning! Follow this pattern for all subsequent groups of numbers.

Listen to the correct pronunciation on your CD and repeat the words.

◀) **CD 1, TR 5, 01:45**

English	Tagalog	Filipino Spanish spelling
eleven	labing-isa	onse
twelve	labindalawa	dose
thirteen	labintatlo	trese
fourteen	labing-apat	katorse
fifteen	labinlima	kinse
sixteen	labing-anim	disisais
seventeen	labimpito	disisiyete
eighteen	labingwalo	disiotso
nineteen	labinsiyam	disinuwebe

Follow the memorizing tip!

Listen to the correct pronunciation on your CD and repeat the words.

◀) **CD 1, TR 5, 02:30**

English	Tagalog	Filipino Spanish spelling
twenty	dalawampu	beinte
twenty one	dalawampu't isa	beinte uno

twenty two	dalawampu't dalawa	beinte dos
twenty three	dalawampu't tatlo	beinte tres
twenty four	dalawampu't apat	beinte kuwatro
twenty five	dalawampu't lima	beinte singko
twenty six	dalawampu't anim	beinte sais
twenty seven	dalawampu't pito	beinte siyete
twenty eight	dalawampu't walo	beinte otso
twenty nine	dalawampu't siyam	beinte nuwebe

Follow the memorizing tip!

For the following numbers, repeat the process as in 21–29 in both Tagalog and Spanish.

◀) **CD 1, TR 5, 03:41**

English	Tagalog	Filipino Spanish spelling
thirty	tatlumpu	treinta
forty	apatnapu	kuwarenta
fifty	limampu	singkwenta
sixty	animnapu	sisenta
seventy	pitumpu	sitenta
eighty	walumpu	otsenta
ninety	siyamnapu	nubenta

Listen to the correct pronunciation on your CD and repeat the words.

◀) **CD 1, TR 5, 04:32**

English	Tagalog	Filipino Spanish spelling
one hundred	isandaan	siyento
two hundred	dalawandaan	dos siyentos
three hundred	tatlongdaan	tres siyentos
four hundred	apatnaraan	kuwatro siyentos
five hundred	limandaan	singko siyentos
six hundred	animnaraan	sais siyentos
seven hundred	pitongdaan	siyete siyentos
eight hundred	walongdaan	otso siyentos
nine hundred	siyamnaraan	nuwebe siyentos
one thousand	isanlibo	mil

Exercise 1
Why not try out your new knowledge of Spanish and Tagalog numbers?

1. What is the Spanish number for **19**?
2. What is the Tagalog number for **64**?
3. What is the Spanish number for **99**?
4. What is the Tagalog number for **27**?
5. What is the Spanish number for **115**?
6. What is the Tagalog number for **480**?

Exercise 2
Louise Cook was delighted to discover that there is also a weekly lottery draw in the Philippines. She chose the numbers 4, 11, 16, 34, 39 and 45. Can you help Louise to check her lottery ticket? Listen to this week's numbers as they are broadcast on the radio.

◀) **CD 1, TR 5, 05:43**

Insight
In English grammar, the adjective describes a noun, thus the adjective precedes the noun: for example: **mahabang pila** (*long queue*), **sirang silya** (*broken chair*). In Tagalog, the noun can also come before the adjective and still mean the same thing: for example: **pilang mahaba** (*long queue*) and **silyang sira** (*broken chair*).

2 Counting money

The Philippine peso comes in the following denominations:

Tagalog	Spanish	English
piso	peso	*one peso*
dalawang piso	dos pesos	*two pesos*
tatlong piso	tres pesos	*three pesos*
apat na piso	kuwatro pesos	*four pesos*
limang piso	singko pesos	*five pesos*
anim na piso	sais pesos	*six pesos*
pitong piso	siyete pesos	*seven pesos*
walong piso	otso pesos	*eight pesos*
siyam na piso	nuwebe pesos	*nine pesos*
sampung piso	diyes pesos	*ten pesos*

Exercise 3

Louise Cook found some peso notes in her purse. Using what you have learned so far in this unit, can you help her count the money? Put the subtotal in the column on the right. How much money does she have in her purse altogether?

Sub-total:

1. Limang piso + sampung piso =
2. Limang piso + limang piso =
3. Dalawampung piso + limampung piso =
4. Limampung piso + limampung piso =
5. Limandaang piso + limandaang piso =

_____

Total

Now try repeating this exercise, this time using Spanish numbers.

3 Anong oras na? *Telling the time*

Now that you feel confident with numbers, you will be pleased to hear that telling the time in the Philippines is done almost exclusively in Filipino Spanish. The hours in Filipino Spanish are as follows:

Filipino Spanish	*English*
Ala-una	*One o'clock*
Alas dos	*Two o'clock*
Alas tres	*Three o'clock*
Alas kuwatro	*Four o'clock*
Alas singko	*Five o'clock*
Alas sais	*Six o'clock*
Alas siyete	*Seven o'clock*
Alas-otso	*Eight o'clock*
Alas nuwebe	*Nine o'clock*
Alas diyes	*Ten o'clock*
Alas-onse	*Eleven o'clock*
Alas dose	*Twelve o'clock*

To say 'half past' the hour, simply mention the hour followed by 'y medya' (pronounced: '*eeh mehd-yah*'). For example, 3.30 would be 'alas tres y medya'.

To say XX minutes <u>past</u> the hour, simply mention the hour followed by the minutes in Filipino Spanish (see table). For example, twenty five minutes past six would be '**alas sais beinte singko**'. Quarter past ten would be: '**Alas diyes kinse**'.

To say XX minutes <u>before</u> the hour, simply say: '**menos XX** _____ [*number of minutes*] **para alas** _____ [*the hour*]'.

For example, twenty minutes to three: '**menos beinte para alas tres**'. Ten minutes to eleven would read: '**menos diyes para alas onse**', and so on.

To ask the time, simply say: '**Anong oras na?**'

Exercise 4
'Anong oras na?' Can you tell the time?

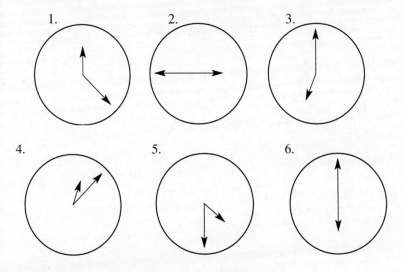

2 *Magkano, magkakano* How much, how much each?

In Dialogue 1 of this unit, Bill Cook purchased some envelopes from the local sarisari store. The question word he used was **magkano** (how much). He said: 'Magkano naman?' (How much is it?). **Magkano** simply means *how much*. For example: 'Magkano ang Tee-shirt?' *How much is the tee-shirt?* **Magkano** may also refer to the total sum of your purchase/s. Be careful, however, not to confuse **magkano** (how much) and **magkakano** which means *how much each*. For example, if there are many mangoes in a basket, unless you want to buy the whole basket of mangoes, you need to ask: 'magkakano ang mangga?' *How much are the mangoes each?*

Responding to *magkano* and *magkakano*

Now that you are confident in asking 'how much' or 'how much each', how do you respond to these questions? There are two basic ways of responding: 1) Replace **magkano** or **magkakano** with the price of the item and then repeat the whole sentence; 2) simply give the price.

Question	Reply	Quick reply
1. **Magkano** ang isang yarda ng lace?	₱35.00 ang isang yarda ng lace.	₱35.00.
How much is a yard of lace?	*A yard of lace costs ₱35.00.*	*₱35.00.*
2. **Magkano** ang sombrero?	₱95.00 **po** ang sombrero	₱95.00 **po.**
How much is the hat?	*The hat costs ₱95.00* (formal)	*₱95.00 sir/madam.* (formal)
3. **Magkakano** ang kandila?	₱15.00 ang isa.	₱15.00.
How much each are the candles?	*The candles are ₱15.00 each*	*₱15.00.*

Haggling

Dialogue 2

◀) CD 1, TR 5, 06:29

While sightseeing Louise Cook finds herself at an open market. She begins speaking with a woman standing behind one of the market stalls.

Tindera	Bili na, bili na. **Murang-mu**ra.
Louise	Magka**ka**no ang som**brero**?
Tindera	Ma'am **mu**ra lang *po*. Tig-siy**en**to sing**kwen**ta **pe**sos *po*.
Louise	**Mu**ra? Kay m**ahal** *nga* eh!
Tindera	A**ba**, magan**da** *po* iyan. Bunt**al** *po*, **ting**nan nin**yo** – i**su**kat *po* nin**yo**.
Louise	(Isinukat) **Medy**o malii**t**. *Wala* bang **ta**wad?
Tindera	**Mu**ra na *po*. Mag**kan**o ba ang **gus**to nin**yo**?
Louise	Si**ten**ta y **sing**ko **pe**sos.
Tindera	Ka**yo** nam**an**! *Hindi po*. Malu**lu**gi *po* ako. **Si**ge, siy**en**to **bein**te **pe**sos *po*.
Louise	**E**to lang ang **pe**ra ko, ot**sen**ta **pe**sos.
Tindera	Isan**daan** *po*, **mu**ra na *po* iy**an**.
Louise	Ot**sen**ta lang tala**ga**.
Tindera	No**ben**ta *po*, ma**ya**man nam**an** ka**yo**.
Louise	O, **si**ge, ot**sen**ta y **sing**ko, kung *hindi*, *hindi* na **ba**le.
Tindera	**Si**ge na *po*, ot**sen**ta y **sing**ko.
Louise	Sal**a**mat, **e**to ang **ba**yad ko.

tindera	*vendor*
bili na	*come and buy*
murang-mura	*very cheap*
tig-siyento singkuwenta pesos	*₱150.00 each*
kay mahal nga	*in fact it's expensive*
buntal	*a kind of Philippine fibre*
tingnan ninyo	*you have a look*
isukat ninyo	*you try*
medyo maliit	*slightly small*
wala bang tawad?	*any chance of a discount?*
gusto ninyo	*you like*
kayo naman	*Oh, you*
malulugi	*I'll lose*
eto lang	*just this*
talaga	*really*
mayaman naman kayo	*anyway you are rich*
o, sige	*all right/okay*
kung hindi	*if not*
hindi na bale	*never mind*

QUICK VOCAB

Translation

Vendor	Come and buy, come and buy. Very cheap.
Louise	How much each are the hats?
Vendor	Ma'am so cheap. (They're) ₱150.00 each.
Louise	Cheap? Actually they're expensive!
Vendor	They're pretty. Made of buntal. Just look at them – why don't you try one?
Louise	(*Trying one on*) A little bit small. No discount?
Vendor	That's ever so cheap. How much do you want to pay (for it)?
Louise	₱75.00.
Vendor	Please! I can't. I'll lose out. (It won't even pay for my overheads!). Okay, ₱120.00 ma'am.
Louise	This is all the money I've got, ₱80.00.
Vendor	One hundred pesos ma'am, that's ever so cheap.
Louise	I can only really pay ₱80.00.
Vendor	₱90.00 ma'am, anyway you are rich.
Louise	Okay, ₱85.00, if not, never mind (I won't buy it).
Vendor	Okay ma'am, ₱85.00.
Louise	Thank you, here you are. (*lit, here's my payment*)

Exercise 5

Imagine you are at a local market in the Philippines. Try asking how much different items are, using both **magkano** and **magkakano**. Use the **Quick vocab** to help you. Why not ask your Filipino friends to help you, too!

Insight

Part of the pleasure of gift-giving is to see the delight on the recipient's face when the gift is opened. But many Filipinos will frown upon opening a gift in the presence of the giver. To do so implies a materialistic concern for the gift itself, rather than valuing their relationship with the giver.

mangga	*mango*
guyabano	*soursop*
dalandan	*oranges*
papaya	*papaya*

pinya	*pineapple*
saging	*banana*
lanzones	*lanzones* (tropical fruit, similar to lychee)
bayabas	*guava*
talong	*eggplant* (aubergine)
ampalaya	*bitter melon*
kalabasa	*squash*
sili	*hot pepper*
kamatis	*tomatoes*
pechay	*pakchoi* (Chinese cabbage)
repolyo	*cabbage*

Changing currency and travellers' cheques at the bank

◀) CD 1, TR 5, 07:58

Dialogue 3

Bill and Louise Cook want to change some money at the bank. Bill strikes up a conversation with one of the bank tellers.

Teller	Maganda**ng** um**a**ga *po*. Ano *po* ang maipag**lilingkod** ko sa in**yo**?
Bill	Maganda**ng** um**a**ga nam**an**. **Gus**to kong **mag**papa**lit** ng sterling pounds.
Teller	Mag**ka**no *po*?
Bill	Lim**an**daang sterling pounds. Mag**ka**no ba ang pa**lit**?
Teller	Sis**en**ta y **ot**so **pe**sos po sa is**ang** sterling pound.
Bill	O **si**ge. **He**to. (Iniab**ot**)
Teller	(Bumil**an**g). O, **he**to *po* ang **pe**ra at re**ci**bo nin**yo**.
Bill	Nag**pa**palit din ba ka**yo** ng travellers cheques?
Teller	Opo. Pero sis**en**ta **pe**sos *po* ang pa**lit**. Kai**la**ngan *po* **na**min ang pasa**por**te nin**yo**.
Bill	**He**to ang travellers cheques at ang pasaporte ko.
Teller	**Si**ge *po*, pirmahan lang *po* nin**yo** ang mga **tse**ke.
Bill	Sa**la**mat.

ano po ang maipaglilingkod ko	*what (service) can I do?*
gusto kong magpapalit ng	*I want to change some*
ang palit	*the exchange rate*
sa isang	*to one/against one*
iniabot	*handed over*
bumilang	*counted*
pera at recibo ninyo	*your money and receipt*
nagpapalit din ba kayo	*do you also change?*
kailangan po namin	*we need*
pasaporte ninyo	*your passport*
pirmahan lang	*(just) please sign*
ang mga tseke	*the cheques*

Translation

Teller	Good morning sir. What can I do for you?
Bill	Good morning to you too. I'd like to change some sterling pounds.
Teller	How much sir?
Bill	£500.00. What (*how much*) is the exchange rate?
Teller	(It's) 68 pesos to a sterling pound.
Bill	Okay. Here you are. (*Handing him the money*)
Teller	(*Counting*) Here's your money and receipt sir.
Bill	Do you also change travellers' cheques?
Teller	Yes sir. But the exchange rate is 60 pesos to a sterling pound. We'll need your passport.
Bill	Here are my travellers' cheques and my passport.
Teller	Kindly (*please*) sign the cheques, sir.
Bill	Thank you.

Exercise 6

How much of the conversation at the bank can you remember? Listen to the CD again and follow Dialogue 3. The following statements or questions appeared in the dialogue.

◀） **CD 1, TR 5, 07:58**

True or false?:

1. Ano po ang maipaglilingkod ko sa inyo?   True/False
2. Magkano ba ang palit?   True/False

3. Sisenta pesos po ang palit.   True/False

4. Nagpapalit din ba kayo ng sterling pounds?   True/False

5. Pirmahan lang po ninyo ang mga tseke.   True/False

Exercise 7

How do you ask the following in Tagalog?

1. I'd like to change some dollars.
2. What is the exchange rate?
3. The exchange rate is 40 pesos.
4. Do you also exchange Australian dollars?

Use the dialogue and the **Quick vocab** provided to help you.

Exercise 8
Listening and understanding

◀) **CD 1, TR 5, 08:59**

A common form of recreation for Filipino men is cockfighting. Many men rear and train fighting cocks in the hope of winning prestige and, of course, making money. Let us now join a group of men at a 'sabungan' (cockfighting pit).

1. How much money are they betting on the red fighting cock? ('sa pula')?
2. How much are they betting on the white fighting cock ('sa puti')?

One-minute phrases

> **Atik** (*ah-teek*) Street word for **pera**, *money*. Someone who has a lot of money is **maatik**.
>
> **Perahin na lang** (*peh-rah-heen nah lahng*) Literally, *just to make into money,* meaning *just give cash/money instead of goods etc.*
>
> **Nakatuntong sa numero** (*nah-kah-toon-tawng sah noo-meh-raw*) Literally, *stepping on numbers.* This Tagalog expression is used to refer to someone who is constantly subject to scrutiny, *making*

him/her feel uneasy. A person who has to constantly *watch his/her ps and qs*.

Isang katutak (*ee-sahng kah-too-tahk*) Literally, *one/a load of/more than plenty*. This phrase is used in connection with surplus or abundance. For example: **Isang katutak ang pagkain sa pinggan ko!** *I've got plenty of food on my plate!*

Nagmimiron (*nahg-mee-mee-rawn*) Derived from the verb **nagmamayroon** meaning *pretending to possess something*. This phrase is often used in connection with a person who is seen to be 'showing off' or 'bragging', or for someone who is ogling.

Insight

As in so many countries around the world, prices often increase when the shopkeeper, vendor or salesperson sees that the customer is a foreigner. Be patient with this. Don't be afraid to try out your Tagalog, even if they speak back to you in broken English. You will find that with a smile and even a little Tagalog, the price will go down. Don't be afraid to haggle in the markets and in small stores. Don't try to haggle in big stores as prices there are fixed.

Summary

1. **Magkano** = '*how much?*'.
2. In response to **magkano**, replace **magkano** with the price.
3. **Magkakano** = '*how much each?*'.
4. **Ilan** = '*how many?*'. Reply in Tagalog or English.
5. Tagalog numbers are normally used in counting.
6. House numbers are in English.
7. Prices in supermarkets and department stores are usually in English.

8. Time is usually **given** in Spanish but **asked** in Tagalog: **Anong oras na?** '*What time is it now?*'
9. In marketplaces, prices can be in Spanish or English.
10. It is possible to haggle in marketplaces but not in big stores as the prices there are fixed.

6

Saan ka nakatira?
Where do you live?

In this unit you will learn how to:

- Use the question word **saan**
- Follow directions

Using the question word *saan*

Dialogue 1

🔊 **CD 1, TR 6**

Roy Cook is waiting at a bus stop. He's off to Makati, the heart of the business and commercial district of Manila. While waiting, Roy notices his old friend Manny and strikes up a conversation with him.

Roy	O, ano Manny, kumusta ka?
Manny	Roy, ikaw ba talaga? Bakasyon ka ba?
Roy	Ako *nga*. Oo kasama ko ang mga magulang ko.
Manny	Saan ang punta mo?
Roy	Sa Makati Mega Mall lang kasi masyadong mainit ngayon.
Manny	Doon din ang punta ko. Sabay na tayo.
Roy	Mabuti. Saan kayo nakatira ngayon?
Manny	Sa Sikatuna Village, malapit sa Diliman.
Roy	Saan sa Sikatuna Village? May kilala ako doon.
Manny	Sa may simbahang Katoliko, numero uno, tres, otso. Pumunta ka sa bahay ha? Heto ang mapa.
Roy	Salamat. O, Makati na pala ito!!!

ikaw ba talaga	*is it really you?*
sa	*in/on/at/in the/on the/at the*
bakasyon ka ba	*are you on vacation?*
nga	*indeed/it's true*
kasama ko	*I'm with*
mga magulang ko	*my parents*
saan	*where* (direction)
ang punta mo	*your destination*
masyadong mainit	*too/very/quite hot*
ngayon	*now/today*
doon	*there*
din	*also/too/as well*
sabay na	*do it together/at the same time*
nakatira	*living/residence*
may kilala ako	*I know someone*
sa may	*near*
simbahan	*church*
numero	*number*
uno, tres, otso	*one, three, eight*
pumunta ka	*you go/you visit/stop by*
sa bahay	*at my place*
ang mapa	*the map*
Makati na pala ito	*ah, we've arrived in Makati already* (literally, so this is Makati already)

QUICK VOCAB

Translation

Roy	Hey, Manny, how are you?
Manny	Roy, is it really you? Are you on vacation?
Roy	I am indeed. I'm with my parents.
Manny	Where are you going?
Roy	To Makati Mega Mall because it's so hot today.
Manny	I'm also going there. Let's go together.
Roy	Good. Where are you living now?
Manny	At Sikatuna Village, near to Diliman.
Roy	Where in Sikatuna Village? I know someone there.
Manny	Near the Catholic Church, number one, three, eight (Why not) Stop by the house? Here's the map.
Roy	Thanks. Ah, we've arrived in Makati already!

Language skills

1 *Saan?* Where?

In Dialogue 1, Roy Cook introduces us to a new question word: **saan** or 'where'. He asks Manny: '**Saan** ang punta mo? (*Where are you going?*). '**Saan** kayo nakatira? (Where do you live?) Be careful not to confuse **saan** with the question word **nasaan** we first met in Unit 4. Although both **saan** and **nasaan** can be translated into English as 'where', both question words perform different functions in Tagalog and so need to be addressed separately.

Saan has two major uses: 1) it represents the place where the action expressed in a sentence occurs. For example: **Saan** ka bumili ng selyo? (*Where did you buy stamps?*); 2) it represents a continuing condition. Example: **Saan** ka nakaupo? (*Where are you seated?*) When using **saan** as a question word, the reply should begin with '**sa**' followed by the place where the action occurred in the sentence.

In summary, the difference between **nasaan** and **saan** is quite simple: whereas both questions may refer to location ('where?'), only **saan** questions refer to either the *place of action*, or to *a continuing condition*. For example: **Nasaan** si Richard? Where [location] is

Richard? **Saan** matutulog si Richard? Where will Richard sleep [action]? Don't worry if this sounds a bit heavy going. It will soon become clear to you. Study the following examples and then re-read the explanation.

Examples:

1. Tagalog: **Saan** tayo kakain?
Literal: Where we will eat?
English: Where are we going to eat?
Reply: **Sa** Dad's (At Dad's)

2. Tagalog: **Saan** ka nagpagupit?
Literal: Where you have a haircut?
English: Where did you have a haircut?
Reply: **Sa** Rudy's Barber Shop (At Rudy's Barber Shop)

3. Tagalog: **Saan** sila matutulog?
Literal: Where they will sleep?
English: Where will they sleep?
Reply: **Sa** bahay ko (At my house)

4. Tagalog: **Saan** mag-aaral si Tessie?
Literal: Where will study Tessie?
English: Where will Tessie study?
Reply: **Sa** St Paul's (At St Paul's)

5. Tagalog: **Saan** nakahiga ang bata?
Literal: Where lying down the child?
English: Where is the child lying down?
Reply: **Sa** kama (On the bed)

6. Tagalog: **Saan** sila nakatayo?
Literal: Where they standing?
English: Where are they standing?
Reply: **Sa** harapan (At the front)

7. Tagalog: **Saan** naupo ang babae?
Literal: Where sat the woman?
English: Where did the woman sit?
Reply: **Sa** bagong silya (On the new chair)

8. Tagalog: **Saan** bumili ng sorbetes ang mga bata?
Literal: Where bought ice cream the children?
English: Where did the children buy ice cream?
Reply: **Sa** Ben & Jerry's (At Ben & Jerry's)

kakain	*will eat*
nagpagupit	*had a haircut*
matutulog	*will sleep*
mag-aaral	*will study*
nakahiga	*lying down*
nakatayo	*standing*
naupo	*sat*
bumili	*bought*
sorbetes	*ice cream*

Insight

The use of **nasaan** is quite different from **saan** in that the **na** in **nasaan** tells us where the *subject* is. **Saan**, on the other hand, is used to let us know where an *action* is or was performed. For example: *Where did you eat?* **Saan ka kumain?** To know where the *subject* is, we use **nasaan**. For example: *Where is London?* **Nasaan ang London?** Here, the subject is London, hence **nasaan** is used.

Exercise 1

Listen to Dialogue 1 again and follow the transcribed conversation. You will notice that the dialogue has been repeated for a second time on the CD, but this time, Manny's voice has been omitted. Using the text provided, why not try out the role of Manny.

◄» **CD 1, TR 6, 01:11**

Exercise 2

Here are some sentences with the words jumbled up. Can you put the words back into the correct order to make a good **saan** sentence? Use the explanation and examples to guide you.

1. nakatira/sila/saan.
   Answer: _____
   Translation: Where do they live?

2. kayo/matutulog/saan.
   Answer: _____
   Translation: Where will you sleep?

3. Nag-aaral/saan/sina Lucy.
   Answer: _____
   Translation: Where do Lucy and her friends study?

4. bumibili/saan/po kayo/ng sorbetes.
   Answer: _____
   Translation: Where do you buy ice cream? (formal)

5. Si Adam/kakain/saan/ng almusal.
   Answer: _____
   Translation: Where will Adam eat breakfast?

nag-aaral	*studying/study*
bumibili	*buying/buy*

QV

Finding an address on a map

Dialogue 2

🔊 CD 1, TR 6, 02:23

Roy decided to call Manny on the telephone. Manny is giving Roy instructions on how to get to his house.

Roy	Hello Manny, si Roy ito.
Manny	Kum**us**ta Roy, **pu**punta ka ba **ri**to?
Roy	Oo, **pe**ro pak**iu**lit mo nga ang ti**ra**han mo. *Hindi* ba mas**ya**dong ma**la**yo iy**an**?
Manny	Okey lang. Mas**ya**dong ma**la**pit nga eh! Ting**nan** mo ang **ma**pa. Naki**ki**ta mo ba ang sim**ba**hang Ka**to**liko?

Roy	Oo. **Na**sa Kalye Vito ito.
Manny	**U**na, *bumaba* ka sa McDonald's. Iyan ay **Ka**lye Sanchez. Dumi**ret**so ka **bu**hat sa McDonald's. Naki**ki**ta mo ba ang **Ka**lye Roxas?
Roy	Oo.
Manny	Tuma**wid** ka do**on** – iyan ang **kal**ye na**min**, **Kal**ye Simeon. Ka**mi** ay **nu**mero **u**no, tres, **o**tso. May ka**sa**ma ka ba?
Roy	*Wala*. Nag-iisa a**ko**. Hinta**yin** mo a**ko**.

pupunta ka ba	*are you going to*
pakiulit mo nga	*please repeat*
tirahan	*residence/address*
nakikita mo	*you see/you are seeing*
Katoliko	*Catholic*
una	*first*
bumaba ka	*you alight/get off*
iyan	*that*
kalye namin	*our street*
kami ay	*we are*
kasama	*companion*
nag-iisa	*alone*
hintayin mo ako	*wait for me*

Translation

Roy	Hello Manny, this is Roy.
Manny	How are you Roy, are you coming over?
Roy	Yes, but can you repeat your address for me? Isn't it very far?
Manny	It's ok. In fact it's quite near. Look at the map. Can you see a Catholic church?
Roy	Yes, it is along Vito Street.
Manny	First, get off at McDonald's. That is Sanchez Street. From McDonald's walk straight ahead. Can you see Roxas Street?
Roy	Yes.
Manny	Cross there. That's our street, Simeon Street
	We are (Our house is) number one three eight. Do you have somebody with you? (literally, *do you have a companion?*)
Roy	No, I'm alone. Wait for me.

More useful words

plaza	*town square*
ospital	*hospital*
munisipyo	*municipal offices*
kapitolyong panglalawigan	*provincial capital*
korte	*court*
istasyon ng pulis	*police station*
sementeryo	*cemetery*
Bulwagang Pambarangay	*Barangay Hall*
palengke	*market*
LRT	*light rail transit*

Exercise 3
Fill in the right word using a word from the box.

bahay	kasama	ka	mapa	nakikita

1. Pupunta _____ ba sa hotel?
2. Sa Kalye Simeon ang _____ namin.
3. Saan sa _____ ang simbahang Katoliko?
4. _____ mo ba ang McDonald's?
5. Sino ang _____ mo?

Exercise 4
Match up the question with the correct answer:

Question

Answer

1. Masyadong malayo ba ang tirahan ni Manny?
2. Saan nakatira si Manny?
3. Saan dapat tumawid si Manny?
4. May kasama ba si Roy?
5. Nasaan ang simbahang Katoliko?

a. Walang kasama si Roy
b. Nasa Kalye Vito ito.
c. Sa Sikatuna Village.
d. Hindi. Masyadong malapit ito.
e. Sa Kalye Roxas.

Language skills

2 *Masyado* *So, very, quite, too, etc.*

Remember the adjectives (describing words) you have already met? Well, the good news is that there are some interesting ways of 'spicing up' your adjectives with small words such as *too, quite, very, so*, etc. These small words are known as 'adverbs'. You can spot them easily because in addition to being small, they always go in front of the adjective. For example, quite (adverb) + handsome (adjective) = quite handsome; so (adverb) + hot (adjective) = so hot, etc. Adverbs give additional information about adjectives. This means that if you want to give extra impact to your adjectives, you need to use an adverb or adverbs. In Tagalog, adverbs such as *so, very, quite, too* are represented by a single word: '**masyado**'. Adverbs work in Tagalog in just about the same way as they do in English. As with English adverbs (e.g. 'quite'), **masyado** can appear on its own. However, when **masyado** is used in connection with an adjective, it is placed before the adjective. In order to help the sentence flow better, '**ng**' is attached to the end of the word '**masyado**'. For example: masyado + ng (very) + marumi (dirty) = masyadong marumi (very dirty); masyadong mataas (too high), masyadong mahaba (very long) and so on. Of course, there are other kinds of adverbs but we will deal with those as they come along.

Here are some examples of adverb + adjective combinations:

Masyado + ng + adjective	=	Combination	English
Masyadong + malaki	=	masyadong malaki	*very big*
Masyadong + malamig	=	masyadong malamig	*too cold*
Masyadong + mabilis	=	masyadong mabilis	*so fast*
Masyadong + mainit	=	masyadong mainit	*very hot*
Masyadong + madaldal	=	masyadong madaldal	*very talkative*
Masyadong + mataas	=	masyadong mataas	*quite high*
Masyadong + madilim	=	masyadong madilim	*very dark*
Masyadong + malakas	=	masyadong malakas	*quite loud, very strong*
Masyadong + mahina	=	masyadong mahina	*too soft (volume), very weak*
Masyadong + mabagal	=	masyadong mabagal	*too slow*
Masyadong + mahaba	=	masyadong mahaba	*quite long*

Insight
The Philippines is full of fascinating sights and sounds for the traveller. To be curious in a new environment is natural, but be careful not to stare. At best, Filipinos regard staring as rude. At worst, staring can be interpreted as aggressive.

Exercise 5 Sentence building
Can you fill in the spaces with the right word or combination of words that you can find in the **Quick vocab**?

> **Magbabakasyon si Phil at si Tina sa Pilipinas!**
> *Phil and Tina will go on Holiday to the Philippines*
>
> Nasa eroplano si Phil at si Tina. _____ sila sa Pilipinas.
> _____ _____ (40 c) sa Pilipinas pero doon sila
> magbabakasyon. _____ _____ daw ang Pilipinas
> (17,000 milya _____ _____ Heathrow). Ang eroplano ay
> _____ _____ na. Sabi ng _____ _____
> _____ alas 9:30 daw nang umaga _____ _____ ng
> eroplano sa paliparan.

masyadong mainit	*very hot*
masyadong mataas	*quite high*
kapitan ng eroplano	*captain of the airplane*
magbabakasyon	*will go on vacation*
ang dating	*time of arrival*
masyadong malayo	*quite far*
buhat sa	*from*

Finding the right Jeepney/bus

◀) CD 1, TR 6, 03:35

Dialogue 3

Roy has decided to take a Jeepney to Manny's place. There are many
Jeepneys in Manila so Roy wants to make sure that he gets on the
right one.

Roy	Papunta ba ito sa Sikatuna Village?
Drayber	Opo. Saan po ba doon?
Roy	Sa McDonald's sa Kalye Sanchez.
Drayber	OK po, hihinto ito sa McDonald's.
Roy	Magkano ang pamasahe hanggang sa Sikatuna?
Drayber	Dos singkwenta lang po.
Roy	Heto ang bayad. Pakipara mo sa Kalye Sanchez ha?
Drayber	Opo.

papunta ba ito sa	*is this going to*
saan po ba	*where sir?*
hihinto ito	*this will stop*
ang pamasahe	*the fare*
hanggang sa	*until*
dos singkwenta	*2.50 pesos*
heto ang bayad ko	*here's my fare*
pakipara mo	*please stop at*

Translation

Roy	Is this going to Sikatuna Village?
Driver	Yes sir, where (in Sikatuna Village)?
Roy	McDonald's on Sanchez Street.
Driver	OK sir, we will be stopping there. (literally, *this will stop*)
Roy	How much is the fare to Sikatuna Village?
Driver	It's 2.50 pesos sir.
Roy	Here's my fare. Please stop at Sanchez Street, OK?
Driver	Yes sir.

Exercise 6

Imagine that you are going to visit a friend in the Diliman area of Metro Manila. Use Dialogue 3 and the **Quick vocab** to help you form your own dialogue. Use your **CD** to make the exercise more realistic and more fun:

◄» CD 1, TR 6, 04:20

Ikaw	_____
Drayber	Opo. Saan po ba doon?
Ikaw	_____
Drayber	Okay po, hihinto ito sa _____
Ikaw	_____ hanggang sa _____
Drayber	Tres singkwenta lang po.
Ikaw	_____
Drayber	Opo.

One-minute phrases

Kilala ko siya (*kee-lah-lah kaw see-yah*) Literally, *I know him/her*. This expression is used to mean that a person knows 'of' someone (has heard of them/shook hands with them or they have been introduced to each other). The expression does not necessarily mean that they know the person as a friend or acquaintance. For example: **Kilala niya ang asawa ng gobernador.** *He/she knows the governor's wife/husband.*

Do not mistake the above with

Kakilala ko siya (*kah-kee-lah-lah kaw-see-yah*) Literally *He/she is an acquaintance*. For example: **Kakilala ko si Bobbie Rodero.** *Bobbie Rodero is my acquaintance.*

Matalik na kaibigan (*mah-tah-leek nah kah-ee-bee gahn*) Meaning *best friend*. For example: **Matalik na kaibigan ko si Jun Terra.** *Jun Terra is my best friend.*

Mabilis magpatakbo (*mah-bee-lees mahg-pah-tahk-boo*) Literally, *fast to run a vehicle*. Meaning: *a fast driver*. For example: **Mabilis magpatakbo ang aming drayber kaya maaga kaming nakarating sa paliparan.** *Ours was a fast driver so we arrived at the airport early.*

Huling biyahe (*hoo-leeng bee-yah-heeh*) Meaning: *last trip*. For example: **Anong oras ang huling biyahe ninyo papunta sa Calapan?** *What time is your last trip to Calapan?*

Insight

The Jeepney is a mode of transport unique to the Philippines. Originally modelled on the US army Jeep, it has since been transformed into the most common form of public transport on Philippine roads. Jeepneys are easily identifiable by their typically colourful and lavish decoration. They are probably the cheapest means of transport available, although not always the most comfortable! If you wish to ride on a jeepney, don't forget that there are few official 'stopping' places and so you will have to inform the driver when and where you want to get off.

Destinations and routes are usually written on both the front and the side of the Jeepney. You can hail Jeepneys in most places except on main roads where stricter traffic regulations apply. If in doubt, ask a local!

Summary

1. **Saan** = *where*. Used when asking the name of a place.
2. **Saan** is used with a main verb. '*Where do you buy..?*
3. **Nasaan** indicates the location of the subject.
4. **Nakatira** = *live/living*.
5. '*Where do you live*' = **Saan ka nakatira.**
6. **Masyado** is an adverb meaning: '*very, quite, so*'.
7. Add **ng** to **masyado** when describing an adjective. **Masyado + ng = Masyadong** e.g., **masyadong malayo** (*very far*).
8. It is possible to intensify by saying **masyadong-masyado**.
9. **Papunta** = *going to* (in the direction of).
10. '*Para*' = *Stop*! Used to ask a driver to stop.

7

Ang pamilya ko
My family

In this unit you will learn how to:

- Introduce the members of your family
- Use **ay** in a sentence
- Use possessive pronouns

Introducing the members of your family

Dialogue 1

◀) **CD 1, TR 7**

At the Abiva house, Tita Abiva is showing her family album to Bill and Louise Cook.

Tita	Ito ay larawan ng pamilya ko. Sa likuran, buhat sa *kaliwa* ay si Tatay, si ate Azon at si Jake ang asawa niya, si Edith ang asawa ni Jose, si Louie ang asawa ni Citta, at ito ay si Nanay.

pinakabunso	*youngest*
larawan	*photograph/picture*
ng pamilya ko	*of my family*
sa likuran	*behind/at the back*
ang pamilya ninyo	*your family*
tatay	*father*
asawa	*spouse*
pero	*but*
ang asawa niya	*her/his partner*
binata	*bachelor*
na katabi ko	*(who's) next to me*
katabi ni	*next to*
nasa likuran	*at the back*
ng pamilya namin	*of our family*
ang asawa ko	*my partner*
malaki-laki	*quite big*
ate	*elder sister*
harapan	*front*
malaking pamilya	*big family*
kapag	*if/when*
masayang pamilya	*happy family*
nasa harapan	*in front*

QUICK VOCAB

Translation

Tita	This is a photograph of my family. At the back, from the left that is (my) father, (my) older sister Azon and her husband Jake, Edith the wife of Jose, Louie, the husband of Citta and this is (my) mother.
Bill	[and] Those in the front?
Tita	The ones in front, from the left are Ely who is unmarried, Dino (who is) seated next to me, (he) is a bachelor and the youngest in our family, and this is Toto my husband.

| **Bill** | Your family is quite big. |
| **Tita** | Yes, but a big family is a happy family. |

Exercise 1

Look at the picture of the Abiva family in Dialogue 1. Imagine that Tita Abiva has asked **you** to explain to the Cooks 'who is who' in the picture. Remember, your answer should begin with '**nasa**' as you will need to show the *location* of the person. In your answers, use the words from the box below. The dialogue and **Quick vocab** may also be of help to you.

nasa likuran	kaliwa	katabi ni	nasa harapan	kanan

Example: Tatay.   Answer: **Nasa likuran, sa kaliwa.**

1. Si Ate Azon at si Jake.   Answer:
2. Si Ely.   Answer:
3. Si Tita.   Answer:
4. Si Citta.   Answer:
5. Si Toto.   Answer:
6. Si Dino.   Answer:

The Filipino family tree

Tagalog	Pronunciation	English
nanay/inay	*nah-nigh/ee-nigh*	*mother*
tatay/itay	*tah-tigh/ee-tigh*	*father*
ate	*ah-te*	*older sister*
kuya	*koo-yah*	*older brother*
kapatid	*kah-pah-teed*	*sibling*
kapatid na lalaki	*kah-pah teed nah lah-lah-kee*	*brother*
kapatad na babae	*kah-pah teed nah bah-bah-ee*	*sister*
tiyo	*tee-yaw*	*uncle*
tiya	*tee-yah*	*aunt*
lolo	*law-law*	*grandfather*
lola	*law-lah*	*grandmother*
apo	*ah-paw*	*grandchild*
bayaw	*bah-yao*	*brother-in-law*
hipag	*hee-pahg*	*sister-in-law*
pamangkin	*pah-mahng-keen*	*nephew/niece*
asawa	*ah-sah-wah*	*husband/wife*

Language skills

1 *Ko, mo, niya, namin, natin, ninyo, nila*
Possessive pronouns

If you look closely at Dialogue 1, you will notice that the words **ko** (*my*), **niya** (*his/her*) and **namin** (*our*) have one thing in common: they express *ownership* or *possession*. These words are known as **possessive pronouns**. Possessive pronouns are used in two basic ways: 1) they tell us about *ownership*, i.e. 'ang pasaporte **ko**' (*my* passport), 'ang guro **namin**' (*our* teacher), 2) they show *relationship* with a person, i.e., 'ang nanay **ko**' (*my* mother), 'ang tatay **namin**' (*our* father). You will notice that in English the possessive pronoun goes in front of the thing (*noun*) it possesses. For example: **your** name, **his** house, **my** father, **our** country and so on. In Tagalog, the order is reversed with the possessive pronoun being placed *after* the word it possesses. For example: pangalan **mo** (*your* name), bahay **niya** (*his* house), tatay **ko** (*my* father), bansa **natin** (*our* country) and so on. One small but important difference to watch out for is the first person plural. In English, we simply say 'our house', 'our street', 'our village'. Tagalog has two possibilities: one which *includes* the listener (**natin**), and another which *excludes* the listener (**namin**). For example, if I were to speak to you about 'tatay **natin**' or 'our father', then the use of the inclusive form (**natin**) makes it clear that he is also *your* father. If however I talk about 'tatay **namin**', then the use of the exclusive form (**namin**) indicates that he is 'our' father (me, my brothers and sisters) while not implying that he is also your father. Look at the following table:

Personal possessive pronouns

Number		English	Tagalog
1st person	(singular)	*my*	**ko**
	(plural)	*our*	**namin** (exclusive of listener/s)
		our	**natin** (inclusive of listener/s)
2nd person	(singular)	*your*	**mo**
	(plural)	*your*	**ninyo**
3rd person	(singular)	*his/her*	**niya**
	(plural)	*their*	**nila**

Here are some example sentences:

English	Tagalog
1. He/she is **my** friend.	*Kaibigan ko siya*
2. Is he **your** driver?	*Drayber mo ba siya?*
3. We are **their** guest.	*Bisita nila kami*
4. Cora is **our** teacher.	*Guro namin si Cora*
5. Are you **his** friend?	*Kaibigan ka ba niya?*

Exercise 2

Translate the following sentences, using the **Quick vocab** to help you:

1. Margaret is my friend.
2. John is his brother.
3. Ann is their visitor.
4. They are my classmates.

Exercise 3 Listening

bisita	*guest*
mga kaklase	*classmates*
guro	*teacher*

Listen carefully to the accompanying recording, then look at the pictures. Can you tell who is related to whom?

🔊 **CD 1, TR 7, 00:59**

1.

2.

3.   **4.**

Language skills

2 *Ng* *Of/of the*
Ni/nina + *Name of person/s*

Another new word used in Dialogue 1 was 'ng' (pronounced *nang*). Ng is also used to show **possession**. For example: 'ang laruan **ng** bata' (literally, *the toy of the child = the child's toy*), 'baso **ng** tubig' (a glass **of** water), 'ang pintuan **ng** bahay' (*the doorway of the house*). These examples show that **ng** can be translated into English as 'of' or 'of the'. Try to remember, however, that in English, the word **of** often disappears completely and is replaced by an **apostrophe** + **s**. For example, 'the mother **of** the bride' becomes 'the bride's mother', 'the book **of** the student' becomes 'the student's book'. When using a person's name, however, we use the word **ni** instead of **ng**, indicating that the person concerned is the *possessor*. For example, 'Ito ang bahay **ni** Mary' *(this is Mary's house)*. If more than one person is involved, then **nina** is used (the plural of **ni**). For example: 'Ka-opisina siya **nina** Tony'. *He is an officemate of Tony and his friend/s.*

Look at the following examples:

Tagalog	English
ni Jose	**of** Jose/Jose's
nina Jose	**of** Jose and his friends/s'
ni Mary	**of** Mary/Mary's
nina Mary	**of** Mary and her friends/s'
ng bata	**of the** child/the child's
ng mga babae	**of the** women/the women's
ng Presidente	**of the** President/the President's
ni Queen Elizabeth	**of** Queen Elizabeth/Queen Elizabeth's

Here are some full sentences to show this expression in use.

1. Anak **ni** Queen Elizabeth si Prince Charles.
   Prince Charles is the son of Queen Elizabeth.

2. Kotse **ng** Presidente ito.
   This is the car of the President.

3. Doktor **ni** Bennie si Doktor Cruz.
   Doctor Cruz is Bennie's doctor.

4. Maleta **ng** mga babae iyan.
   That is the women's suitcase.

Exercise 4
Fill in the blank with the correct word. Refer to the Language skills above.

1. Kailangan mo ba _____ (ng/ni) tulong ko?
2. Hindi _____ (namin/nina) alam ang tirahan ni Phil.
3. Anak _____ (ni/ng) ginoong Abiva si Jobert.
4. Sino ang kapatid _____ (ng/ng mga) guro?
5. Gusto _____ (ko/nina) ang bagong kotse mo.
6. Nasa mesa ang pagkain _____ (ng/ni) mga bisita.
7. Bukas, narito ang guro _____ (niya/nina).

Exercise 5
Look at the pictures and write a sentence about each using either *ng*, *ni* or *nina*.

Using *ay* in a sentence

Dialogue 2

◀) CD 1, TR 7, 01:50

At the Abiva house, Bill, Louise and Tita continue their conversation.

Louise	Ilan ang anak ninyo?
Tita	Lima. Isa lang ang walang asawa. Heto ang larawan ng mga anak at mga apo ko.
Louise	Sila ay magaganda.
Tita	Kayo, ilan ang anak ninyo?
Louise	Dalawa lang. Si John at si Roy.
Tita	May anak ba si John?
Bill	Oo. Dalawa. Si Adam at si Lucy.
Tita	Maliit ang pamilya ninyo!

Louise	Oo *nga*.
Katulong	Eto *po* ang **pam**palam**ig**.
Tita	Sa**la**mat. **Ta**yo ay **ma**gpalamig **mu**na.

Insight

Oo nga is translated as *I agree*. But **nga** (glottalized) can be used for non-emphatic requests: for example: **Magluto ka nga ng kape.** *Please make some coffee.* **Nga** when added to an imperative sentence changes the imperative from a command to a polite request. **Kumain ka nga.** *Please eat.*

QUICK VOCAB

ilan	*how many*
ang anak ninyo	*your child*
lima sila	*there are five*
isa lang	*only one*
walang asawa	*not married*
ng mga anak	*of the children*
pampalamig	*refreshment*
mga apo ko	*my grandchildren*
dalawa lang	*only two*
anak ninyo	*your children*
pamilya ninyo	*your family*
oo nga	*I agree*
eto po	*here you are*
magpalamig muna	*have some refreshments first*

Translation

Louise	How many children do you have?
Tita	Five. Only one is not (yet) married. Here is a photo of my children and my grandchildren.
Louise	They are beautiful.
Tita	How many children do you have? (literally, *and you, how many children do you have?*)
Louise	Just two. John and Roy.
Tita	Does John have children?
Bill	Yes. Two. Adam and Lucy.
Tita	Your family is small!

Louise	I agree.
Maid	Here is your refreshment ma'am!
Tita	Thank you. Let's have something to drink first (literally, *refreshments*).

Exercise 6

Read the following story. You will notice that several words are missing from the Tagalog dialogue. Using the **Quick vocab** provided, fill in the missing words. Use the English translation to help you.

Donna visits Chit's family in Batangas

Donna	Magandang araw po. Kumusta po kayo? Si Donna po ako. _____ ako ni Chit.
Host	Ikaw ba si Donna? Pasok ka. _____ ka pala. Ilan kayong _____ ?
Donna	Tatlo po. Ako, ang _____ , si Eloisa ang pangalawa, at si Mila, ang _____ . Lahat po kami walang asawa.
Host	Ganoon ba? Kumusta ang mga magulang mo?
Donna	Mabuti po naman sila. Kayo po, ilan po ang _____ _____?
Host	Apat ang _____ _____ .
Donna	_____ ang may asawa?
Host	Isa lang _____ _____. Si Zeny at dalawa na _____ _____ _____. Magpalamig ka muna.
Donna	Maraming salamat po. Ang sarap nito! Kung gayon may _____ na pala kayo.
Host	Oo at maligaya naman ako!
Donna	Mabuti naman at nakilala ko kayo sa wakas.
Host	Ako rin!

Translation

Donna	Good morning (*polite*). How are you? I am Donna – Chit's friend.
Host	Are you Donna? Ah, please come in! You are indeed tall! How many brothers and sisters do you have?
Donna	Three ma'am. I'm the eldest, Eloisa the second and Mila is the youngest. We are all still single.
Host	I see. And how are your parents?
Donna	They are fine ma'am. And how about you ma'am, how many children do you have?

Host	I have four children.
Donna	Are any of them married yet?
Host	Only one so far. Zeny. She has two children. Please have some refreshments.
Donna	Thank you. This is delicious! So, you now have grandchildren!
Host	Yes, and I am very happy about that!
Donna	It is so nice to meet you at last.
Host	You too!

QUICK VOCAB

pinakabunso	*youngest*
matangkad	*tall*
magkakapatid	*siblings*
apo	*grandchild*
pinakamatanda	*eldest*
ang anak niya	*her children*
ang may-asawa	(the) *married* (one)
anak ko	*my children*
ilan	*how many*

Exercise 7

Which question matches which answer?

1. Anak mo ba siya?

    A. Oo. Asawa yata ni Azon si Jake.

2. Nasa silangan ng Pilipinas ang Davao.

    B. Kuya.

3. Ano ang tawag sa matandang kapatid na lalaki?

    C. Hindi. Sa tindahan tayo bumibili ng selyo.

4. Asawa kaya ni Azon si Jake?

    D. Hindi. Hindi ko siya anak.

5. Sa ospital tayo bumibili ng selyo.

    E. Wala. Nasa Timog ito.

Exercise 8 Speaking and listening activity

Listen to the dialogue on the CD. How many of the words or phrases from the conversation between Pepot and Donna can you remember? Listen to the CD again. Here are some snatches from the dialogue. Fill in the missing parts. When you have completed the task, why not ask one of your Filipino friends to help you act out the dialogue?

Donna	O, tuloy ba _____ _____ _____ kina Peps? (*our picnic*)
Pepot	Sino ba ang _____ _____ _____ _____? (*older of the two?*)
Donna	_____ _____ ang tanda ni Romy kay Peps. (*three years*)
Pepot	_____ _____ si Peps. (*younger*)
Donna	_____ _____ng anak ni Romy. (*what is the name*)
Pepot	_____ _____ _____ _____ . (*Don't you know?*)
Donna	Oo. _____ _____ _____ _____ _____. (*she is my mother's sister*).
Pepot	Bibili ako _____ _____ _____ _____ . (*some cold drinks*)
Donna	Sa palagay ko, magiging masaya _____ _____ _____ _____ (*this picnic*).

Language skills

3 *Ay*

Life and language would seem rather boring if we had only one set way of communicating correctly with one another. Fortunately, we can vary sentences in order to add spice, variety and colour to our language. For example, '*Hello Bob, how are you this morning?*' becomes '*Morning Bob, how are you?*' or perhaps '*How are you this morning, Bob?*'. All of these simple sentences communicate the same message, but all are slightly different. Tagalog does much the same thing with the simple word **ay** (pronounced *eye*). This little word has no direct English translation but is useful when it comes to adding variety to our spoken Tagalog. The good news for English speakers is that the word **ay** follows the normal English language sentence structure. It *inverts* the usual sequence of Tagalog words making it resemble its English equivalent. For example, *he is good* (**mabuti siya**) becomes *siya ay mabuti*. You may be forgiven for thinking that **ay** means 'is' or that **ay** is the equivalent of the English verb 'to be', but this is not so. A sentence involving the use of **ay** does not differ in meaning from the sentence without **ay**. It simply offers variety and assists the flow of the sentence. **Ay** can also be used as a more formal style and as such is commonly found in writing, lectures, sermons and so on, although this is only used after vowels. You will no doubt have noticed the use of **ay** in Dialogue 1. **Ay** is often shortened to **'y**. Both forms are correct. You will notice that the shortened **'y** form is most commonly used when following words which end with a vowel. This is not always the case however. For example: **Ito'y maganda,** *This is pretty.* **Ikaw'y guro,** *You are a teacher.*

Here are some more examples.

English	Tagalog	Inverted (*ay* sentence)
They are Americans	Amerikano sila	Sila *ay* Amerikano
The queue is long	Mahaba ang pila	Ang pila *ay* mahaba
Is the chair clean?	Malinis ba ang silya?	Ang silya ba *ay* malinis?
Ann is industrious	Masipag si Ann.	Si Ann *ay* masipag
They are nurses	Mga narses sila.	Sila*'y* mga narses
The vegetable is fresh	Sariwa ang gulay	Ang gulay *ay* sariwa.
The mango is sour	Maasim ang mangga	Ang mangga*'y* maasim
The car is at the garage	Nasa garahe ang kotse	Ang kotse*'y* nasa garahe
He is a doctor here	Doktor siya dito	Siya *ay* doktor dito

Exercise 9

Convert the following standard Tagalog sentences into their equivalent **ay** form sentences:

1. Anak mo siya.
2. May tiket ako.
3. Malamig ang tubig.
4. Mainit ngayon.
5. Masarap ang handa mo.

tiket	*ticket*
malamig	*cold*
tubig	*water*
masarap	*delicious*
handa	*food preparation*

Insight

Filipinos are skilled at declining a request without using a direct refusal. **Hindi** is a perfect example of this. Where refusal has the potential to cause offence or disrupt the harmony of the present moment, Filipinos will commonly find a way around this. To smooth over the situation, you may even hear **Oo** (*yes*). The trick is to listen to the *way* in which *yes* was said. Was there hesitation or reluctance? **Oo** can therefore mean *yes*, *perhaps*, or even *no* (**hindi**).

One-minute phrases

Maghabol sa tambol mayor (*mahg-hah-bawl sah tahm-bawl mah-yor*) Literally, *to chase the principal drum (of a marching band)*. This expression is applied to somebody who has been cheated (i.e. in money, relationships, financial deals, etc.). The expression implies that the victim has no chance of finding justice. Marching bands are a common sight in the Philippines, especially during fiestas, funerals and weddings. *To chase the principal drum*, as the saying goes, takes some doing, as it is a heavy instrument to run away with! The phrase is similar in meaning to the English expressions, *caught napping* or *caught with his pants down!*

Mukhang Biyernes Santo (*mook-hahng beeyer-ness sahn-taw*) Literally, *a face like Good Friday!* This expression is applied to a person who looks gloomy. As a Christian country, the Philippines traditionally observes the celebration of Holy Week. Part of Holy Week is the observance of Good Friday, the solemn remembrance of the day Jesus died. Filipinos tend to disapprove of festivities on Good Friday as a sign of respect for the **Santo Intiero** or *Dead Christ*. Anyone who wears a solemn expression on their face at other times may find themselves on the receiving end of the comment, **Mukhang Biyernes Santo ka!** *You've got a face like Good Friday!*

Parang pinagbiyak na bunga (*pah-rahng pee-nahg-bee-yahk nah boo-ngah*) Literally, *Looks like a fruit chopped in two*. When a piece of fruit is chopped into two halves, the two halves are generally identical. This expression is commonly used therefore to refer to twins.

Kaibigang matalik/matalik na kaibigan (*kah-ee-bee-gahng mah-tah-leek/mah-tah-leek na kah-ee-bee-gahn*) a term which means *best friend*.

Kasa-kasama (*kah-sah-kah-sah-mah*) This expression is used to identify a person commonly seen with another person. For example: **Laging kasa-kasama ni Jun si Bobbie.** *Bobbie is always seen in Jun's company.*

Insight

Show an interest in learning more about the family of your Filipino friends. If you ask politely about children, grandparents, aunts, uncles and cousins, etc., this is understood as a genuine desire to know them and to build friendship. Be ready to talk about your own family too.

Summary

1. **Kapatid** = *sibling*.
2. **Kapatid na lalaki** = *brother*. **Kapatid na babae** = *sister*.
3. **Tatay at Nanay** = *Father and Mother*.
4. **Ko** = *my*, **Mo** = *your*, **niya** = *his/her*.
5. **Namin** = *our* exclusive of listener, **Natin** = *our* inclusive of listener.
6. **Nila** = their.
7. **Ni** used before a person's name, **Nina** is used if more than one person.
8. **Ng** = *of/of the.*
9. For variety, **Ay** is used to reverse the structure of a sentence. e.g., **Guro ako** may become **Ako ay guro.** Both mean: '*I am a teacher.*'
10. **Ay** is often contracted (shortened) **Ako'y guro. Siya'y nars. Tayo'y huli na sa klase.**

8

Sa restawran
At the restaurant

In this unit you will learn how to:

- Order your drinks
- Choose some typical Filipino food
- Ask for your bill
- Make words plural using 'mga'

Ordering your drinks

Dialogue 1

◀) CD 1, TR 8

Bill, Louise and Roy have decided to eat dinner at the local *Kamayan* restaurant.

Waiter	Magan**dang** ga**bi** *po*. Mali**gay**ang pagda**ting** sa 'Kam**ay**an'.
Bill	May **me**sa ba ka**yo** para sa tat**lo**?
Waiter	**May**roon *po*. **He**to *po* ang **me**sa ni**nyo**.
Bill	Sa**la**mat. (*Naupo* ang mag-**a**nak)
Waiter	Sir, **he**to *po* ang menu **na**min. A**no** *po* ang **gu**sto niny**ong** inu**min**?
Bill	Sanda**li** lang. Louise?
Louise	Mala**mig** na **tu**big lang **mu**na. May mineral water ba ka**yo**?
Waiter	**May**roon *po*. Ka**yo** *po* sir?
Bill	San Miguel beer.
Waiter	(kay Roy) Sa in**yo** *po*, sir?
Roy	White wine ang sa **a**kin.
Waiter	Okey *po*. Pulu**tan** sir, **I**big *po* ba nin**yo**.

Bill	Oo. **Ano** ang pulutan nin**yo**?
Waiter	**Ta**pa at lit**son** *po*. Is**ang pla**to o is**ang** plat**i**to *po*?
Bill	Parang masarap. O sige. Isang plato. Salamat.
Waiter	Wala pong anuman.

maligayang pagdating	*welcome*
may mesa ba kayo	*do you have a table*
para sa tatlo	*for three*
malamig na tubig	*cold water*
ang mesa ninyo	*your table*
ang menu namin	*our menu*
ang gusto ninyo	*what you like*
platito	*saucer*
muna	*first/for the time being*
parang	*seems/like*
kay	*to (+ name)*
ang sa akin	*mine*
pulutan	*finger food to go with drinks*
tapa	*sliced fried beef*
litson	*suckling pig*
plato	*plate*

Translation

Waiter	Good evening sir. Welcome to *Kamayan*.
Bill	Do you have a table for three?
Waiter	Yes sir. Here is your table, sir.
Bill	Thank you. (The family sits down)
Waiter	Sir, here's our menu. What would you like to drink?
Bill	Just one moment. (You) Louise?
Louise	I'll have cold water (for the time being). Do you have any mineral water?
Waiter	Yes, we have ma'am. And you sir?
Bill	San Miguel beer.
Waiter	(to Roy) And you, sir?
Roy	I'll have a white wine.
Waiter	OK sir. Finger foods (to go with the drinks) sir, would you like some?
Bill	Yes. What are your pulutan?

Waiter	Sliced fried beef and suckling pig sir. One plate sir, or one saucer?
Bill	Seems delicious. OK, one plate (of finger foods). Thank you.
Waiter	You're welcome sir.

Exercise 1

Can you say the following?

1. There are four of us. (We are four)
2. Do you have a table for four persons?
3. I want (a glass of) cold water.
4. I would like (a bottle of) San Miguel beer.
5. Do you have a big table?

Exercise 2

Look at Dialogue 1 again. Based on this dialogue, can you tell which of the following sentences are true and which are false?

1. Para sa dalawa ang mesa.
2. Ang mesa ay para sa tatlo.
3. Mabuti para kay Louise ang malamig na tubig.
4. Gusto ni Louise ng malamig na beer.
5. Hindi gusto ni Bill ang inumin.
6. San Miguel Beer yata ang gusto ni Bill.

Language skills

1 *Mga* Making words plural

Dialogue 1 introduced us to the word 'mga' (pronounced *mah-ngah*). In jargon, this word is known as a pluralizer. A pluralizer is a word which lets us know that more than one person, place or thing is being referred to. In English, there are three basic ways of indicating the plural: 1) by adding the letter 's' to the end of the pluralized word. Hence, suitcase becomes 'suitcases'; 2) by changing a single letter in the pluralized word. Here, woman becomes women; 3) by adding 'es' to the pluralized word. Here, mango becomes mangoes. Tagalog has a far less complex way of making words plural. Simply add the word mga before the noun you wish to pluralize. For example: **tiket** (*ticket*) becomes **mga** tiket (*tickets*); **babae** (*woman*) becomes **mga babae** (*women*); **Pilipino** (*Filipino*) becomes **mga Pilipino** (*Filipinos*). What could be easier?!

Insight

If the pluralizer **mga** is used in conjunction with **ito**, it precedes the other noun in all cases: for example: **itong mga damit** *these dresses*; **mga damit na ito** *these dresses*.

Exercise 3

Find the correct Tagalog words for the following and then pluralize them.

Did you know . . . ?

Sometimes Tagalog will pluralize adjectives, too. For example **mabuti** (*good*) can become **mabubuti**, **malaki** (*big*) can become **malalaki**. Here the **mga** pluralizer is dropped in favour of repeating the second syllable of the word. In this type of sentence the plural adjective must always precede a plural noun or pronoun.

For example: **maliit siya – maliliit sila.** Don't worry if this seems too complicated for you at this time – you can come back to it later when you feel more confident. Just stick to the **mga** form for the moment.

Exercise 4

Using the **Quick vocab** provided arrange the following muddled up words into correct Tagalog sentences.

1. bisita/sa bahay/na/mga/may.
2. kayo/mga/ba/estudyante?
3. pilipino/sila/mga/hindi.
4. kailangan/ang/ko/at mesa/mga silya.
5. sariwa/mga prutas/na ito/ang.

na	*already*
estudyante	*student*
hindi	*no*
kailangan	*need*
silya	*chair*
sariwa	*fresh*
prutas	*fruit*

Choosing some typical Filipino food

Dialogue 2

◀) **CD 1, TR 8, 01:23**

The Cook family are ready to order. The waiter approaches them.

Waiter	Ibig n'yo na *po* bang um**or**der?
Bill	O**o**. A**ko**, **gus**to ko ng a**do**bong pus**it**, me**cha**do at gini**sang gu**lay. Ik**aw**, Louise? A**no** ang order mo?
Louise	A**ko**, **gus**to ko ng apri**ta**da, sinig**ang** na ban**gus** at **ka**nin. May na**pi**li ka na ba, Roy?
Roy	Op**o**. Muk**hang** mas**arap** ang a**do**bong ma**nok**. **Gus**to ko rin ng pan**sit** at pini**ri**tong **lum**piya.
Waiter	A**no** *po* ang starter nin**yo**? **May**roon pong **so**pas man**ok** o ka**ya**'y sa**ri**wang **lum**pia.
Bill	Sa**ri**wang **lum**pia!

Waiter	Sariwang **lum**pia, sir. Masa**rap** *po* ang **sar**sa.
Bill	**Sa**lamat.
Waiter	*Wala* pong anu**man**.

QUICK VOCAB

ibig n'yo na	*would you like now*
umorder	*to make your order*
sopas manok	*chicken soup*
adobong pusit	*squid adobo*
mechado	*mechado (larded)*
ginisang gulay	*sauteed vegetables*
ano	*what*
apritada	*apritada (a kind of main dish, fried)*
sinigang na bangus	*fish*
kanin	*boiled rice*
may napili	*has selected/chosen*
mukhang masarap	*seems tasty*
abobong manok	*chicken adobo*
starter ninyo	*your starter*
o kaya'y	*or*
sariwa(ng) lumpia	*fresh spring rolls*
rekomendado	*recommended*
sarsa	*sauce/dressing*
gusto ko rin	*I also like*

Translation

Waiter	Would you like to order now?
Bill	I would like squid adobo, mechado and sauteed vegetables. (And) You Louise? What would you like to order?
Louise	I would like apritada, sinigang na bangus [fish] and rice. Have you chosen, Roy?
Roy	Yes, mum. The chicken adobo looks tasty. I would also like noodles and fried lumpia.
Waiter	Sir, what would you like for your starter? There is chicken soup or fresh lumpia.
Bill	Fresh lumpia!
Waiter	Fresh lumpia sir. The salad dressing is delicious!
Bill	Thank you.
Waiter	You're welcome.

Mang Simeon's Kamayan Restaurant
Roxas Boulevard, Manila

Starter:

Tapang baka	₱175.00
Sopas Manok	₱100.00
Lumpiang ubod	₱125.00
Sariwang lumpia	₱125.00
Ensaladang seafood	₱200.00
Pansit luglog	₱125.00

Ulam:

Adobong manok sa gata	₱250.00
Adobong baboy at baka sa toyo	₱300.00
Pansit bihon	₱280.00
Pansit miki	₱280.00
Pansit miki at bihon	₱280.00
Kaldereta	₱300.00
Sinigang na bangus	₱280.00
Pritong tilapia	₱280.00
Ginisang pusit	₱300.00
Menudo	₱200.00
Sinigang na bakang may saging	₱250.00
Kanin	₱100.00
Chinese fried rice	₱120.00

Gulay:

Ginisang munggo	₱65.00
Chop suey	₱150.00
Inihaw na talong	₱60.00

Pamutat:

Leche Flan	₱100.00
Halo-halo	₱150.00
Sorbetes	₱150.00
Minatamisang saging na may yelo	₱150.00

Inumin:

San Miguel beer	₱35.00
Soft Drinks	₱25.00
Fruit Shake	₱40.00
Kape	₱25.00

Service charge not included

Exercise 5

Choose from the list of condiments in the **Quick vocab** and tell the waiter what you would like to have. Use the dialogue to help you.

Waiter	Para sa inihaw na bangus po ba?
You	(Clue: ask for some vinegar for your bangus.)
Waiter	Bakit, matabang po ba?
You	(Clue: ask for some salt.)
Waiter	Ito po ay para sa ensalada?
You	(Clue: ask for some sauce/salad dressing.)
Waiter	Ibig po ba ninyo ito para sa pansit?
You	(Clue: ask for some soy sauce.)

toyo	*soy sauce*
paminta	*pepper*
suka	*vinegar*
sarsa	*sauce/salad dressing*
asin	*salt*
ibig po ba ninyo	*would you want*
gusto ko ng	*I would like/I want*

Insight

Whether at corner stores or in small (**turo-turo**) restaurants along the highway, some delicacies are always on the menu and are sure to tickle Filipino taste buds. Here are a few of the most popular dishes:

Leche flan – A sweet dish consisting of evaporated milk, condensed milk, egg yolks, sugar, lemon peel and vanilla essence. Similar in appearance and taste to *crème caramel*. It is always the main attraction on the buffet table at fiestas and celebrations.

Bilobilo – This popular snack is prepared by mixing water and sticky rice flour. The mixture is then shaped into small balls which in turn are dropped into a pan quarter filled with boiling coconut milk where sugar, shredded jack fruit, pineapple and vanilla have already been added.

Bibingka – Cooked in smouldering coconut husks, **bibingka** has its own unique taste. It is prepared from rice flour, sugar and the flesh of a young (i.e. unripe) coconut. **Bibingka** is placed under a smouldering coconut husk until it turns a slightly brownish colour. Sometimes the top of the **bibingka** is decorated with chopped cheese. Nice to eat when warm, but tends to harden when cold.

Adobong manok – Made by marinating pieces of chicken in vinegar, pepper, garlic, then cooked in coconut milk until tender and aromatic. Seasoned with soy sauce. Served hot as a side dish. **Masarap!**

Language skills

2 Other uses of *Mga*

Mga is also used in Tagalog to express approximation. When used in connection with numbers, it can be understood to mean 'approximately', 'about' or 'around'.

Examples:

Tagalog:	**Mga** apat na kilo ang kailangan ko.
English:	*I need about 4 kilos.*

Tagalog:	**Mga** pito siguro ang darating.
English:	*Perhaps around seven* (people) *will be arriving.*

Tagalog:	Mga isang yarda ang bilhin mo.
English:	*You* [need to] *buy around one yard.*

Mga can also be used when approximating time.

Examples:

Tagalog:	Mga alas dos nang hapon ako babalik.
English:	*I'll be back by around 2.00 p.m.*

Tagalog:	**Mga** alas onse sila natulog kagabi.
English:	*They slept at about 11.00 last night.*

Tagalog: **Mga** alas sais nang umaga ang simula ng misa.
English: *The mass starts at around 6.00 a.m.*

Exercise 6
Complete the following sentences:

1. Gusto ko ng (around 2 kilos) dalanghita.
2. Kailangan namin ng (approximately 3 yards).
3. (Around 2 o'clock) ba ang alis ng bus?
4. (Approximately nine) ang mga bisita nila.
5. Siguro (about eight people) are in the Jeepney.

gusto ko	*I like/want*
dalanghita	*oranges*
kailangan	*need*
alis	*departure*
siguro	*perhaps*

Dialogue 3

The Cook family are enjoying their meal, but they would like to order some more food.

◀) CD 1, TR 8, 02:35

Bill	U**mo**rder pa **ta**yo ng pan**si**t. U**bos** na.
Louise	U**bos** na rin ang **gu**lay at **hi**pon.
Roy	At *saka* a**do**bong ma**nok**. **Tu**big rin.
Bill	(to waiter) **Gu**sto pa **na**min ng: isang **pla**tong pan**si**t, i**sang pla**tong **gu**lay, i**sang pla**tong **hi**pon at a**do**bong ma**nok**.
Waiter	**Ka**nin rin *po* sir?
Bill	Oo. At *saka* mala**mig** na **tub**ig.
Waiter	O**po** sir. Sa**la**mat *po*.
Bill	Wa**lang** anu**man**.

umorder pa tayo	*let's order some more*
ng pansit	*some noodles*
ubos na	*ran out/consumed*
tubig rin	*water too*
gulay at hipon	*vegetables and prawns*

at saka	*and also*
gusto pa namin ng	*we want some more*
isang plato(ng)	*a plate of*
gulay	*vegetables*

Translation

Bill	Let's order some more noodles. (There's) Nothing left!
Louise	No more vegetables and prawns either.
Roy	And chicken adobo too! Water also.
Bill	(to waiter) We would like another plate of noodles, some more vegetables, also prawns and chicken adobo.
Waiter	Rice as well sir?
Bill	Yes, and some cold water too.
Waiter	Yes sir. Thank you.
Bill	You're welcome.

Exercise 7

On the CD you can hear people ordering different dishes at a Manila Kamayan restaurant. Did you notice what each person ordered? Look at the waiter's order slip. Write down what each person has ordered.

◄》 CD 1, TR 8, 03:25

Mang Simeon's Kamayan Restaurant
Roxas Boulevard, Manila

Customer 1: *Miss Buyco* _____

_____

Customer 2: *Mrs Vito* _____

_____

Customer 3: *Miss Guanzon* _____

_____

Table *14*   Waiter *Domingo*

Asking for the bill

Dialogue 4

🔊 CD 1, TR 8, 04:41

The Cook family have enjoyed their meal. Bill Cook now wants to pay.

Bill	Ang chit *nga* **na**min.
Waiter	Aba **o**po. *Sandali* lang *po*. (Waiter returns and hands him the bill)
Bill	(Pointing at something) A**no** ito?
Waiter	I**yan** *po* ang starter ni**nyo**.
Bill	Iy**an**, a**no** iyan?
Waiter	Iy**an** *po* ang i**nu**min ni**nyo**.
Bill	Gano**on** ba? Ka**sa**ma ba ang service charge **di**to?
Waiter	Hindi po.
Bill	O, a**no** na**man** ang mga i**to**?
Waiter	Ang mga i**yan** *po* ang pulu**tan** ni**nyo**.
Bill	Gano**on** ba? Okey, ma**bu**ti. **He**to ang **ba**yad ko.
Waiter	Sa**la**mat *po* sir.
Bill	Wa**lang** anu**man**.

QUICK VOCAB

ang chit nga namin	*our bill please*
aba opo	*sure, sir*
medyo nagulat	*somewhat surprised*
ano ito	*what is this?*
ang mga ito	*these*
ang mga iyan	*those*
magkano	*how much*
pangalawang order	*second order*
kasama ba	*is it included*
heto ang bayad	*here's the payment*

Translation

Bill	(May we have) Our bill please.
Waiter	Of course sir. One moment please.
Bill	(Checking bill) What is this?

Waiter	That's your starter sir.
Bill	And that, what is that?
Waiter	That is (those are) your drinks, sir.
Bill	Is that so? Is the service charge included here?
Waiter	No, sir.
Bill	What are these here?
Waiter	Sir, those are your side dishes that came with the drinks.
Bill	Is that so? Ok, that's fine. Here's the payment.
Waiter	Thank you sir.
Bill	You're welcome.

Ito   Iyan

Iyon

Language skills

3 *Ito, iyan, iyon* *This, that, that (over there)*

Ito (pronounced *ee-taw*) 'This' refers to something close to the speaker, approximately within arm's reach. For example: **Relos ko ito.** *This is my watch*.

Iyan (pronounced *ee-yahn*) 'That' is used to refer to anything close to the person/s addressed (approximately within arm's reach) but not too close to the speaker. For example: **Sariwa ba iyan?** *Is that fresh?*

Iyon (pronounced *ee-yawn*) '*that*' is used to refer to things at a distance from both the speaker and the person/s addressed. For example: **Anong halaman iyon?** *What* [kind of] *plant is that* [over there]?

Practise reading the following sentences:

Tagalog	Literal	English
Pasaporte ko ito	Passport my this	*This is my passport*
Ito ba ang pila?	This ? the queue	*Is this the queue?*
Ilog Pasig iyan	River Pasig that	*That is Pasig River*
Bulkang Mayon iyon	Volcano Mayon that	*That (over there) is Mayon Volcano*
Masarap ito	Delicious this	*This is delicious*
Bolpen ko rin iyan	Pen my also that	*That is also my pen*
Hindi ba barko iyon?	Not ? ship that	*Isn't that a ship (over there)?*

4 *Mga + ito, iyan, iyon*

Remember **mga**? By adding the pluralizer **mga** to **ito**, **iyan**, and **iyon**, we get **mga ito**, **mga iyan**, **mga iyon**. Strictly speaking, as **ito**, **iyan** and **iyon** are pronouns, it is theoretically correct just to add **mga**. In practice however, this does not happen. The problem is solved by simply annexing **ang** before **mga**, thus **mga ito** becomes **ang mga ito**, **mga iyan** becomes **ang mga iyan** and **mga iyon** becomes **ang mga iyon**. Look at the explanation:

	Process	Meaning
ang **mga** ito	the/pluralizer/this	= *these*
ang **mga** iyan	the/pluralizer/that	= *those*
ang **mga** iyon	the/pluralizer/that	= *those* (over there)

Here are some further examples:

Singular	Plural
1. Tagalog: Maleta ko ito.	Maleta ko ang mga ito *or* Mga maleta ko ang mga ito.
English: *This is my suitcase.*	*These are my suitcases.*
2. Tagalog: Malinis ba iyan?	Malilinis ba ang mga iyan?
English: *Is that clean?*	*Are those clean?*
3. Tagalog: Bahay iyon.	Mga bahay ba ang mga iyon? Bahay ba ang mga iyon?
English: *Is that a house (over there)?*	*Are those houses (over there)?*

One-minute phrases

Dala-dala (*dah-lah dah-lah*) Literally, *load-load*. Meaning *a load carried around*. For example: **Laging maraming dala-dala si Bing.** *Bing has always a lot to carry around.*

May padala (*meh pah-dah-lah*) Literally, *has something* (an item) *to be delivered*. Meaning *a delivery*. Something sent either through the post or delivered in person. **May padala(ng) Barong Tagalog si Ate Ely sa akin.** *Ate Ely sent me a Barong Tagalog.*

Mabuting makisama (*mah-boo-teeng mah-kee-sah-mah*) Literally, *nice to conform with others*. Meaning *a person who gets along well with everybody*. For example: **Mabuting makisama si Doktor Rivera.** *Doctor Rivera gets along well with everybody.*

Tirhan mo ako (*teer-hahn maw ah-kaw*) Meaning *leave some* (food) *for me*. **Tirhan** is derived from the verb **tira** meaning *to portion out*. For example: **Tirhan mo ako ng leche flan.** *Leave some leche flan for me.*

Sabi-sabi (*sah-bee sah-bee*) Literally, *say-say/talk-talk*. This phrase is used to refer to *idle gossip*. A common and very popular Tagalog saying is as follows: **Ang maniwala sa sabi-sabi walang bait sa sarili.** *You are not kind to yourself if you believe in gossip.*

Insight

In rural Philippines, it is still very common for people to eat with their hands. This was the way Filipinos ate for hundreds of years before the arrival of the Spanish. *Kamayan* restaurants (**kamayan** comes from the Tagalog word **kamay** which means *hand*) offer people the opportunity to sample local delicacies in this traditional way. Why not try it out for yourself? If you show a willingness to enter into Filipino traditions, it can only serve to strengthen the ties with your Filipino friends.

Summary

1. **Mga** is used to pluralize in Tagalog, e.g. **libro** = *book*, **mga libro** = *books*. **Kutsilyo** = *knife*. **Mga kutsilyo** = *knives*.
2. Adjectives can be pluralized. **Malaki** to **malalaki**.
3. **Mayroon ba kayong . . . ?** Is normally used to ask about what is *not* on the menu.
4. **Pulutan** is the term used when ordering something to go with alcoholic drinks.
5. **Mga** is also used to express number approximation: **mga pito** (around seven).
6. **Mga** is also used to express time approximation: **mga alas siyete** (around seven o'clock).
7. You may also ask: **Mga anong oras?** *Around what time?*
8. **Ito, iyan, iyon** = *this, that, that yonder*.
9. The plural of **ito** = **ang mga ito**; the plural of **iyan** = **ang mga iyan**; the plural of **iyon** = **ang mga iyon**.
10. Always use **ang** before pluralizing **ito, iyan** or **iyon**.

9

Sa botika
At the pharmacy

In this unit you will learn how to:

- Ask for medication
- Consult a doctor
- Name the parts of the body

Asking for medication

Dialogue 1

◄) CD 1, TR 9

Louise Cook is at the pharmacy. She wants to buy some medicine for Roy who has been experiencing stomach trouble.

Louise	May ga**mot** ba ka**yo** pa**ra** sa **pag**tatae?
Pharmacist	**Me**ron *po*. **Pa**ra sa in**yo** *po* ba?
Louise	*Hindi*. **Pa**ra sa a**nak** ko.
Pharmacist	A**nong** ed**ad** po ang a**nak** ni**nyo**?
Louise	Dalawam**pung** ta**on** siya.
Pharmacist	**He**to *po* ang ga**mot** sa **pag**tatae. Masa**kit** din *po* ba ang u**lo** ni**ya**?
Louise	*Hindi* na**man**. Kai**lan**gan ba ni**ya** ng re**se**ta ng dok**tor**?
Pharmacist	*Hindi* na *po*. I**inumin** *po* ni**ya** i**to** tat**long be**ses i**sang ar**aw. I**wa**san lang *po* ni**yan**g umin**om** ng **tu**big na may **ye**lo.
Louise	Ma**ra**ming sa**la**mat. **He**to ang **bay**ad.
Pharmacist	*Wala* pong anu**man**.

may gamot	*has/have medicine*
(para) sa pagtatae	*for diarrhoea*
anong edad	*how old*
anak ninyo	*your child*
dalawampung anyos	*20 years old*
ang gamot	*the medicine*
masakit	*hurting/painful*
ang ulo niya	*his/her head*
hindi naman	*not quite*
reseta ng doktor	*doctor's prescription*
hindi na po	*not anymore*
iinumin	*will swallow*
tatlong beses isang araw	*three times a day*
iwasan lang	*please avoid*
uminom	*to drink*
tubig na may yelo	*water with ice*

Translation

Louise	Do you have anything for diarrhoea?
Pharmacist	Yes ma'am. Is it for you?
Louise	No. It's for my son.
Pharmacist	How old is your son?
Louise	Twenty years old.
Pharmacist	Here's the medicine for diarrhoea. Does he have a headache too?
Louise	No. Does he need a doctor's prescription?
Pharmacist	No. He must take this three times a day. He needs to avoid drinking water with ice.
Louise	Thank you very much. Here's the payment.
Pharmacist	Don't mention it.

Exercise 1

How much do you remember from the dialogue between Louise Cook and the pharmacist? Can you match column A and column B?

A	B
1. gamot	a. para sa anak ko
2. reseta	b. tubig
3. edad	c. ulo

4. para sa inyo po ba?   **d.** doktor

5. masakit   **e.** dalawampung anyos

6. uminom   **f.** sa pagtatae

Other items commonly found at the pharmacy can be found in the Quick vocab.

termometro	*thermometer*
'band aid'	*sticking plaster*
antiseptik krema	*antiseptic cream*
gamot sa pagtatae	*medicine for diarrhoea*
gamot sa sakit ng ulo	*headache tablet*
gamot sa sipon	*medicine for colds*
bulak	*cotton wool*
gamot sa nagsusuka	*medicine for vomiting*
'bandage' or pantapal	*bandage*
tintura de yudo	*iodine*
gamot sa ubo	*cough medicine*

Language skills

1 *Para sa* For

When Louise Cook asked the pharmacist for some medicine for her son, she said: 'May gamot ba kayo **para sa pagtatae?**' Do you have (any) medication for diarrhoea? The Tagalog words '**Para sa**' used in this example are translated into English as 'for'. **Para sa** can be used in three different ways:-

1. To indicate where or who something is for: for example, '**Para sa guro ang bolpen**', *The ballpen is for the teacher*. '**Para sa kusina ang mga silya**', *The chairs are for the kitchen*. Sometimes Tagalog drops the word '**para**' and so the sentence becomes simply '**sa guro ang bolpen**' or '**sa kusina ang mga silya**'. When **para** is deleted, however, the resultant sentence is often ambiguous, since the **sa** phrase may be interpreted as a possessive **sa** phrase '**sa guro ang bol pen**' may also mean *the pen belongs to the teacher*. **Para**, therefore, cannot be dropped. When the name of an individual is involved, then **para sa** becomes **para kay**, for example, '**Para kay Amy ang silid na ito**' or simply '**kay Amy ang silid na ito**', *This room is for Amy*.

2. To indicate favour or support for an individual or group: for example, 'Para sa Partido Mabuhay si Ignacio', *Ignacio is for the Mabuhay Party*', 'Para sa Newcastle United F.C. si John', *John is for Newcastle United F.C.* Once again, sometimes the word 'para' is dropped and the sentences become 'sa Partido Mabuhay si Ignacio' and 'sa Newcastle United F.C. si John'.

3. To indicate the purpose of or for something: for example, 'Para sa paglalaba ang sabon', *The soap is for washing clothes*; 'Para sa pagtulog ang kulambo', *The mosquito net is for sleeping*; 'Para sa pagsulat ang lapis', *The pencil is for writing*. Notice that in this type of sentence, the word **para** cannot be dropped.

2 *Para kanino* For whom
   Para saan For what

The related Tagalog question words are '**para kanino**' (for whom?) and '**para saan**' (for what?). Both question words look for an answer in the '**para sa**' form. For example: '**Para kanino ang pasalubong?**' (*for whom is the gift?*), '**para kay Alice ang pasalubong**' (*the gift is for Alice*). '**Para saan ang gatas?**' (*what is the milk for?*), '**para sa kape ang gatas**' (*the milk is for the coffee*). Use the following table to guide you through the different variations of the '**para sa**' form:

	Tagalog	English	Question word
1st person	para sa akin	*for me*	Para kanino
	para sa amin	*for us* (exclusive)	Para kanino
	para sa atin	*for us* (inclusive)	Para kanino
2nd person	para sa iyo	*for you*	Para kanino
	para sa inyo	*for you* (plural and singular formal)	Para kanino
3rd person	para kay	*for* + person's name =	para kanino
	para kina	*for* + person's and friend/s' names =	para kanino
	para sa kaniya	*for him/her*	para kanino
	para sa kanila	*for them*	para kanino
	para sa tao	*for a person* (personal noun)	para kanino
	para sa paa	*for the foot* (thing)	para saan
	para sa bintana	*for the window* (place)	para saan

Take a look at the following examples:

Tagalog: Para sa bata ang gatas
English: *The milk is for the child*

Tagalog: Para sa lola ang pamaypay
English: *The fan is for grandmother*

Tagalog: Para kay Patricia ang mga bulaklak
English: *The flowers are for Patricia*

Tagalog: Para sa akin ba ang mga ito?
English: *Are these for me?*

Tagalog: Hindi para sa kanila ang pagkain
English: *The food is not for them*

Tagalog: Para sa bagong meyor ako
English: *I am for the new mayor*

Tagalog: Para sa mga bata ang mga laruan
English: *The toys are for the children*

Tagalog: Para sa organisasyon ko ba si Liam?
English: *Is Liam for my organization?*

Insight

Tagalog speakers have a tendency to drop **para** when speaking. For example: **(Para) sa titser ang lapis**. *The pencil is for the teacher*. When **para** is dropped, the sentence is often ambiguous, since the **sa** may be interpreted as a possessive phrase.

Exercise 2

Now try answering the questions by saying what each item is for. Choose the correct answer from the **Quick vocab** provided.

Example:
Para saan ang mantikilya?   Para sa tinapay ang mantikilya.

1. Para saan ang gatas?   _____
2. Para saan ang kurtina?   _____

3. Para saan ang selyo? _____
4. Para saan ang payong? _____
5. Para saan ang kama? _____
6. Para saan ang maleta? _____
7. Para saan ang yelo? _____

ulan	*rain*
mantikilya	*margarine*
gatas	*milk*
silid-tulugan	*bedroom*
kurtina	*curtain*
selyo	*stamp*
tsaa	*tea*
bintana	*window*
biyahe	*travel*
kama	*bed*
maleta	*suitcase*

QUICK VOCAB

Consulting a doctor

Dialogue 2

🔊 **CD 1, TR 9, 01:07**

Roy Cook's stomach trouble had still not cleared up by the following day and so he decided to pay a visit to the doctor. We now join him at the surgery.

Doktor	**Ano**ng masa**kit** sa i**yo**?
Roy	Masa**kit** *po* ang ti**yan** ko at nag**tatae** a**ko**. May bini**li** a**kong** ga**mot** sa bo**tika pa**ra sa **pagtatae**.
Doktor	Ma**buti**. **Ano** ba ang ki**nain** mo?
Roy	Pan**sit**, lits**on** at San Miguel beer.
Doktor	**Ting**nan ko nga ang ma**ta** mo.
Roy	(Ibinu**ka** ang ma**ta**)
Doktor	**Ting**nan ko na**man** ang bi**big** mo at i**la**bas mo ang **di**la mo.
Roy	(Ibinu**ka** ang bi**big** at inila**bas** ang **di**la).
Doktor	**Ilang be**ses kang nag**tatae** sa i**sang** a**raw**?

124

Roy	Mga li**mang be**ses *po*.
Doktor	**Sob**ra si**gu**ro ang na**ka**in mo. **Bi**bigyan ki**ta** ng dalaw**ang** re**se**ta. **Isa pa**ra sa sa**kit** ng ti**yan**.
Roy	**Pa**ra sa**an** *po* it**on**g i**sa**?
Doktor	**Pa**ra sa **pa**gtatae. Toasted bread lang **mu**na ang ka**in**in mo.
Roy	Sal**a**mat *po*.
Doktor	Wa**lang** anum**an**.

ang tiyan ko	*my stomach*
nagtatae ako	*I'm having diarrhoea*
may binili ako(ng)	*I bought*
ang kinain mo	*what you ate*
tingnan ko nga	*let me see/examine*
ang mata mo	*your eyes*
ibinuka	*opened*
ang bibig mo	*your mouth*
ilabas	*show*
ang dila mo	*your tongue*
ilang beses	*how many times*
sa isang araw	*in one day*
mga lima	*about five*
sobra siguro	*perhaps too much*
ang nakain mo	*what you have eaten*
bibigyan kita	*I'll give you*
dalawang reseta	*two prescriptions*
para sa sakit ng tiyan	*for stomach ache*
para sa pagtatae	*for diarrhoea*
lang muna	*first*
ang kainin mo	*what you have to eat*

QUICK VOCAB

Translation

Doctor	Where are you feeling the pain?
Roy	I have a stomach ache and I've got diarrhoea. I bought some medication for diarrhoea from the pharmacy.
Doctor	Good. What have you eaten?
Roy	Noodles, suckling pig and San Miguel beer.

Doctor	Let me examine your eyes.
Roy	(Opening his eyes)
Doctor	Now let me look in your mouth. Show me your tongue.
Roy	(Opening his mouth and showing his tongue).
Doctor	How many times a day are you going to the toilet?
Roy	About five times sir.
Doctor	Perhaps you've over eaten. I will give you two prescriptions. One for your stomach ache.
Roy	What is the other one for?
Doctor	For your diarrhoea. Just eat toast for the meantime.
Roy	Thank you.
Doctor	Don't mention it.

Naming the parts of the body

◀) CD 1, TR 9, 02:28

Mga bahagi ng katawan Parts of the body

Listen to the **CD** for the correct pronunciation of each word. Use the pronunciation guide to help you remember the words.

	English	Tagalog	Pronounced
1.	*ankle*	bukongbukong	*boo-kawng-boo-kawng*
2.	*arm*	bisig	*bee-seeg*
3.	*back*	likod	*lee-kawd*
4.	*backside*	puwit	*poo-weet*
5.	*breast*	dibdib	*deeb-deeb*
6.	*cheek*	pisngi	*pees-ngee*
7.	*chin*	baba	*bah-bah*
8.	*ears*	tainga/tenga	*teh-ngah*
9.	*elbow*	siko	*see-kaw*
10.	*eye(s)*	mata	*mah-tah*
11.	*eyebrow*	kilay	*kee-ligh*
12.	*eyelashes*	pilikmata	*pee-leet-mah-tah*
13.	*face*	mukha	*mook-hah*
14.	*foot*	paa	*pah-ah*
15.	*fingers/toes*	daliri	*dah-lee-ree*
16.	*hand*	kamay	*kah-migh*

ulo
braso
balikat
kamay
bisig
daliri
pulso
balakang
tiyan
binti
tuhod
sakong
bukongbukong

kilay
buhok
mata
tainga/
tenga
ilong
pisngi
bibig
ngipin
baba

17.	*hair*	buhok	*boo-hawk*
18.	*head*	ulo	*oo-law*
19.	*heel*	sakong	*sah-kawng*
20.	*hips*	balakang	*bah-lah-kahng*
21.	*jaw*	panga	*pah-ngah*
22.	*knee*	tuhod	*too-hawd*
23.	*leg*	binti	*been-tee*
24.	*lower arm*	braso	*brah-saw*
25.	*mouth*	bibig	*bee-beeg*
26.	*nape*	batok	*bah-tawk*
27.	*neck*	leeg	*leh-ehg*
28.	*nose*	ilong	*ee-lawng*
29.	*palm*	palad	*pah-lahd*
30.	*penis*	buto	*boo-taw*
31.	*scalp*	anit	*ah-neet*
32.	*shoulder*	balikat	*bah-lee-kaht*
33.	*sole*	talampakan	*tah-lahm-pah-kahn*
34.	*stomach*	tiyan	*tee-yahn*
35.	*teeth*	ngipin	*ngee-peen*
36.	*tongue*	dila	*dee-lah*
37.	*vagina*	puki	*poo-kee*
38.	*waist*	baywang/bewang	*beh-wahng*
39.	*wrist*	pulso	*pool-saw*

Insight

Body image, grooming and cleanliness are priorities to most Filipinos. Both men and women take time to ensure that they present themselves at their best. Fingernails may come in for discreet inspection, not to mention toenails for those wearing sandals or **tsinelas**.

Exercise 3 Understanding and speaking

Imagine that you are at the pharmacy. Complete your part of the following dialogue. Once you have completed the dialogue, why not ask one of your Filipino friends to act out the dialogue with you?

Parmasyotika	Magandang umaga po, sir.
Ikaw	_____ _____ . (Say good morning)
Parmasyotika	Ano po ang kailangan nila, sir?
Ikaw	Masakit ang _____ _____ . (Say: I have a toothache) May _____ (medicine) ba kayo para dito?
Parmasyotika	Opo. Mayroon po.
Ikaw	____ _____ . _____ __ (Say all right. Thank you (formal).)
Parmasyotika	Gusto po ba ninyo ay yung iinumin?
Ikaw	(Say Yes, that's fine)
Parmasyotika	O sige po. heto po ang tabletas. Iinumin ninyo ito tatlong beses isang araw.
Ikaw	_____ _____? (Ask how much it is)
Parmasyotika	Treynta pesos po.
Ikaw	Heto _____ _____ . (Say here's the payment)
Parmasyotika	Maraming salamat po.
Ikaw	_____ _____ . (Say don't mention it)

Exercise 4

Can you place the following list of body parts in their correct order? For the correct order, begin with the top of the body and work down to the feet.

1. ulo
2. paa
3. mata
4. daliri
5. binti
6. kamay
7. buhok
8. panga
9. talampakan
10. tiyan

Exercise 5

Say whether the following statements are **tama** (*true*) or **mali** (*false*). Use the **Quick vocab** to help you. **Remember**: a **mali** answer should follow this format: Nasa _____ ang _____.

Example: Nasa kamay ang mata.   Answer: Mali. Nasa mukha
                                          ang mata.

1. Nasa gitna ng binti ang tuhod.   Answer:
2. Nasa likuran ang dibdib.   Answer:
3. Nasa kamay ang mga daliri.   Answer:
4. Nasa bisig ang talampakan.   Answer:
5. Nasa tenga ang labi.   Answer:
6. Nasa bisig ang kamay.   Answer:

nasa harapan	*at the front*
nasa tabi ng	*beside/next to the*
nasa gitna ng	*in the middle of*
nasa pagitan ng	*between the*
nasa ilalim ng	*at the bottom of*
nasa ibaba ng	*below the*
nasa itaas ng	*above the*
nasa likuran	*at the back/behind*

Exercise 6
Listening and understanding

Look at the pictures. On the CD you will hear a number of people complaining about their ailments. Can you match up the picture with the ailment?

◀)) CD 1, TR 9, 04:36

1.   2.   3.

One-minute phrases

Parang kabute pronounced (*pah-rahng kah-boo-teh*) Literally, '*like mushroom*'. This term is applied to a person who seems to have the ability to *appear and disappear*. In Filipino tradition, mushrooms are said to appear almost overnight. An example of this is the child who regularly plays truant from school, attending class only occasionally.

Ang sakit ng kalingkingan ay damdam ng buong katawan (*ang-sah-keet nahng kah-leeng-kee-ngahn igh dahm-dahm nahng booawng kah-tah-wahn*) This is a popular Filipino saying which can be translated as *the pain of the little finger is felt by the whole body*. For example, in a situation where a worker makes a mistake, the consequences of that mistake may be experienced by all or many of his/her co-workers.

Ganito 'yon *(gah-nee-taw 'yawn)* Literally, *it's like this* . . . A phrase roughly equivalent to the English expression, 'beating around the bush'. The expression is often used when someone wants to give a long (boring?) explanation. Example: **Saan ka galing? Ganito 'yon. . . .** *Where have you been? Well, it's like this. . . .*

Nakapamburol *(nah-kah-pahm-boo-rawl)* Literally, *dressed in funeral attire*. This is a very common Tagalog expression applied to a person dressed in his/her Sunday best (best clothing). Similar in meaning to the English expressions, *dressed to the nines* or *dressed to kill*. Example: **Nakapamburol si Mario kasi abay siya sa kasal.** *Mario is dressed to kill because he will be a sponsor at the wedding.*

Dedbol na ako *(ded-bol-nah-ahkaw)* literally, *I'm like a dead bull*. Similar in meaning to the English expressions *I'm exhausted, I'm shattered*.

Insight

Filipino people are generally very modest about their bodies, particularly the women. Revealing swimming costumes and other garments are not commonly worn, especially in rural areas. In Filipino culture, modesty and respectability go hand in hand. Respecting local culture in this regard will ensure a healthy respect for the visitor too! Tourist beaches and resorts do, however, offer a more relaxed environment for the sun worshipper. Don't forget the after-sun lotion!

Summary

1. **Para sa** = *for* in English; when someone or something is a beneficiary, e.g.: **Para sa guro.** *For the teacher.*
2. **Para sa akin, para sa iyo, para sa kaniya** = *For me, for you* and *for him/her.*
3. **Para kay** is used with a person who is named as a beneficiary, e.g.: **Para kay Lucy.** *For Lucy.*
4. **Para kina** is used when more than one person is named as a beneficiary, e.g.: **Para kina Paul.** *For Paul and friends.*
5. **Para saan** = *for what/for where.*
6. **Para kanino** = *for whom.*
7. **Para sa** is also used to indicate favour or support.
8. **Para sa** is also used to indicate purpose.
9. **Ulo, buhok, mata, pisgni, ilong, bibig** = *head, hair, eye, cheek, nose, lips.*
10. **Bisig, braso, kamay, daliri, binti, paa** = *upper arm, lower arm, hand, fingers/toes, leg, foot.*

10

Tulong?
(Need) Help?

In this unit you will learn how to:

- Ask for help
- Use the **sa** possessives and **kanino** (*whose*)
- Shop for a gift
- Use **sa** as a preposition

Asking for help

Dialogue 1

◀) **CD 1, TR 10**

Bill Cook needs some assistance. He bought a tee-shirt but it doesn't fit him. He's gone back to the department store.

Tindera	Magand**ang ha**pon *po*. A**no** pong maipag**lil**ingkod ko sa in**yo**?
Bill	Magand**ang ha**pon na**man**. I**tong** T-shirt na binili ko dito, mali**it** sa **a**kin. Size L lang ito.
Tindera	Gano**on** *po* ba? Sa in**yo** *po* ba? Ano pong size nin**yo**?
Bill	Size XXL ako. Oo sa **a**kin. May XXL ba ka**yo**?
Tindera	Sa pala**gay** ko *po*. Sumun**od** *po* ka**yo** sa **a**kin sa T-shirt depart ment. **Di**to *po* ba nin**yo** k**inu**ha i**yan**?
Bill	Oo. **Di**to sa lu**gar** na i**to**.
Tindera	Pu**mili** *po* ka**yo** ng size nin**yo** at **pa**palitan **na**min i**yan**.
Bill	Mar**ami**ng sa**la**mat.
Tindera	*Wala* pong anu**man**.

tindera	*assistant* (female)
itong T-shirt	*this tee-shirt*
na binili ko dito	*that I bought here*
maliit sa akin	*small for me*
lang ito	*this is only*
ganoon po ba	*is that so*
sa palagay ko	*in my opinion*
sumunod po kayo sa akin	*please follow me*
ninyo kinuha iyan	*you got that*
sa lugar na ito	*here in this place*
pumili po kayo	*please choose*
ng size ninyo	*your size*
papalitan namin iyan	*we will replace that*

Translation

Tindera	Good afternoon sir. What can I do for you?
Bill	Good afternoon to you, too. The tee-shirt I bought here, it's small for me. (It's) Only size L.
Tindera	Is that so sir? Is it yours sir? What size do you take?
Bill	I take XXL. Yes it's mine. Do you have size XXL?
Tindera	I think so sir. Please follow me to the tee-shirt department. Did you get that from this department?
Bill	Yes. Here in this area.
Tindera	Please choose your size and we'll exchange it.
Bill	Thank you.
Tindera	You're welcome sir.

Exercise 1

Can you supply the correct question to Bill's answer?

1. Bill: 'Itong T-shirt na binili ko dito, maliit sa akin.'

   Did the tindera ask:

   a. Gusto po ba ninyo ng T-shirt?
   b. Ano pong maipaglilingkod ko sa inyo?
   c. Magandang hapon po.

2. Bill: 'Size L lang ito.'

Was he asked:

   a. Sa inyo po ba?
   b. Anong size po?
   c. Ganoon po ba?

3. Bill: 'Size XXL ako.'

Did the tindera ask:

   a. Ganoon po ba?
   b. Size L po ba?
   c. Ano pong size ninyo?

4. Bill: 'Oo. Dito sa lugar na ito.'

The tindera asked:

   a. Saan po ninyo kinuha iyan?
   b. Dito ba ninyo kinuha iyan?
   c. Dito mo ba kinuha iyan?

Language skills

1 *Sa akin, sa iyo, sa kaniya* Mine, yours, his/hers

The words mine, yours, his/hers, ours, yours, and theirs all tell us about who owns or possesses something. In English these words are known as possessives (see also Unit 7). There are two main ways in which the possessive is expressed in Tagalog: 1) by the use of **may** or **mayroon** (see Unit 2), 2) by the use of the possessive **sa** form. In the possessive **sa** form (**sa akin, sa iyo, sa kaniya, sa amin, sa atin, sa inyo, sa kanila** and **sa** + personal/common noun) **sa** is used together with the possessor in order to express possession of the subject. For example: **Sa akin ang aklat.** *The book is mine.* **Sa inyo ba ang maletang ito?** *Is this suitcase yours?* **Sa babae ang payong.** *The umbrella belongs to the woman.* **Remember:** the **sa** form changes depending on who or what is the possessor. For example, **sa** becomes **kay** or **kina** when used with a person or people's names. Try not to worry about this. You will pick up more as you go along. Just look at the following examples:

1. **Sa bata** ang bisikleta — *The bicycle belongs to the child*
2. **Kay Joe** ang malamig na inumin — *The cold drink is Joe's*
3. **Kina Ely** ang regalo — *The gift belongs to Ely and her friends*
4. **Sa atin** ba iyan? — *Is that ours?*
5. **Sa Amerikano** daw ang lapis — *Apparently the pencil belongs to the American*

Sa possession table

	Tagalog	English
1st person	sa akin	mine
	sa amin	ours (exclusive)
	sa atin	ours (inclusive)
2nd person	sa iyo	yours
	sa inyo	yours (plural and singular polite)
3rd person	kay Sally	Sally's
	kina Gary	Gary's and his friend's/s'
	sa kaniya	his/hers
	sa kanila	theirs
	sa + personal noun	belong/s to
	sa + common noun	belong/s to

Insight

Whereas **Kanino** is translated as *whose*, **Kanino ang** becomes *whose is the*. **Kanino ang** can be contracted to become **kanino'ng**: for example: **Kanino ang bahay?/Kanino'ng bahay?** Both translate as: *Whose is the house?* This is not to be confused with **kaninong + noun** which has a different meaning: for example: **Kaninong bahay ito?** *Whose house is this?*

Exercise 2

Using what you have learned so far in this Unit, re-arrange the following jumbled up sentences into their correct form. The literal English translation should give you a clue.

1. Tagalog: maletang/ito/ang/sa akin
   Correct order: _____
   Literal: Mine the suitcase this.

2. Tagalog: Sa bata/bisikleta/ang/ba?
Correct order: _____
Literal: Belonging to the child the bicycle?

3. Tagalog: ang/Jeepney/bagong/sa kanila.
Correct order: _____
Literal: Belongs to them the new Jeepney.

4. Tagalog: sa/iyan/hindi/iyo.
Correct order: _____
Literal: Not yours that.

5. Tagalog: tsinelas/Beth/ang/kay.
Correct order: _____
Literal: Beth's the slippers.

6. Tagalog: ito/kina/ba/Philip?
Correct order: _____
Literal: Belong to Philip and his friend/s does this?

2 *Mga kulay* Colours

We have already met some of the Tagalog words for colours. Here is a fuller list:

Tagalog	Pronunciation	English
berde	behr-deh	*green*
azul	ah-sool	*blue*
pula	poo-lah	*red*
puti	poo-tee	*white*
dilaw	dee-lao	*yellow*
itim	ee-teem	*black*
rosas	raw-sahs	*pink*
kayumanggi	ka-you-mang-gee	*brown*
kulay dalandan	koo-lie da-lan-dan	*orange*
kulay-abo	koo-lie-ah-bo	*grey*
biyoleta/murado	bee-yaw-let-ah	*purple*
kulay-pilak	koo-lie-pee-lak	*silver*
kulay-ginto	koo-lie-gin-taw	*gold*

Exercise 3

Read through the list of Tagalog colour words again. Now cover the list up and line up the English words with their correct Tagalog equivalents:

1. yellow   berde   _____
2. white   kulay-pilak   _____
3. red   itim   _____
4. blue   puti   _____
5. silver   biyoleta   _____
6. purple   kulay ginto   _____
7. black   dilaw   _____
8. green   pula   _____
9. gold   azul   _____

Exercise 4 Reading and listening

Listen to the CD. Margaret, Bob and family are on a visit to Mines View Park in Baguio. They are trying to decide who will carry each of the bags. Follow the text then try to answer the questions that follow.

◀) CD 1, TR 10, 10:07

Sa Mines View Park sa Baguio

Nasa Mines View Park sa Baguio si Margaret at ang asawa niyang si Bob. Marami silang bag dahil kasama nila si Stephen, Amy, Lucy at Paul. Pakinggan natin sila:

Margaret	Kanino itong pulang bag?
Amy	Sa akin po.
Bob	Kanino naman ang itim na tote bag?
Stephen	Hindi sa akin. Kay Paul iyan.
Margaret	Kanino ang dilaw na plastic bag?
Paul	Kay Lucy yata.
Bob	Itong itim na duffel bag, sa iyo ba ito, Stephen?
Stephen	Opo. Salamat po.
Margaret	Sa iyo ba ang denim na tote bag, Paul?
Paul	Hindi po. Kay tatay iyan.

nasa parke	*at the park*
ang asawa niyang	*her husband*
marami	*many/plenty*
dahil sa	*because*

138

kasama nila	*accompanied by*
kanino	*whose*
pulang handbag	*red handbag*
itim	*black*
hindi sa akin	*not mine*
dilaw	*yellow*
yata	*I think*
itong itim	*this black* (one)

Translation

Margaret	Whose red bag is this?
Amy	(It's) mine mum.
Bob:	(And) who does this black tote bag belong to?
Stephen	Not mine. That is Paul's.
Margaret	Whose is the yellow plastic bag?
Paul	I think that's Lucy's.
Bob	This black duffel bag, is this yours, Stephen?
Stephen	Yes sir. Thank you.
Margaret	Is the denim tote bag yours, Paul?
Paul	No ma'am. That belongs to Dad.

Answer in complete sentences.

1. Kay Paul ba ang itim na tote bag?
2. Kay Stephen ba ang pulang plastic bag?
3. Kay Paul ba ang duffel bag?
4. Kanino ang denim na tote bag?
5. Kay Lucy ba ang dilaw na plastic bag?

Shopping for a gift

Dialogue 2

◀) **CD 1, TR 10, 02:08**

The Cook family are at a handicraft shop shopping for **pasalubong**.

Louise	Magaganda ang mga panyolito, pamaypay at burdadong napkins dito. Bibili ako ng isang dosenang panyolito.
Bill	Tama. Para kanino ang mga panyolito?
Louise	Para sa mga ka-opisina ko.
Bill	Kanino ang mga pamaypay?
Louise	Sa akin. Bibili ako ng tatlo.
Bill	Bibili naman ako ng laruang Jeepney.
Louise	Kanino ang laruang Jeepney?
Bill	Kanino pa? 'di sa akin at kay Roy.
Louise	Kanino naman ang burdadong napkins?
Bill	Sa kapitbahay natin. Pasalubong!
Louise	Tama.

magaganda	*beautiful* (plural)
ang mga panyolito	*the handkerchiefs*
mga pamaypay	*fans*
burdado(ng)	*embroidered*
sa kapitbahay natin	*for our neighbours*
bibili ako ng	*I'll buy/I'm going to buy*
isang dosenang	*one dozen*
tama	*that's right*
para kanino	*for whom*
para sa	*for*
mga ka-opisina ko	*my officemates*
laruan(g)	*toy*
kanino pa	*whose else*
'di sa akin	*of course it's mine*
pasalubong	*gift*

Translation

Louise	The handkerchiefs, fans and embroidered napkins here are gorgeous. I'm going to buy a dozen handkerchiefs.
Bill	All right. For whom are the handkerchiefs?
Louise	For my officemates.
Bill	Whose are the fans?
Louise	Mine. I'm going to buy three.

Bill	I'm going to buy a toy Jeepney.
Louise	Whose is the toy Jeepney?
Bill	Who else's? Of course, it's for Roy and me.
Louise	And whose are the embroidered napkins?
Bill	They are for our neighbours. Homecoming gifts!
Louise	Exactly!

Insight

Food is so central to Filipino thinking that many people use **kumain ka na?** (*have you eaten yet?*) as an informal greeting, rather than the more formal **kumusta ka?** or **kumusta po kayo?**

Language skills

3 *Kanino* Whose

Whenever we use a **sa** form sentence to express possession by a person or persons, then the accompanying question word is always **kanino** (*whose*). For example, '**Kanino ang payong?**', *Whose is the umbrella?/To whom does the umbrella belong?* or *Who does the umbrella belong to?* You will notice that there are three variations given in English. The Tagalog form is much simpler using only **kanino**. To form a **kanino** question, simply use **kanino** in place of the **sa** possessor. Note that Tagalog sometimes uses **kanino** in connection with **ng** as a linker, thereby becoming **kanino + ng = kaninong**. The main difference is that **kanino** is used on its own to represent the question word '*whose*', whereas **kaninong** may only be used when followed by the noun it describes or modifies. It can never stand alone. Here are some examples of this form:

1. **Kaninong** sombrero (noun) iyan? *Whose hat is that?* **Kaninong** kotse (noun) ang nasa garahe? *Whose car is in the garage?* **Kaninong** anak (noun) si Sophie? *Whose child is Sophie?*
2. **Kanino** ang lapis? *Whose is the pencil?* **Kanino** ang kotseng itim? *Whose is the black car?*

Look at the following examples:

Question: **Kanino** ang mga maleta?
Reply: **Sa amin** ang mga maleta.

Question: **Kanino** ang bansang Pilipinas?
Reply: **Sa mga Pilipino** ang bansang Pilipinas.

Question: **Kaninong anak** si Prince Charles?
Reply: **Kay Queen Elizabeth na anak** si Prince Charles *or*
Kay Queen Elizabeth.

Question: **Kaninong pamasahe** ito?
Reply: **Sa aking pamasahe** ito.

Question: **Kaninong pasaporte** ang nasa mesa?
Reply: **Kay Corang pasaporte** ang nasa mesa.

Question: **Kanino** ang computer dito?
Reply: **Sa mga estudyante** ang computer dito.

Exercise 5
Translate the following sentences into Tagalog? Use **kanino** or
kaninong + noun.

Example: Whose is this?   **Kanino** ito?
        Whose child is Beth?   **Kaninong anak** si Beth?

1. Whose are those?
2. Whose house is this?
3. Whose teacher is Cora?
4. Whose is that?
5. Whose are these vegetables?
6. Whose are the green mangoes?
7. Whose is this suitcase?
8. Whose child is Joanna?
9. Whose is this suitcase?
10. Whose camera is that?

Exercise 6 Listening and speaking
Listen to the CD. You will hear items mentioned that belong to one
of the groups of people in the cartoons. Can you identify which item
belongs to which group? You will be asked: **Kanino ang** [+ item]?
Your reply should be:

1. sa mga tao sa beach, **2.** sa mga turista or **3.** sa mga bata.

Use the **Quick vocab** provided to help you.

beach ball	*beach ball*
pala	*spade*
balde	*bucket*

QV

tuwalya	*towel*
pasaporte	*passport*
tiket	*ticket*
lapis	*pencil*
notbuk	*notebook*
pisara	*blackboard*
kamera/Kodak	*camera*
sunglasses	*sunglasses*
radyo	*radio*
alimango	*crab*
desk	*desk*

Language skills

4 Sa *To/to the, in/in the, on/on the, at/at the*

We have already met **sa** and looked at its uses in connection with other words. A further use of **sa** is that it represents the place where the action expressed in a sentence occurs. For example: **Bumili si Roy ng posporo sa tindahan.** *Roy bought some matches from the store.* By far the most common usage of **sa** is when it represents the English words *in/in the, on/on the, at/at the.* English refers to these words as prepositions. Prepositions tend to be used in two main ways: 1) to represent a place, 2) to represent time. We can try to make this a little clearer by looking at a few examples of each: **Lumalangoy si Louie sa dagat,** *Louie is swimming in the sea.* **May kumakain ba sa kusina?,** *Is someone eating in the kitchen?* **May pagkain na sa mesa,** *There is food on the table now.* **Umiyak siya sa simula ng tula,** *He/she cried at the beginning of the poem.* All of these are prepositions of place. Prepositions can also be used to express the time in which an action occurred. For example: **Matutulog ako sa hapon,** *I will sleep in the afternoon.* **Mananahi ako sa Sabado,** *I will do some sewing on Saturday.* **Nagtatrabaho si Greg sa gabi,** *Greg works at night.*

Study these further examples:

Tagalog: Bibisita ka ba **sa kamakalawa?**
English: *Will you be visiting in a fortnight?*

Tagalog: Wala kami **sa bahay** kahapon.
English: *We weren't at home yesterday.*

Tagalog: Pupunta ka ba **sa kaarawan ko?**
English: *Are you coming to my party?*

Tagalog: Kayo ba ang manedyer **sa tindahang ito?**
English: *Are you the manager in this store?*

The **Quick vocab** contains some useful time words and phrases.

ngayon	*today*
kahapon	*yesterday*
bukas	*tomorrow*
noong isang araw	*the day before yesterday*
sa isang araw	*the day after tomorrow*
ngayong linggo	*this week*
noong isang linggo	*last week*
sa isang linggo	*next week*
ngayong umaga	*this morning*
ngayong hapon	*this afternoon*
mamayang gabi	*tonight*
kahapon nang hapon	*yesterday afternoon*
kagabi	*last night*
bukas nang umaga	*tomorrow morning*
bukas nang gabi	*tomorrow night*
bukas nang hapon	*tomorrow afternoon*
bukas nang tanghali	*tomorrow midday*
mamaya	*later*
linggo-linggo	*every week*
tuwing Linggo	*every Sunday*

QUICK VOCAB

Exercise 7

Fill in the space with the correct **sa** (preposition of place) reply. Use the **Quick vocab** to help you.

dagat	*sea*
tindahan	*store*
palengke	*market*
palaruan	*playground*
kalye	*street/road*
tindahan ng laruan	*toy store*
paliparan	*airport*

1. Bibili (buy) si Boy ng sorbetes _____ .
2. Maraming eroplano (aeroplanes) _____ .
3. Maliligo (bathe) ka ba _____ .
4. Magaganda ang mga laruan (toys) _____ .
5. Sariwa (fresh) ang mga gulay (vegetables) _____ .
6. Naglalaro (play) sina Eileen _____ .
7. Tumatakbo (run) ang mga sasakyan (transportation)
   _____ .

Exercise 8

This time, provide a **sa** (preposition of time) reply. Use the **Quick vocab** to help you.

tanghali	*midday*
gabi	*at night*
hapon	*afternoon*
umaga	*morning*
Sabado	*Saturday*
Linggo	*Sunday*
hatinggabi	*midnight*

Example: Aalis daw siya **sa umaga**.
 Appparently he/she is leaving in the morning.

1. Narito ang mga magulang (parents) ni Elizabeth _____ .
   (afternoon)
2. _____ kami sisimba. (will go to church)

3. Maraming bituin (stars) _____ .

4. Mainit (hot) ang araw _____ . (midday)

5. Lumulubog (sets) ang araw _____ .

6. Sumisikat (shine) ang araw _____ .

7. Pupunta (will go) si Jayne at si John dito _____ .

One-minute phrases

Sigurado ka ba? (*see-goo-rah-daw kah bah*) Literally, *sure you are?* This phrase is commonly used to express doubt about information. For example: **Sigurado ka bang darating ang bisita mo mamaya?** *Are you sure your visitor will be arriving later?*

Palabiro (*pah-lah-bee-raw*) Literally, *fond of joking.* A person with a good sense of humour! For example: **Palabiro si Juanito kaya laging masaya ang barkada niya.** *Juanito is fond of cracking jokes; that's why his friends are always in a happy mood.*

Tayo-tayo (*tah-yaw tah-yaw*) Literally, *we-we* or *us-us.* First person plural. This phrase seems grammatically unusual. Anybody who uses the expression 'tayo-tayo' automatically excludes other people from their group. For example: **Sinu-sino ang iimbitahin mo sa party mo?** *Who are you going to invite to your party?* Reply: **Wala. Tayo-tayo lang.** *No-one. Just ourselves.*

Sila-sila (*see-lah-see-lah*) Literally, *they-they*, exactly the same connotation as 'tayo-tayo' except that this time, it is in the third person plural. For example: **Sila-sila lang ang nag-uusap.** *They themselves are just talking to one another.*

Maasim ang mukha (*mah-ah-seem ahng mook-hah*) Literally, *the face is sour.* This applies to someone whose facial expressions indicate disapproval. For example: **Parang galit si Mister Cruz, maasim ang mukha eh.** *I think Mr Cruz is angry, his face looks sour.*

Insight

For the visiting westerner, clothing in the Philippines can seem very good value for money. Be careful, however, as things may not always be as they seem! Always check a garment carefully. As regulations tend to be more relaxed, there are plenty of 'fake' goods on the market. Check the size carefully, too. Filipinos tend to be smaller in physical stature than their western cousins. A good rule of thumb would be to always try the next size up. For example, if you normally buy XL tee-shirts at home, look for a Filipino size XXL.

Summary

1. **Ano po ang maipaglilingkod ko sa inyo?** = *What can I do for you?*
2. **Sa akin, sa iyo, sa kaniya** = *is mine, is yours, is his/hers* (possessives).
3. **Sa amin, sa inyo, sa kanila** = *is ours, is yours, is theirs.*
4. **Kay** is used before a person's name to indicate ownership. **Kay Stanley** = *Stanley's.*
5. The plural form of **kay** is **kina. Kina Basilia** = Belonging to Basilia and her friends.
6. **Kanino** = *whose.*
7. **Kaninong + noun** Kaninong sapatos = *whose shoes?*
8. **Sa** as a preposition = *at, to, in, on,* etc.
9. **Sa** is never used before **bukas, ngayon, mamaya, kahapon, kagabi.**
10. *Every day* = **araw-araw;** *every week* = **linggo-linggo;** *every month* = **buwan-buwan.**

11

Gusto kong magpagupit
I want a haircut

In this unit you will learn how to:

- Make an appointment
- Describe what you want done
- Use pseudo-verbs

Making an appointment

Dialogue 1

🔊 **CD 1, TR 11**

Bill Cook wants to have his hair cut. He telephones a nearby barber shop.

Bill	Magand**ang** um**a**ga. **Gus**to kong **mag**pagu**pit**.
Barbero	Magand**ang** um**a**ga *po* na**man**. A**non**g **o**ras *po* ang **i**big nin**yo**?
Bill	Kail**a**ngan kong **mag**pagupit ngay**ong** al**as** dos. **Puwe**de ba?
Barbero	**Tit**ingnan ko *po*. A**ba**, may ba**kant**e *po* ka**mi**. **Puwe**de *po*. Kung **gust**o *po* nin**yo**, mas ma**a**ga.
Bill	**Ay**aw ko nang mas ma**a**ga. Al**as** dos na lang.
Barbero	**O**po. Mar**a**ming sa**la**mat *po*.
Bill	Wa**lang** anu**man**.

gusto ko(ng)	*I like/want*
magpagupit	*have a haircut*
ang ibig ninyo?	*what you want?*
ngayon(g) alas dos	*today at two o'clock*
puwede ba	*is it possible*
titingnan ko	*let me see*
aba	*oh!/say!*
may bakante	*has/have a vacancy*
ayaw ko	*I don't like*
mas maaga	*earlier*

Translation

Bill	Good morning. I want to have a haircut.
Barber	Good morning to you, too. What time do you have in mind?
Bill	I need to have a haircut today at 2.00 p.m. Is this possible?
Barber	Let me see. Yes, we have a vacancy. It's possible sir. If you like, we have an earlier time.
Bill	I don't want an earlier time. 2.00 p.m. would be all right.
Barber	Yes sir. Thank you very much.
Bill	Don't mention it.

Trish & Lucy Styling Salon
Iriga
Camarines Sur
Telephone: 6354-299-6146

Price List

Gupit (lalaki)	₱100.00
Kulot (perm)	₱350.00
Manicure	₱120.00
Pedicure	₱120.00
Masahe	₱150.00
Hair Colour & Wash	₱450.00
Wax	₱500.00
Cut & Wash	₱300.00

Tumatanggap kami ng Home Bookings

Exercise 1

Listen once again to Dialogue 1 on the CD. Try playing the part of the barber, then reverse roles and play the part of Bill Cook.

Language skills

1 Pseudo-verbs

kailangan	need(s) (to), ought to, must, should
dapat	ought to, must, should
maaari	can, may, could, might
puwede	can, may, could, might
gusto	like(s) (to), would like (to), want(s) (to)
ibig	like(s) (to), would like (to), want(s) (to)
nais	like(s) (to), would like (to), want(s) (to)
ayaw	do(es)n't like (to), wouldn't like (to)

Although the above list looks complicated, it is in fact quite straightforward. All of the words in the list appear at first glance to be ordinary verbs (doing words). However, although they do have verb-like meanings, they do not change in the same way that genuine verbs do and are therefore called pseudo-verbs. As the translations show, some of the pseudo-verbs are similar to one another in meaning: **kailangan** and **dapat**; **maaari** and **puwede**; **gusto**, **ibig** and **nais**. There are however certain subtle differences.

For example, in sentences where **kailangan** or **dapat** occur, **kailangan** suggests internal necessity or need, whereas **dapat** suggests external necessity or appropriateness. Look at the following sample sentences: a. **Kailangan** matalino ang estudyante b. **Dapat** (na) matalino ang estudyante, may be translated as *The student must be intelligent*. Sentence (a) suggests that the student feels the need to be intelligent, whereas sentence (b) requires that the student be intelligent.

In sentences where **maaari** or **puwede** occur, both denote ability, permission or possibility. **Maaari** is common in both formal and informal contexts; **puwede** is common only in informal contexts.

Gusto, **ibig** and **nais** all denote preference or desire. The three differ from one another in level of usage and in some cases, in connotation as well. **Gusto** is the most common. **Ibig** is more formal than **gusto**, and occurs more frequently in writing than in speech. **Nais** is the most formal and is rare in ordinary conversation.

Ayaw is the contrary of **gusto, ibig** and **nais** in that it expresses dislike.

These pseudo-verbs are commonly used in conjunction with **ng** which we first met in Unit 7 (more on this later in this Unit). The usage table will help you to decide which is the most appropriate pseudo verb to use:

Usage table

Pseudo-verb	English	Use
gusto	*like(s) (to), would like (to), want (s)*	most common; mild inclination to a stronger desire
ibig	*like(s) (to), would like (to), want (s)*	more formal than **gusto** and occurs more frequently in writing than in speech; a fairly strong desire
nais	*like(s) (to), would like (to), want (s)*	specifies stronger preferences than **gusto**; a strong desire
ayaw	*do(es)n't like (to), wouldn't like (to)*	contrary of **gusto, ibig, nais** (similar in meaning to **hindi**)
dapat	*ought to, must, should*	connotes external necessity or appropriateness
kailangan	*need(s) (to), ought to, must, should*	connotes internal necessity or need
maaari	*can, may, could, might*	denotes ability, permission, or possibility; common in both informal and formal contexts
puwede	*can, may, could, might*	denotes ability, permission, or possibility; common only in informal contexts

Examples:

Tagalog: **Kailangan** mo ba ito?
English: *Do you need this?*

Tagalog: Hindi ko **gusto** ang pagkain kagabi.
English: *I didn't like the food last night.*

Tagalog: **Puwede** tayong matulog doon.
English: *We can sleep (over) there.*

Tagalog: Ito ba ang **nais** mo?
English: *Is this what you want?*

Tagalog: Iyan ang **ibig** ko sa kaniya.
English: *That's what I like about him.*

Tagalog: **Ayaw** ko ng kapeng walang gatas.
English: *I don't like coffee without milk.*

Tagalog: **Dapat** na narito sila bukas.
English: *They should be here tomorrow.*

Tagalog: **Maaari** bang dito muna tayo?
English: *Might we stop here first?*

Exercise 2

Complete the following sentences with an appropriate pseudo-verb.

1. Ano ang (gusto, kailangan, ibig, nais) [like] mo?
2. (Kailangan, nais, ibig) [need] namin ng malamig na tubig.
3. Bakit (ayaw, ibig, gusto) [doesn't like] niya ng halo-halo?
4. (Dapat, nais, ayaw) [should] nasa bahay na ang mga bata.
5. Ano ang (ibig, puwede, dapat) [want] kainin ng bisita?

Describing what you want done

Dialogue 2

◀) CD 1, TR 11, 00:55

Bill Cook is at the barber's. He is describing to the barber the haircut he wants.

Barber	Sir, ano **pong** gu**pit** ang **gus**to nin**yo**?
Bill	**Gus**to ko *hindi* mas**ya**dong ma**ha**ba.
Barber	I**big** *po* ba nin**yo** hang**gang** ita**as** ng **ba**tok?
Bill	Puwe**de** na, **pe**ro *hindi* ko **gus**to ang crew cut.
Barber	**Nai**s *po* ba nin**yo** *maikli* sa ta**bi**?
Bill	Oo. **Pe**ro kai**lan**gan **med**yo maka**pal** sa tuk**tok**.
Barber	Okay lang *po*. **Hu**hugasan ko lang *po* ang inyong bu**hok**.
Bill	O **si**ge, **gus**to ko rin ng **kon**ting ma**sa**he.
Barber	Opo sir.
Bill	Sala**mat**.
Barber	*Wala* pong anu**man**.

QUICK VOCAB

ano pong gupit	*what (kind of) haircut*
sa tabi	*at the sides*
hindi masyado(ng)	*not very*
mahaba	*long*
ibig po ba ninyo	*do you want*
hanggang itaas	*reaching the top*
batok	*nape*
puwede na	*will suffice*
gusto ko rin	*I'd also like*
hindi ko gusto	*I don't like*
nais po ba ninyo	*do you want*
medyo	*slightly*
maikli	*short*
makapal	*thick*
sa tuktok	*at the top*
huhugasan ko lang	*I'll just wash*
ang inyong buhok	*your hair*
konting masahe	*a little massage*

Translation

Barber	Sir, what kind of haircut would you like?
Bill	I like it not too long.
Barber	Would you like it just above the nape of the neck?
Bill	That would do, but I don't want a crew cut.
Barber	Would you like it to be short at the sides?
Bill	Yes. But it needs to be thick on top.

Barber	That's OK sir. I just have to wash your hair.
Bill	OK, I'd also like a massage.
Barber	Yes sir.
Bill	Thank you.
Barber	You're welcome sir.

Exercise 3 Writing and speaking

Sagutin sa Tagalog (respond in Tagalog):

1. Anong klaseng gupit ang gusto ni Bill?
2. Gusto ba ni Bill ng crew cut?
3. Saan dapat maikli ang gupit?
4. Ano muna ang gagawin ng barbero?
5. Ano pa ang gusto ni Bill na gagawin ng barbero?

Language skills

2 More about pseudo-verbs

Since **kailangan, gusto, ibig, nais, maaari, puwede, ayaw** and **dapat** are considered action words, it is clear that they have to be used in connection with a word which identifies those actually 'doing' the 'action' ('subjects' or, perhaps more appropriately, we can refer to them as 'actors').

In Tagalog, the general rule is as follows: pseudo-verbs take only **ng** form 'actors'. The **ng** form consists of the following: **ni** (of/singular – personal), **nina** (of/plural – personal), **ko** (my), **mo** (your), **niya** (his/her), **namin** (our/exclusive), **natin** (our/inclusive), **ninyo** (your/plural), **nila** (their), **nito** (of this), **niyan** (of that), **noon** (of that over there) and **ng** (of). These pseudo-verbs may also need an object or objects.

Remember the difference between a definite and an indefinite object? A definite object is always preceded by the word 'the', whereas an indefinite object is always preceded by the word 'a'. The connecting word used with an indefinite object is **ng** whereas **ang** is used for definite objects. Look carefully at the table below and then study the examples:

Pseudo-verb	Actor	Object	
		Definite	or indefinite
	A	B	C
kailangan (**ng**)	ni, nina, ko,	(**ang**) si sina,	(**ng**)
gusto	mo, niya,	ako, ka, siya,	same as A
ibig	namin, natin	kami tayo,	
nais	ninyo, nila,	kayo, sila ito,	
puwede	nito niyan,	iyan, iyon	
ayaw	noon	**ang** + noun	
dapat	**ng** + noun		
maaari			
(**Note: ko + ka = kita**)			

To produce a pseudo-verb sentence: 1. Choose a pseudo-verb. 2. Choose an 'actor' from column A. 3. Choose a definite object from column B or 4. Choose an indefinite object from column C.

The basic formula is as follows:

Pseudo-verb + A + B or C = sentence

Look at the following example sentences. Note the differences between a pseudo-verb and actor used in connection with a definite object, then with an indefinite object.

Pseudo-verb	Actor	Indefinite object	Definite object
Ayaw	ni Judy	**ng hilaw na mangga**	
Judy doesn't like unripe mangoes			
Ayaw	ni Judy		**ang hilaw na mangga**
Judy doesn't like the unripe mango			
Gusto	mo [ba]	**ito?**	
Do you want/like/Would you want/like this?			
Gusto	mo [ba]	**nito?**	
Do you want/like/Would you want/like some of this?			
Kailangan	ko	**ng bagong sapatos**	
I need a new (pair of) shoes			
Kailangan	ko		**ang bagong sapatos**
I need the new (pair of) shoes			

Did you notice . . . ?

The first example could be literally translated as 'doesn't like of Judy unripe mangoes'. However, as explained earlier, all pseudo-verbs require **ng** form actors. Although these **ng** form actors are required in Tagalog, we do not need to translate them into English. The correct translation of the sentence thus reads, *Judy doesn't like unripe mangoes*.

Insight

ayokongkumain literally means *I don't want me to eat*, so we translate it as *I don't want to eat*. What is happening here is that the 'pseudo-verb' has to take an **ng** form actor, in this case **kong**, 'me'. In the natural English translation this 'me' is dropped. Meanwhile **kailangang** + noun/adjective is understood to mean *it is necessary*. **Kailangang panalo si Stephen.** *Stephen needs to be a winner*.

Exercise 4

Match up columns A (pseudo-verb with **ng** actor) and B (definite/indefinite object) correctly. When you have done this, use a preposition of time or space from the box to expand the sentence further.

Example:

A	B	Place
Gusto namin	ng malamig na Pepsi	sa bahay

A (pseudo-verb with 'actor')	B (definite or indefinite object)
1. Gusto ni Tessie	magpagupit
2. Kailangan nila	ng malamig na kape
3. Nais po ba ninyo	ang bagong kotse
4. Hindi ko gusto (ng)	ng katulong
5. Ayaw ng mga bisita	ng aking tulong

Exercise 5

Fill in the space with a pseudo-verb and then translate your sentence into English.

1. _____ mo ba ng lapis (pencil)?

Translation:

2. _____ bumili ni Baby ng saging (banana) sa palengke.
   Translation:
3. Bakit mo _____ ng malaking pisara (blackboard)?
   Translation:
4. Sino ang _____ mong isama (go with you) sa sine?
   Translation:
5. _____ mo ba ng malamig (cold) na Pepsi?
   Translation:

Dialogue 3

Louise Cook is at the hairdresser's. She is discussing hairstyles with the hairdresser (HD).

◄)) **CD 1, TR 11, 01:50**

HD	Ma**gan**da *po* ang bu**hok** nin**yo** ma'am, **A**no *po* ang **gus**to nin**yong** ga**win** ko?
Louise	Pu**wed**e bang cut, and blow dry?
HD	Ma**aa**ri *po*. **Gus**to *po* ba nin**yo** ng *maikli*?
Louise	**Ba**gay ba sa **a**kin ang maik**ling** gu**pit**?
HD	**O**po. Ba**ba**gay *po* sa in**yo**. Ma**gan**da *po* sa in**yo** ang maik**ling** bu**hok**.
Louise	Mas **ba**gay **ya**ta sa **a**kin ang ma**ha**ba.
HD	**Ba**gay *po* sa in**yo** ang ma**ha**ba at maik**li**.
Louise	O **si**ge, maik**li**.
HD	**O**kay *po*. Huhu**ga**san ko **mu**na ang bu**hok** nin**yo**.
Louise	Sa**la**mat.
HD	*Wala* pong anu**man**.

maikling buhok	*short hair*
ang buhok ninyo	*your hair*
ang mahaba	*a longer one*
gawin ko	*I'd do*
puwede ba(ng)?	*is it possible?*
maaari po	*it's possible* (formal)
bagay ba sa akin	*does it suit me*
ang maikling gupit	*short cut*
babagay po sa inyo	*it will suit you*
mas bagay	*suits better*

158

huhugasan ko muna   *I will wash first*
maganda sa inyo   *beautiful/nice on you*

Translation

HD	Your hair is pretty madam. What would you like me to do?
Louise	Can I have a 'cut and blow dry'?
HD	It's possible ma'am, would you like a short cut?
Louise	Does a short cut suit me?
HD	Yes ma'am, it would suit you. A short cut would be nice on you.
Louise	I think a longer (one) is prettier.
HD	Long hair and short hair both suit you.
Louise	OK, a short one.
HD	OK ma'am. I'll have to wash your hair first.
Louise	Thank you.
HD	Don't mention it.

Exercise 6

Try playing the part of the hairdresser. Based on the dialogue, tell Mrs Cook the following:

1. Her hair is very long.
2. Long hair suits her too.
3. You'll have to wash her hair.

More words used at the barber shop/hairdresser can be found in the Quick vocab.

magpakulot	*to have a perm*
magpagupit	*to have a cut*
putulin/gupitin	*to cut* (the hair)
putulan/gupitan	*to give the hair/person a cut*
i-set	*to set the hair*
gunting	*scissors*
tuwalya	*towel*
silya	*chair*
tuwid na buhok	*straight hair*
minamanikyur	*being given a manicure*
pinipedikyur	*being given a pedicure*

Exercise 7

Listen carefully to the CD. You will hear three different people explaining to their hairdresser/barber what they want. Use Dialogue 3 and the **Quick vocab** to help you understand. Write down on the task sheet what each customer is asking for:

◀) **CD 1, TR 11, 02:53**

Toto Mario's Unisex Hair Salon

476 Pereira Street
Quezon City

Phone 01915-5550

Stylist: *Mario*   Date: *March 19, 2000*

Customer 1 _____
Pangalan: _____
Kailangan: _____
_____
_____

Customer 2 _____
Pangalan: _____
Kailangan: _____
_____
_____

Customer 3 _____
Pangalan: _____
Kailangan: _____
_____
_____

Exercise 8 Understanding and speaking

You are off to the stylist to have your own hair cut. Listen to the CD and respond to your stylist's questions:

◀) **CD 1, TR 11, 04:05**

Stylist	Magandang umaga po. Welcome sa Toto Mario's.
Ikaw	(Say good morning)

Stylist	Ano po ang maitutulong ko sa inyo?
Ikaw	(Tell him you want to have your hair cut)
Stylist	Ibig n'yo na po bang magpagupit ngayon o gumawa ng appointment para bukas?
Ikaw	(Tell him you would like it now, if possible)
Stylist	Aba opo. Gusto rin po ba ninyong hugasan ko ito?
Ikaw	(Tell him no thank you. You just want it cut)
Stylist	Ibig po ba ninyo mahabang gupit o maikli?
Ikaw	(Tell him you want it cut short)
Stylist	Ibig rin po ba ninyo ng masahe?
Ikaw	(Tell him politely you just want the haircut)
Stylist	Okay lang po sir.
Ikaw	(Say thank you very much)

Insight

1. Don't forget to tip 10–15%.
2. Ask if they have worked with non-Asian hair before (if you are non-Asian).
3. Ask them to repeat what you have requested (to make sure they have understood).
4. Stylists often love to chat. Don't lose the opportunity to practise your Tagalog!

Language skills

3 More on the *sa* preposition

During the conversation between Louise Cook and the hairdresser, the hairdresser said: **Babagay po sa inyo. Maganda po sa inyo and maikling buhok.** It will suit you ma'am. A short cut would be nice on you. In this example, the word 'sa' was used in yet another way. It wasn't used as a preposition of time or place, but rather with the describing word **maganda. Sa** can also be used with adjectives. For example: **Mabait sa akin si Cora.** *Cora is nice to me.* **Mabuti sa kanila ang mga guro.** *The teachers are good to them.* **Mapagmahal si Jonathan sa mga kapatid niya.** *Jonathan is affectionate to his brothers.* When **sa** is used as an ordinary preposition, then it is translated into English as either **to, for, on, in, into, about,** or **at.**

Some further examples:

1. Tagalog: Malaki **sa iyo** ang blusa mo
   English: *Your blouse is big on you*

2. Tagalog: Maliit **sa bata** ang sapatos
   English: *The shoes are small on the child*

3. Tagalog: Maluwang **kay Larry** ang sombrerong ito
   English: *This hat is loose (big) on Larry*

4. Tagalog: Mabuti raw **sa iyo** ang gamot
   English: *Apparently, the medicine is good for you*

Insight

Food is a strong social component of Filipino culture. Food and sharing go hand-in-hand. Visit someone while they are eating and the invitation, kain tayo! (*Let's eat!*), will almost certainly follow. While you are not seriously expected to tuck in, a polite response is expected, such as *No thank you; I've just eaten!*

Exercise 9

Why don't you see how much you have remembered – choose the correct answer from the box:

1. Magalang _____ (to the old people) si Rosita.
2. Mabuti _____ (to you) ang magpahinga.
3. Malaki yata _____ (on him) ang tsinelas.
4. Hindi ba maliit _____ (on me) ang pantalong ito?
5. Mabait _____ (to us) ang bisita ni Margaret.
6. Masyadong mahaba _____ (on her) ang damit na ito.

One-minute phrases

Matigas ang ulo (*mah-tee-gahs ahng oolaw*) Literally, *hard the head*. Meaning hardheaded/stubborn. For example: **Matigas ang ulo ni Boy.** *Boy is stubborn.*

Hindi yata pupuwede (*heen-dee yah-tah poo-poo-weh-deh*) Literally, *not I think it will do*. Meaning *I don't think it's possible./I don't think it can.*

Pagbutihin mo (*pahg-boo-tee-heen maw*). Meaning *make it good*. This phrase is commonly used when offering encouragement. For example: **Pagbutihin mo ang pag-aaral para maging doktor ka pagdating ng araw.** *Study hard so that you'll become a doctor in the future.*

Lakad-takbo (*lah-kahd tahk-baw*). Literally; *walk-run*. Meaning a brisk walking pace. For example: **Lakad-takbo ang ginawa ko para maabot ko ang huling biyahe ng tren.** *I half walked, half-ran in order to catch the last train.*

Mabilis pa sa alas-singko (*mah-bee-lees pah sah ah-lahs-seeng-kaw*). Literally, *faster than five o'clock*. This phrase goes back to the time in the 1950s and 1960s when Filipino employees in Manila used to listen out for the five o'clock whistle from the port area of the city. The whistle signalled the end of the shift for the dock workers. Anyone finishing their work before the five o'clock whistle was deemed by his or her workmates to be *faster than the five o'clock* [whistle].

Insight

Whether you want to make an appointment with a hairdresser or buy something from a department store, you may sometimes find it difficult to attract the attention of a shop assistant. Invariably, they know that you are there but are hesitant to give you eye contact or approach you because of a lack of confidence in their own English. The assumption is always that foreigners do not understand Tagalog. This is just shyness and can easily be overcome with a warm and friendly smile, coupled with a few words of Tagalog. Never be afraid to try out your Tagalog. Even a few words will go a long way towards giving you a positive and memorable experience of the Philippines.

Summary

1. Pseudo-verbs are also known as quasi-verbs; words with verb-like meanings.
2. Pseudo verbs use **ko, mo, niya, namin, natin, ninyo, nila** as actors (doers).
3. Pseudo verbs use **ng** for an indefinite object and **ang** for a definite object.
4. **Kailangan** = *need, necessary.*
5. **Gusto** = *like.*
6. **Ibig** = *like,* but is more formal than gusto.
7. **Nais** = a strong desire.
8. **Dapat** = *should* or *must.*
9. **Maaari/puwede** denotes ability, permission.
10. **Sa** is translated into English as *to, for, on, in, into, about* or *at* when used as an ordinary preposition.

12

Bagay ba sa akin?
Does this suit me?

In this unit you will learn how to:

- Try something on in a store
- Use the passive
- Describe the weather

___

Trying something on in a store

Dialogue 1

◀) **CD1, TR 12**

Louise Cook is trying something on in the changing room of a departmental store.

Store assistant	**Gus**to *po* ba nin**yo** i**yan**? Mag**su**kat pa *po* ka**yo** ng i**ba**. **Pal**da at **blu**sa po kung **a**yaw nin**yo** ng di**ret**so. May i**bang ku**lay rin po. Mag**su**kat *po* ka**yo** ng **pal**da at **blu**sa.
Louise	**Si**ge. (Isinukat) **Med**yo masi**kip ya**ta ang **blu**sa **pe**ro malu**wang** na**man** ang **pal**da. **Gus**to kong pu**mi**li pa.
Store assistant	**Si**ge *po*. Pu**mi**li pa *po* ka**yo**. I**to** pong may bulak**lak**? Di**ret**so po ito.
Louise	**Na**pakagan**da** niy**an** at kung **ta**ma ang **su**kat, **bi**bili ak**o** ng dala**wa**. **Gus**to ko ring bumi**li** ng ban**da**na.
Store assistant	Ma**ra**mi *po* ka**ming** ban**da**na. **Na**sa kabi**lang** departa**men**to *po* ang mga i**to**.
Louise	Ma**ra**ming sa**la**mat.
Store assistant	*Wala* pong anu**man**.

QUICK VOCAB

gusto po ba ninyo	*do you like/would you like*
magsukat pa	*try some more*
ng iba	*other ones*
may palda at blusa	*we have blouses and skirts*
kung ayaw ninyo	*if you don't like*
diretso	*straight* (dress)
ibang kulay rin	*other colours also*
bibili ako	*I will buy*
isinukat	*tried it on*
medyo masikip	*slightly small*
ng bandana	*a scarf*
pero maluwang	*but loose*
pumili pa	*choose some more*
may bulaklak	*with flowers*
napakaganda	*so pretty*
niyan	*that*
kung tama	*if right*
ang sukat	*the size*
ang kamay	*the arms*
nasa kabila(ng) departamento	*in the department store*

Translation

Store assistant	Do you like that ma'am? Why not try a few others. We have skirts and blouses if you don't want a dress. They come in other colours too. Why not try on a skirt and a blouse ma'am.
Louise	All right. (*trying it on*) I think the blouse is a little tight but on the other hand the skirt is loose.
Store assistant	Okay ma'am. Please try on some others. How about this flowery dress?
Louise	That is so pretty, and if it's my size, I will take two. I would also like to buy a scarf.
Store assistant	We have many scarves. They're in the department next door.
Louise	Thank you very much.
Store assistant	You're welcome.

166

Exercise 1

Drawing from what you have learned so far, replace the words in italics with a different adjective, verb, noun or pronoun, to form coherent Tagalog sentences.

Example: Gusto po ba ninyo *iyan*?
            Answer: Gusto po ba ninyo *ito*?

1. May palda at blusa po kung *ayaw* ninyo ng diretso.
2. Magsukat po kayo ng *palda at blusa*.
3. Medyo *masikip* yata ito.
4. Ito pong may *bulaklak*?
5. Napakaganda niyan at kung *mabuti* ang sukat, bibili ako ng dalawa.
6. Gusto ko ring *bumili* ng bandana.
7. Marami po kaming *bandana*.

Language skills

1   Verbs: Active voice/passive voice
Transitive/intransitive

When forming a simple sentence, action words play a key role: they let us know what is being done. These action words are known as verbs. Verbs have two distinct ways of indicating an action, each giving a different flavour or 'voice' to the sentence. We can call these distinct flavours the active voice and the passive voice. The 'voice' of a sentence tells us something about the relationship between: 1) the subject of the verb; 2) the 'doer' of the verbal action; 3) the person or thing that the verbal action is done to.

We use the active voice when the subject of the verb is the 'doer' of the action. The active voice is used in most English speech and writing, because we usually want to inform our listeners or our readers about who or what carried out the action of the verb. For example: Roy read a book yesterday. Jack and Jill carried a pail of water. I bought a pair of slippers.

The passive voice is used when the subject is not the person or thing 'doing' the action of the verb. It is the person or thing that is acted upon by the verb. For example: The ball was thrown by the boy. The ribbon was cut by the mayor. These words were said by him. We also use the passive voice to direct our listener's attention to the most important part of our message. The passive voice can be used when we do not know who carries out the action expressed by the verb. For example: The food has been eaten.

Before moving on to **um** verbs, it is important for us to understand the difference between transitive and intransitive verbs. Very simply, a transitive verb is a verb that has a direct object. For example: **Bumili si Roy ng sombrero** (*bumili* is the verb while **ng sombrero** is the direct object). *Roy bought a hat.* An intransitive verb, by way of contrast, is a verb that has no direct object. For example: **Namili si Mary**. *Mary went shopping.* Some verbs are always transitive (with an object), others are always intransitive (without an object), but just to keep us on our toes, many verbs are used both transitively and intransitively. We will further explore both transitive and intransitive verbs as we go along.

2 The *um* verb

We now turn to the first active verb type, known as the **um** verb. The **um** verb type forms major transitive and intransitive verbs. There are two major ways of forming **um** verbs: 1) by adding **um** in front of a verb stem or 'root' that begins with a vowel. (A verb root is a verb in its simplest form. For example, the verb **kumain** *to eat*. The root/stem of **kumain**, is **kain** = *eat*); or 2) by inserting **um** inside a verb root that begins with a consonant (non-vowel). Look at some examples.

How to change the tense of an **um** verb stem beginning with a vowel:

Example: Verb stem: **alis** (*leave*)

um + alis	= umalis (to leave)	infinitive
a + alis	= aalis	future
um + a + alis	= umaalis	present
um + alis	= umalis	past

Note: Did you notice that in the **um** verb the infinitive and past tense look the same? They are distinguished only by their use. While the infinitive is only used in commands, suggestions and requests, (For example: Umalis ka! 'You go'), the past tense usually takes a time element in the sentence (for example: Kumain kami kagabi, We ate last night).

Four major ways of changing verb tenses in Tagalog

1. Infinitive (used in commands, suggestions and requests only)
   For example:
   Command: Huwag kang **tumayo** diyan! *Don't* [you] *stand there!*
   Suggestion: **Kumain** na tayo. *Let's eat now*
   Request: Puwede bang **kumuha** ka ng plato sa kusina? *Could you fetch a plate from the kitchen?*
2. Future: will/shall + infinitive, the future perfect tense (will have + past participle), be going to + infinitive the future progressive tense (will be + present participle)
   For example: **Uuwi ako.** *I am going home. I will/shall go home*
3. Present: the simple present tense, the present progressive tense
   For example: **Kumakain** ako ng gulay araw-araw. *I eat vegetables every day*
4. Past: the simple past tense, the past progressive tense
   Example: **Bumili** si Ronald ng sorbetes. *Ronald bought some ice-cream*

Listen to the pronunciation of each of the following verbs, then try to pronounce each word yourself, without the help of the CD.

◄) **CD 1, TR 12, 01:20**

Verb root	Meaning	Infinitive	Future	Present	Past
akyat	climb	umakyat	aakyat	umaakyat	umakyat
asa	rely upon	umasa	aasa	umaasa	umasa
inom	drink	uminom	iinom	umiinom	uminom
iyak	cry	umiyak	iiyak	umiiyak	umiyak
uwi	go home	umuwi	uuwi	umuuwi	umuwi
utang	borrow money	umutang	uutang	umuutang	umutang

How to change the tense of an **um** verb stem beginning with a consonant:

Example: Verb stem: **basa** (*read*)

b + um + asa	= bumasa (to read)	infinitive
ba + basa	= babasa	future
b + um + abasa	= bumabasa	present
b + um + asa	= bumasa	past

Listen to the pronunciation of each of the following verbs, then try to pronounce each word yourself, without the help of the CD.

🔊 **CD 1, TR 12, 02:39**

Verb root	Meaning	Infinitive	Future	Present	Past
bili	*buy*	bumili	bibili	bumibili	bumili
kain	*eat*	kumain	kakain	kumakain	kumain
kuha	*get*	kumuha	kukuha	kumukuha	kumuha
gawa	*make*	gumawa	gagawa	gumagawa	gumawa
hiram	*borrow*	humiram	hihiram	humihiram	humiram
lakad	*walk*	lumakad	lalakad	lumalakad	lumakad

More verbs can be found listed at the back of this book.

This is the formula:

Verb	+ actor		
Kumain	si Louie		
Ate	Louie		

Louie ate

Verb	+ actor	+ object	
Kumain	si Louie	ng sorbetes	
Ate	Louie	ice cream	

Louie ate (some) ice cream

Verb	+ actor	+ object	+ place
Kumain	si Louie	ng sorbetes	sa restawran
Ate	Louie	ice cream	at the restaurant

Louie ate (some) ice cream at the restaurant

Verb	+ actor	+ object	+ place	+ time
Kumain	si Louie	ng sorbetes	sa restawran	kahapon
Ate	Louie	ice cream	at the restaurant	yesterday

Louie ate (some) ice cream at the restaurant yesterday

Did you notice how you are able to expand a very simple sentence easily? You can lengthen a sentence by merely adding a preposition of time or place or an adverb, etc.

Exercise 2

Using the sentence structure provided (verb + actor + object + place + time), build a Tagalog sentence around each of the following verbs. Use the **Quick vocab** to help you:

1. Bibili
2. Kumakain
3. Gumawa
4. Humihiram
5. Iinom

kahapon	*yesterday*	
ngayon	*today*	
humihiram	*borrowing*	
ng kape	*coffee*	
kumakain	*eating*	
iinom	*will drink*	
ng laruan	*toy*	
araw-araw	*every day*	
gumawa	*to make*	
bibili	*will buy*	

QUICK VOCAB

A note about recent action

There is a minor, yet important, aspect of active Tagalog verbs known as the recent action. The recent action is used to express events in the very recent past. It is formed by prefixing **ka** to the future tense of the verb. For example, the future tense of the **um** verb **alis** is **aalis**. To form the recent action aspect of the verb, we simply add **ka** + **aalis** = **kaaalis**. Remember, however, that the recent action takes the **ng** form as the 'doer' of the action. In order to underline how recent the action is, the word **lang** (*only/just/only just*) is always used with the recent action form. For example, **Kaaalis lang ni Stephen at ni Amy**, *Amy and Stephen have only just left*. **Huwag na tayong magmeryenda, kakakain** lang natin ng tanghalian, *Let's not have a snack as we've only just eaten lunch*. **Kadarating mo lang ba?**, *Have you just arrived?*

Asking about alterations

Dialogue 2

◀) CD 1, TR 12, 04:02

Louise Cook is at the dressmaker's.

Louise	Magan**dang ha**pon.
Modista	Magan**dang ha**pon *po* na**man**.
Louise	Bumi**li** a**ko** ng **te**la**ng** pambis**ti**da sa pal**eng**ke, at **gus**to kong *magpatahi* ng bes**ti**da.
Modista	A**ba o**po. **Na**saan *po* ang **te**la n'yo?
Louise	**He**to. A**yo**kong mas**ya**dong *maikli* ito.
Modista	*Hindi po*. Pu**we**de *po* bang su**ka**tan ko ka**yo**?
Louise	A**ba oo** na**man**.
Modista	Ang **suk**at *po* ng dib**dib** ay tatlum**pu't an**im na pul**ga**da. Ang **bay**wang *po* ay dalawam**pu't** wa**long** pul**ga**da. Ang hips *po* ay tatlum**pu't** wa**long** pul**ga**da. Ang mang**gas** *po* ay wa**long** pul**ga**da. Ang ba**lik**at ay labing-**an**im na pul**ga**da. Ang **ha**ba ng **pal**da ay dalawam**pu't a**pat na pul**ga**da. Iyan lang *po*.
Louise	Kai**lan** ko maa**a**ring ma**ku**ha ang da**mit**?
Modista	Sa Biyernes *po*. Mga a**las kwa**tro nang **ha**pon.
Louise	Ma**ra**ming sa**la**mat.
Modista	*Wala* pong anu**man**.

QUICK VOCAB

ang sukat ko	*my measurement*
bumili	*bought*
telang pambistida	*dress material*
haba	*length*
sukatan	*to measure*
pulgada	*inches*
paikliin	*be shortened*
nasaan	*where*
heto	*here*

ayoko(ng)	*don't like*
sukat ng dibdib	*bust line*
palengke	*market*
kailan	*when*
magpatahi	*have clothes made*
bukas nang hapon	*tomorrow afternoon*
baywang	*waistline*
hips	*hips*
manggas	*sleeves*
balikat	*shoulders*
palda	*skirt*
makuha	*to collect/get*

Translation

Louise	Good afternoon.
Dressmaker	Good afternoon to you, too.
Louise	I bought some cloth at the market and I would like to have a dress made up.
Dressmaker	Yes ma'am. Where is your cloth?
Louise	Here. I don't want it to be too short.
Dressmaker	No ma'am. Can I take your measurements?
Louise	Of course.
Dressmaker	Your bust line is 36. Your waist line is 28. Your hips are 38. Sleeve length is 8 inches. Armhole is 14 inches. Shoulders are 16. Skirt length is 24 inches. That's all ma'am.
Louise	When will I be able to collect the dress?
Dressmaker	On Friday ma'am, at about 4.00 in the afternoon.
Louise	Thank you very much.
Dressmaker	You're welcome.

Some useful words for a visit to the **sastre** (*tailor*) can be found in the **Quick vocab** below.

medida	*tape measure*
sinulid	*thread*
karayom	*needle*
iklian	*to make short*

habaan	*to make long*
lakihan	*to make big*
liitan	*to make small*
palitan	*change*
terno	*go together*
itupi	*to fold*
kalsahan	*to lower the hemline*

Exercise 3

Listen to the list of items on the CD. The tailor has misplaced his spectacles and can't see where he has left things. Can you help him find them? With a pen or pencil, circle each item mentioned as you hear it.

◀) **CD 1, TR 12, 05:32**

Exercise 4

How do you say the following in Tagalog?

1. You want a green skirt.
2. You don't want a long skirt.
3. You need it on Monday.
4. Your skirt is at home.

174

Insight

There are four major tenses in Tagalog verbs: the infinitive, future, present and past. There is however a fifth tense, known as current action. Represented by the prefix **ka** added to the future tense, this is unique in that it takes **ng** as the actor, while **lang** *always* accompanies the verb: for example: **Katutulog lang ni Jose.** *Jose has just slept.*

Language skills

3 Verbalization of adjectives

Louise Cook used the word **umikli** in her conversation with the dressmaker, **ayokong masyadong umikli ito. Umikli** is derived from the adjective **maikli** (*short*). In Tagalog, adjectives can also become action words (verbs). When this happens, the resulting meaning of the newly formed action word is 'to become ____'. To do this, simply drop the prefix 'ma' from the adjective, e.g., **maikli** (*short*), add '**um**' = **um + ikli = umikli** (*to become shorter*). When the adjective root begins with a vowel (e.g. **asim**, '*sourness*'), simply add '**um**' before the root word to produce the infinitive (e.g. **um + asim = umasim** *to become sour*). When the adjective root begins with a consonant (e.g. **ganda** *beauty*), then '**um**' is placed after the first letter (e.g. **g + um + anda = gumanda**, *to become beautiful*). Here are some more examples:

Example: Adjective stem: **sama** (*badness*) source: **masama** (*bad*)

s + um + ama = sumama (to become/get worse)	infinitive
sa + sama = sasama (will become/get worse)	future
s + um + asama = sumasama (becoming/getting worse)	present
s + um + ama = sumama (became/got worse)	past

Listen to the pronunciation of each of the following verbalized adjectives on the CD. Why not try to repeat them without the help of the CD.

Adjective	Meaning	Infinitive	Future	Present	Past
(ma)laki	*big*	lumaki	lalaki	lumalaki	lumaki
(ma)ganda	*pretty*	gumanda	gaganda	gumaganda	gumanda
(ma)liit	*small*	lumiit	liliit	lumiliit	lumiit
(ma)sarap	*delicious*	sumarap	sasarap	sumasarap	sumarap
(ma)layo	*far*	lumayo	lalayo	lumalayo	lumayo
(ma)buti	*good*	bumuti	bubuti	bumubuti	bumuti
(ma)linis	*clean*	luminis	lilinis	lumilinis	luminis

A further list can be found at the back of this book.

Some example sentences:

Tagalog: **Gumaganda** ang hardin ni Patricia
Literal: becoming more beautiful the garden of Patricia
English: *Patricia's garden is becoming more beautiful*

Tagalog: **Lumilinis** ang kotse mo
Literal: becoming cleaner the car your
English: *Your car is becoming cleaner*

Tagalog: Hindi **bumuti** ang panahon
Literal: (did) not improve the weather
English: *The weather did not improve*

Tagalog: **Bumibilis** yata ang takbo ng relos mo
Literal: becoming fast I think the running of watch your
English: *I think your watch is running fast*

Exercise 5

Provide the correct tense of the following verbalized adjectives. The stem of each adjective is given in the bracket:

1. _____ ang problema ni Jose araw-araw. (laki, present)
2. Ang bahay ni Aling Maria ay _____ . (ganda, present)
3. Hindi ba _____ ang kotse ni Les? (linis, past)
4. Kailangang _____ tayo sa gulo. (layo, infinitive)

Exercise 6

See how many verbalized adjectives you can find in the crossword.

		S	A	K	A	L	I	D
	L	U	M	A	L	A	K	I
L	U	M	I	W	A	N	A	G
	M	A		A	H	A	S	H
H	I	R	A	P		P	M	A
I	N	A	K	B	A	Y	A	A
	A	P	A	N	D	A		
A	W		T	A	N	O	T	N

Describing the weather

Dialogue 3

◆ CD 1, TR 12, 07:49

The weather is bad. Bill, Louise and Roy Cook are talking about it in their hotel room.

Bill	Muk**hang** *sumasama* ang pana**hon**. **Bab**agyo **yat**a!
Louise	Kaga**bi**, umu**lan** nang mala**kas** at hu**mang**in din.
Roy	No**ong isang** ling**go**, **ka**hit u**mu**ulan, sumi**sik**at ang **a**raw.
Louise	Ma**buti** kung ganoo**on**.
Bill	Ma**hir**ap ka**si** di**to** sa Pili**pi**nas, ka**pag** u**mu**lan, **ba**ba**ha** kaa**gad**.
Roy	Du**mi**dilim na na**man** ang **la**ngit.
Louise	Ma**buti ya**ta di**to mu**na **ta**yo sa hotel hang**gang** sa guman**da** ang pana**hon**.
Bill	Sang-**a**yon sa radyo, bu**but**i raw ang pana**hon ba**go guma**bi**.
Roy	Mag**ba**basa a**ko** ng ak**lat**.

umulan	*to rain*
sumasama	*becoming/getting worse*
ang panahon	*the weather*
babagyo	*there will be a typhoon*
na naman	*again*
ang langit	*the sky*
umulan	*rained*
humangin	*was windy*
noong isang linggo	*last week*
kahit	*even though*
umuulan	*raining*
sumisikat	*shining*
ang araw	*the sun*
gumabi	*to become night*
kung ganoon	*if that's the case*
mahirap	*difficult*
kapag	*if/when*
babaha	*will flood*
kaagad	*immediately*
dumidilim	*becoming dark*
dito muna	*here* (for the moment)
hanggang	*until*
gumanda	*to become fine*
sang-ayon sa	*according to*
radyo	*radio*
bubuti	*will become better*
bago	*before*
magbabasa	*will read*

Translation

Bill	The weather seems to be getting worse. I think a typhoon is coming.
Louise	Last night, it rained hard and there was wind too.
Roy	The other week, even though it was raining, the sun was shining.
Louise	It's good (when it's) like that.
Bill	The trouble here in the Philippines is that when it rains there are floods.
Roy	The sky is getting darker again.

178

Louise	It might be a good idea to stay in the hotel until the weather settles.
Bill	According to the radio, the weather will be fine by tonight.
Roy	I will read a book.

Exercise 7

The following sentences need to be expanded. Can you add an adverb of time (e.g. **bukas**, *tomorrow*) or preposition (e.g. **sa** *in, at*) to expand each sentence? Use the **Quick vocab** to help you:

Example: Kumikidlat kanina *add*: **pero** hindi yata uulan.

1. Bumubuti ang panahon **kasi**
2. Umuulan nang malakas **lagi**
3. Hindi bumabaha sa Pilipinas **kung**
4. Lumiliwanag ba ang langit **kahit na**
5. Sasama ang panahon bago gumabi **sapagka't**

kasi	*because*
lagi	*always*
kung	*if/when*
kahit na	*even though*
sapagka't	*because*

QUICK VOCAB

Insight

Filipinos typically display respect for authority through use of formal titles or honorific terms: for example, *Mr Sanayan the engineer* will commonly be addressed as **Engineer Sanayan**, even by long-standing friends or colleagues. The balance between familiarity and respect is commonly expressed by a shortening of the formal title for example, *Doctor* becomes **Doc**, *Father* becomes **Pads**.

Language skills

4 Verbalization of acts of nature

Most Tagalog words describing acts of nature can also be made into verbs. For example, if the sun is shining, Filipinos merely say

'Umaaraw!' (from **araw** = the sun). If there is a flash of lightning, they exclaim: 'Kumikidlat!' (from **kidlat** = lightning). **Umulan kasi kaya hindi kami sumimba**, *It rained; that's why we didn't go to church*. The following list gives further examples of other verbalized acts of nature. Notice that they also form their tenses in the same manner as the **um** verb.

Examples:

	Infinitive & past tense		Present continuous	Future
baha – *flood*	bumaha	*to flood*	bumabaha	babaha
araw – *sun*	umaraw	*to shine* (sun only)	umaaraw	aaraw
ulan – *rain*	umulan	*to rain*	umuulan	uulan
kidlat – *lightning*	kumidlat	*to flash* (lightning)	kumikidlat	kikidlat
kulog – *thunder*	kumulog	*to thunder*	kumukulog	kukulog
sikat – *shine*	sumikat	*to shine* (sun, moon)	sumisikat	sisikat
lubog – *set*	lumubog	*to set* (sun, moon)	lumulubog	lulubog
bagyo – *typhoon*	bumagyo	*to have a typhoon*	bumabagyo	babagyo
hangin – *wind*	humangin	*to become windy*	humahangin	hahangin
ambon – *drizzle*	umambon	*to drizzle*	umaambon	aambon
lindol – *earthquake*	lumindol	*to have an e'quake*	lumilindol	lilindol

Changing the tenses of the *um* acts of nature

	Infinitive	Future	Present	Past
	umulan	uulan	umuulan	umulan
Example:		*It's going to rain*	*It is raining*	*It rained*

Sample sentences:

Tagalog:	Sumisikat ang araw sa silangan
Literal:	Shine/shining the sun in the east
English:	*The sun shines in the east*

Tagalog:	Bumabagyo lagi sa may China Sea
Literal:	Typhoon always near the China Sea
English:	*There's always a typhoon near the China Sea*

Tagalog: Kapag umaambon may bahag-hari daw
Literal: If/when drizzling there is rainbow apparently
English: *Apparently, when it drizzles, a rainbow appears*

Exercise 8

Basing your answers on the verb in italics, supply an appropriate reply to the following questions:

1. Hindi ba *bumabaha* sa Maynila?
2. *Lumulubog* ba ang araw sa silangan?
3. Mga anong oras *sumisikat* ang araw sa Pilipinas?
4. Wala bang ingay kung *kumukulog at kumikidlat*?
5. *Umaaraw* ba kung *sumisikat* ang buwan?

Exercise 9

Look at the pictures showing some acts of nature. Can you say them in Tagalog using the tense or form indicated?

1. Present continuous   2. Past/infinitive   3. Past/infinitive

Exercise 10

Listen to the radio weather forecast on the CD. In your own words, try to give the following weather forecast. Use the **Quick vocab** to help you:

◀) **CD 1, TR 12, 08:53**

Today's weather: Cloudy, possible rain in northern Luzon.
        Tonight: Warm
      Tomorrow: Plenty of sunshine

makulimlim	*cloudy*
maaaring umulan	*it might rain*
hilagang Luzon	*northern Luzon*
mainit	*warm*
mainit ang araw	*plenty of sunshine*

QUICK VOCAB

mamayang gabi   *tonight*
sa hapon   *in the afternoon*

One-minute phrases

Ilista sa tubig (*ee-lees-tah sah too-beeg*) Literally, *list in water*. Meaning not to make a note of something, to forget all about it. This phrase is commonly used in connection with a 'conveniently forgotten' debt.

Di-mahulugang karayom (*dee mah-hoo-loo-gang kah-rah-yawm*) Literally, *cannot drop a needle*. Meaning a crowded area/a tightly packed space. For example: **Napakaraming tao noong dumalaw ang Papa sa Luneta at ito'y di mahulugang karayom.** *Luneta was so crowded when the Pope visited that it was so difficult to move around* (find a needle).

Sisikat din ang araw (*see-see-kaht deen ahng ah-rao*) Literally, *the sun will also rise*. Similar in meaning to the English proverb: 'Every cloud has a silver lining'. **Kalimutan mo na ang nangyari sa iyong pananim dahil sa baha. May kasabihan tayong: sisikat din ang araw,** *Try to forget what happened to your crops because of the flood. We have a saying: every cloud has a silver lining.*

Isukat mo nga (*ee-soo-kaht maw ngah*) Literal and true meaning *why don't you try it on?* Trying an article of clothing or something on in a shop.

Bahag-hari (*bah-hahg-haa-ree*) Literally, *the king's loin cloth*. This is the Tagalog word for rainbow!

Insight

In Filipino culture dress sense is very important. When you don't know what to wear for a particular occasion your Filipino friends will advise you. You could get yourself a 'Barong Tagalog' (Filipino national dress) which is suitable for formal occasions.

Summary

1. There are two voices in Tagalog verbs: the Active and Passive voice.
2. The Active verbs are **um/ma**, **mag** and **mang** verbs.
3. The Passive verbs are **in**, **i** and **an** verbs.
4. The doer or actor of Active verbs is the **ang** group.
5. The object in Active verbs is the **ng** group.
6. Active verbs contain a special category known as 'recent action': **Katutulog ko lang.** *I have just slept.*
7. Transitive verbs are verbs with an object. *I ate an apple.* **Kumain ako ng mansanas.**
8. Intransitive verbs are verbs that do not take an object: *I slept.* **Natulog ako.**
9. Acts of nature can be verbalized in **um** verbs. *It rained.* **Umulan.**
10. Adjectives can be verbalized in **um** verbs, meaning *to become.* *Their house became bigger.* **Lumaki ang bahay nila.**

13

....

Sa istasyon ng bus
At the bus station

In this unit you will learn how to:

- Ask about tickets, destinations, departures and arrivals
- Express days of the week, etc.
- Use **mag** and **ma** verbs

Asking about tickets, destinations and departures

◀) CD 2, TR 1

Dialogue 1

The Cook family are going to the north of Luzon. They are at the ticket office enquiring about departures.

Bill	Magandang umaga. **Gus**to kong bumi**li** ng **ti**ket **pa**ra sa tat**lo** papun**tang** Bana**u**e.
Opisyal	Magandang umaga po na**man. Ib**ig po ba nin**yo ti**ket na papun**ta la**mang do**on** o ba**li**kan?
Bill	Kung puwede ba**li**kan at sa Bi**yer**nes ika-**li**ma ng Ab**ril** ang ba**lik**.
Opisyal	Kai**lan** po nin**yo ib**ig magbi**ya**he?
Bill	Kung puwede sa Mar**tes**.
Opisyal	*Sandali* lang po at **ti**tingnan ko.
Bill	OK lang, mag**hi**hintay a**ko**.

Opisyal	Tatlo *po* ang biyahe sa Martes, ika-dalawa ng Abril. Ang una ay aalis sa alas 4.30 nang umaga, tapos alas 10.30, at alas 2.30 nang hapon. Mabuti *po* ang alas 4.30 nang umaga kung maaari kayong magbiyahe nang maaga.
Bill	Oo. Puwede kaming magbiyahe nang maaga. Saan kami puwedeng mag-almusal?
Opisyal	Hihinto *po* ang bus nang mga alas 7.30 sa Pampanga upang makapag-almusal kayo.
Bill	Mabuti kung ganoon.
Opisyal	Eto *po* ang tiket ninyo para sa tatlong pasahero. Maligayang paglalakbay *po*!
Bill	Maraming salamat.
Opisyal	*Wala* pong anuman.

balikan	*return*
kung puwede sana	*if possible*
dating	*arrival*
gusto kong bumili	*I want to buy*
ng tiket	*tickets*
para sa tatlo	*for three*
papunta sa	*going to*
naman	*too, also*
hihinto	*will stop*
aalis	*will go etc.*
kung puwede sana	*if possible*
ang biyahe	*the trip*
sa araw	*during the day*
nang umaga	*in the morning*
tapos	*afterwards/then*
nang hapon	*in the afternoon*
magbiyahe	*to travel*
maghintay	*to wait*
alis	*departure*
nang maaga	*early*
mag-almusal	*to have breakfast*
upang	*in order to/so that*
makapag-almusal	*can have breakfast*

QUICK VOCAB

kung ganoon	*if that's the case*
eto po	*here sir*
tiket ninyo	*your tickets*
maligaya(ng)	*happy*
paglalakbay	*trip*

Translation

Bill	Good morning. I'd like to buy tickets for three (persons) to Banaue.
Official	Good morning sir. Do you want single tickets or return?
Bill	Return tickets, please, if possible coming back on Friday April 5.
Official	When do you want to travel sir?
Bill	If possible, on Tuesday.
Official	Please wait sir while I check.
Bill	Yes. I'll wait.
Official	Sir, there are three trips on Tuesday April 2. The first is at 4.30 in the morning, then at 10.30 and at 2.30 in the afternoon. The 4.30 (departure) is the best (one) if you can travel early.
Bill	Sure. We can travel early. Where can we have breakfast?
Official	Sir, the bus is going to make a stop at 7.30 at Pampanga so that you can have your breakfast.
Bill	That's good.
Official	Sir, here are your tickets for three passengers. Have a good trip!
Bill	Thank you very much.
Official	You're welcome.

Other useful vocabulary for travelling can be found in the **Quick vocab** below.

pasahero	*passenger*
tiket	*ticket*
pamasahe	*fare*
biyahe	*trip*
pang-isa	*single*
sasakay	*will board*
bababa	*will alight/get off*
sukli	*change*
upuan	*seat*
bakante	*vacant*

parahin	*to stop* (a public vehicle)
konduktor	*conductor*
drayber	*driver*
umangkas	*to get a lift*
siksikan	*packed to capacity*
mama	term a passenger uses to call driver's attention
barya	*change*

QUICK VOCAB

Exercise 1 Listening and understanding

Listen carefully once again to the conversation between Bill Cook and the clerk. Based on the dialogue, identify which of the following statements are true and which are false.

1. Gustong bumili ni Bill ng tiket papuntang Davao.
2. Kung puwede sana gustong umalis nang maaga ni Bill.
3. Sabi ng opisyal: 'Mag-almusal kayo at titingnan ko.'
4. Sabi ni Bill sa opisyal: 'Maghihintay ako.'
5. Tatlo ang biyahe sa araw.
6. May biyahe sa gabi at maaga ito.
7. Hindi puwedeng magbiyahe sina Bill nang maaga.
8. Maaari silang mag-almusal nang maaga.
9. Sa Pampanga hihinto ang bus.
10. Hindi sila mag-aalmusal sa Pampanga.

Exercise 2

Can you say the following sentences in the negative?

1. Gusto kong bumili ng tiket.
2. Puwede bukas nang umaga.
3. Humihinto ang bus nang mga alas 7.30.
4. Malapit ang Babauae buhat sa Maynila.
5. Mabuti ang alas 4.30 nang umaga.

Days, months and dates

In Dialogue 1, Bill Cook mentions that he wants to travel on Tuesday April 2. To give the date in Tagalog, simply use **ika** + Tagalog number. For example: **ika-apat ng Disyembre** = *December 4*.

Question: **Kailan ang kaarawan mo?** *When is your birthday?*
Answer: **Sa ika-apat ng Disyembre.** *On December 4.*

Here is a complete list of the days of the week and months of the year:

Days of the week		Months of the year	
Lunes	*Monday*	Enero	*January*
Martes	*Tuesday*	Pebrero	*February*
Miyerkoles	*Wednesday*	Marso	*March*
Huwebes	*Thursday*	Abril	*April*
Biyernes	*Friday*	Mayo	*May*
Sabado	*Saturday*	Hunyo	*June*
Linggo	*Sunday*	Hulyo	*July*
		Agosto	*August*
		Septyembre	*September*
		Oktubre	*October*
		Nobyembre	*November*
		Disyembre	*December*

Exercise 3

What comes after _____? Can you fill in the blank with the correct answer?

1. Miyerkoles _____
2. Agosto _____
3. Oktubre _____
4. Sabado _____
5. Martes _____
6. Mayo _____
7. Biyernes _____

Exercise 4

Can you translate the following into Tagalog? Use the **Quick vocab** to help you:

Example: July 4   Answer: Ika-apat ng Hulyo

1. His birthday is on August 30.
2. School begins on Monday.
3. We will be visiting you on Saturday, May 10.

4. The conference was last Tuesday, June 14.
5. We are going to the zoo on Sunday, September 3.
6. Are you leaving on Saturday?
7. Who is arriving on Thursday, January 5?

QUICK VOCAB

simula	*start*
bibisita	*be visiting*
kumperensiya	*conference*
pupunta	*going*
aalis	*leaving*
darating	*arriving*
paaralan	*school*

Language skills

1 *Mag* verbs

Most Tagalog verbs begin with **mag**. Like the **um** verbs we met in Unit 12, **mag** verbs can also be transitive (with an object) or intransitive (without an object). You will remember that **um** verbs take either a prefix (an addition before the verb root), or an infix (an addition within the verb root). **Mag** verbs are easier in that they take only a prefix. As with the **um** verbs, the connecting word '**ng**' is used before the object. For example: **Magbili ng bigas.** *Sell rice.* **Mag** verbs need a subject, but they do not always need: 1) a time element; 2) a preposition; 3) an adverb.

The **mag** verb is very versatile in that while it forms both major transitive verbs (verbs with a direct object) and intransitive verbs (verbs without a direct object), it continues to carry the word that the verb suggests. For example: **magtennis** (*to play tennis*), **maglaba** (*to wash clothes*), **magbihis** (*to put clothes on*), **magdasal** (*to pray*), etc. Although most verb stems can be used with the **mag** prefix, it is important to remember that some verbs are **um** verbs only, while some verbs are **mag** verbs only. Listen carefully to how each verb is used by native Tagalog speakers. Through listening and repeating what you hear, you will soon be able to distinguish between the different verb types. If you are unsure, check out the verb list at the back of this book or check your Tagalog dictionary.

The versatility of the **mag** verb becomes clear when we see the variety of ways in which it can be used:

1. **mag** + noun, e.g. mag + bus = magbus, *to go by bus*
2. **mag** + noun designating a member of a profession, e.g. abogado (*lawyer*) = mag-abogado, *to become a lawyer*
3. **mag** + article of clothing, e.g. mag + kamiseta = magkamiseta, *to wear a tee-shirt*
4. **mag** + language, e.g. mag + Tagalog = magTagalog, *to speak Tagalog*
5. **mag** + item designated by the noun, e.g. magbunga, *to bear fruit*
6. **mag** + noun expressing action involving two or more actors, mag + salubong (*greet one another*) = magsalubong, *to meet*
7. **mag** + adjective, e.g. mag + mabagal (*slow*) = magmabagal, *be slow in*, mag + mayaman = magmayaman, *to pretend to be rich*
8. **mag** + times of day, e.g. mag + madaling-araw (*dawn*) magmadaling-araw, *be dawn*

Changing the tense of the **mag** verb is easy. Take for example the verb stem **laba** (*wash clothes*):

mag + laba	=	maglaba	infinitive (used only in requests, commands and suggestions)
mag + la + laba	=	maglalaba	future
*nag + la + laba	=	naglalaba	present
*nag + laba	=	naglaba	past
kapag + la + laba	=	kapaglalaba	recent action

(*__Note__: the prefix **mag** is used in the infinitive and future tenses and changes to **nag** in the present and past tense.)

Here are a few commonly occurring **mag** verbs. Listen to how they are pronounced on the CD:

◀) **CD 2, TR 1, 01:47**

mag-ayos	*to arrange*
mag-alis	*to remove*
mag-abang	*to wait for someone*
mag-aral	*to study*
magbantay	*to guard*
magbigay	*to give*
magbili	*to sell*

magbintang	*to accuse*
magdasal	*to pray*
maghain	*to serve food on the table*
maghugas	*to wash*
maglaba	*to wash clothes*
maglakad	*to walk*
maglaro	*to play*
maglinis	*to clean*
magluto	*to cook*
magmana	*to inherit*
magmasid	*to watch*

A further selection of **mag** verbs can be found at the back of this book.

Exercise 5

Look at the pictures and try to find the correct verb to describe each activity. Give your answers in the **mag** verb form:

1. **2.** **3.**

A guide to expanding the *mag* sentence

A) Transitive verbs (with object)

Verb	+ actor	+ object
Nagbibili	si Jose	ng lumang alahas
Selling/sells	Jose	old jewellery

Jose is selling/sells old jewellery.

Verb	+ actor	+ object	+ place
Nagluto	kami	ng pansit	sa bahay ni Letty
Cooked	we	noodles	at Letty's home

We cooked some noodles at Letty's home.

Verb	+ particle	+ actor	+ object	+ place + time
Nagdala	pala	sila	ng pagkain	sa party kagabi
Brought	so	they some	to the party	last night food

So they brought some food to the party last night.

B) Intransitive verbs (without an object)

Verb	+ actor
Maglalaba	si Margaret
Will wash/will be washing clothes	Margaret

Margaret will be washing clothes.

Qualifier/Verb	+ actor	+ place and/or time
Hindi nagsalita	si Gener	sa pulong kahapon.
Did not talk/speak	Gener	at the meeting yesterday.

Gener didn't talk/speak at the meeting yesterday.

Exercise 6

Using the verb, form and scenario provided, see if you can do the following in Tagalog:

1. Suggest to a friend to play. (laro) (infinitive)
2. Say that you cleaned the car already. (linis) (past)
3. Say that Maria is washing the dishes. (hugas) (present)
4. Suggest to everyone you want to pray. (dasal) (infinitive)
5. Say that Lina and her friends will be cooking. (luto) (future)

Mag and recent action

Just to keep us on our toes, when using the recent action with **mag** verbs, we must be careful to remember that **mag** changes to **pag**. For example:

ka +	future	= recent action
ka +	maglalaro (will play)	= kapaglalaro
ka +	maglilinis (will clean)	= kapaglilinis
ka +	mag-aaral (will study)	= kapag-aaral

See Unit 12.

Enquiring about arrivals

Dialogue 2

🔊 **CD 2, TR 1, 03:01**

Jobert is enquiring about the arrival of the Cook family on the bus from Banaue.

Jobert	Anong oras ang dating ng bus ngayon galing sa Baguio?
Manager	Alas 7.45 po nang gabi.
Jobert	Bakit, anong oras ba itong umalis buhat sa Baguio?
Manager	Kanina pong alas 9.00 nang umaga.
Jobert	Saang mga lugar ba ito hihinto?
Manager	Sa Ilocos po, sa, Tarlac, Pampanga at Bulacan.
Jobert	Ganoon ba? Maraming salamat.
Manager	*Wala* pong anuman.

ang dating	*the arrival*
ngayon	*today/now*
galing sa	*from*
mga lugar	*places*
bakit	*why*
umalis	*departed*

Translation

Jobert	What time will the bus from Baguio arrive?
Manager	Sir, 7.45 in the evening.
Jobert	(Why) What time did it leave/depart from Baguio?
Manager	A while ago at 9.00 this morning.
Jobert	What places will it make a stopover?
Manager	At Ilocos, Tarlac, Pampanga and Bulacan
Jobert	Is that so? Thank you very much.
Manager	You're welcome sir.

Exercise 7

Use Dialogue 2 to answer the following questions:

1. Ilang oras ang biyahe ng bus galing sa Baguio?
2. Hihinto ba ang bus sa Zambales?

3. Alin ang ikatatlong probinsiya na hihintuan ng bus?
4. Ilan lahat-lahat ang probinsiya?

ilan(g)	*how many*
alin	*which one*
ikatatlo(ng)	*third*
lahat-lahat	*altogether*

Exercise 8

Give a Tagalog summary of the schedule in Dialogue 2 in the second column.

English	Tagalog
1. Departure from Baguio:	*9.00 a.m*
2. Arrival from Baguio:	*7.45 p.m*
3. Stopover:	*Ilocos, Pangasinan, Tarlac Pampanga & Bulacan*

Exercise 9

Look at the bus ticket. Can you answer the following questions?

1. Magkano ang halaga ng tiket?
2. Ang numero ng tiket ay: anim, dalawa, dalawa, apat, apat, anim.
3. May petsa ba ang tiket ng bus?
4. Ilang kilometro ang layo ng biyahe?
5. Sinasabi ba sa tiket kung anong oras ang alis?
6. Sinasabi ba sa tiket kung anong oras ang dating?

Insight

A number of **um** verbs can be verbalized under **mag** verbs. One very common verb which creates a problem for some Visayan speakers is the verb stem **bili**. In Tagalog, **bumili** is *to buy* and **magbili** is *to sell*. In the Visayas, **magbili** means *to buy*!

Language skills

2 *Ma* verbs

maligo	*to have a bath*
matulog	*to sleep*
maupo	*to sit down*
makinig	*to listen*
mahiga	*to lie down*

There are five special verb stems that are neither **um** verbs nor **mag** verbs. These verbs are known as **ma** verbs due to them taking the prefix **ma**. The five **ma** verbs are intransitive and their tenses cannot be formed by using **um** or **mag**. As there are so few **ma** verbs, the best approach is simply to try to memorize them. Like **um** and **mag** verbs, **ma** verbs can be used with pseudo-verbs. Example: **Gusto kong maligo** *I'd like to have a bath*.

Forming tenses with ma

Ma + ligo = maligo   =   infinitive (used with requests, suggestions and commands)

Ma + li + ligo	=	future
Na + li + ligo	=	present
Na + ligo	=	past

Example sentences:

| Verb | + actor | + time |
| Naliligo | ako | araw-araw |

I have a bath every day

| Question marker | + verb | + direction |
| Sino | ang nakikinig | sa kaniya? |

Who is listening to him/her?

| Verb | + actor | + particle | + preposition |
| Naupo | ka | ba | sa silyang ito? |

Did you sit on this chair?

Exercise 10

Choose the correct form from the brackets:

1. Ayaw mo bang (maligo, naliligo, naligo) tayo sa dagat? (infinitive)
2. (Makikinig, nakikinig, nakinig) ako sa awitin niya. (present)
3. Maraming (naupo, nauupo, maupo) sa sahig kagabi sa awditoryum. (past)
4. Gusto po ba ninyong (mahiga, nahiga, mahihiga) sa kamang iyan? (infinitive)
5. Si Patricia yata ang (natutulog, natulog, matulog) sa bahay ni John kagabi. (past)

Finding out what your journey will be like

Dialogue 3

◀)) CD 2, TR 1, 03:46

The Cook family are on the bus from Banaue to Manila. Bill Cook is talking to the conductor.

Bill	**Anon**g **o**ras **ta**yo **da**rating sa May**ni**la?
Konduktor	Mga alas-si**ye**te y **med**ya *po* nang ga**bi**.
Bill	Sa**an ta**yo *hihinto* **u**pang makapag**ba**nat ng kata**wan**?

Konduktor	Sa Pam**pa**nga po at **me**ron ding ku**be**ta at **pa**liguan do**on**.
Bill	Magda**dag**dag ba ka**yo** ng gaso**li**na?
Konduktor	Opo.
Bill	May te**le**pono ba do**on pa**ra makat**a**wag a**ko**?
Konduktor	**Me**ron *po.*
Bill	Sal**a**mat.
Konduktor	*Wala* pong anu**man**.

magdadagdag	*will add*
darating	*will arrive*
mga alas siyete y medya	*around 7.30*
nang gabi	*at night*
makatawag	*be able to call*
makapagbanat	*be able to stretch*
kubeta	*toilet*
paliguan	*shower/bathroom*
gasolina	*petrol*
telepono	*telephone*
para	*so that/in order to*

Translation

Bill	What time are we arriving in Manila?
Conductor	Around 7.30 in the evening.
Bill	Is there any place where we can stop to stretch ourselves (lit, our body)?
Conductor	In Pampanga sir. There are also bathroom facilities there.
Bill	Are you going to top up your petrol?
Conductor	Yes sir.
Bill	Are there any telephones there for me to make a call?
Conductor	There are (telephones there) sir.
Bill	Thank you.
Conductor	You're welcome sir.

Exercise 11
Using the dialogue as your guide, can you do the following?

1. Ask the conductor what time the bus is stopping at Pampanga. (use Anong oras)

Unit 13   At the bus station   197

2. Ask him where else you will be stopping. (use pa)

3. Ask the conductor if there are bathroom facilities at the stop. (use Mayroon)

4. Tell the conductor you want to use the bathroom. (use Gusto kong)

Exercise 12 Understanding and speaking

Imagine that you are on a bus bound for Batangas, south of Manila. Why not have a go at speaking with the conductor. Listen carefully to the conductor's responses. Using the hints and the **Quick vocab** to help you, write out your part of the dialogue and then practise speaking it:

Ikaw	(greet the conductor, saying good morning)
Konduktor	Magandang umaga po. Didiretso po ba kayo sa Batan-gas?
Ikaw	(say yes, but that you are unsure about what time the bus returns to Manila)
Konduktor	Babalik po ba kayo pa-Maynila bukas?
Ikaw	(we will return tomorrow afternoon)
Konduktor	Ganoon po ba? Mayroon pong bus na paalis sa istasyon sa alas 3.00
Ikaw	(three o'clock, that's fine)
Konduktor	Ibig po ba ninyong bumili ng tiket na papunta lamang doon o balikan?
Ikaw	(just singles please. Three adults)
Konduktor	Iyan po ay tres siyentos treynta pesos.
Ikaw	(Say here you are/here's my payment)
Konduktor	Maraming salamat po. Marunong kayong managalog!
Ikaw	(say thank you very much, too)

didiretso	*straight on*
babalik	*will return*
bukas	*tomorrow*
ganoon po ba?	*is that so ma'am/sir?*
paalis	*leaving*
istasyon	*station*
balikan	*return*
tres siyentos treynta	*330*
marunong	*know/knows how to*
managalog	*to speak Tagalog*

QUICK VOCAB

Insight

Rice plays such a central role in the Filipino diet that it is served for breakfast, lunch and dinner. No matter how much food is served, without rice, a meal is down-graded to a mere snack. A meal is not a meal unless rice is included!

Language skills

3   *Maka + um* **verb stem** *To be able to, to happen to, to come to, to manage to*
    Makapag + mag **verb stem** *To be able to, to happen to, to come to, to manage to*

In Dialogue 3, Bill Cook used the words **makapagbanat** and **makatawag**. These verb forms seem new and in jargon are known as circumstantial verbs. These verb forms above all give us a glimpse into Filipino culture. According to Filipino beliefs, some actions are brought about purely by circumstance, by accident or by occurrences beyond the actor's/s' control. The active **um** and **mag** verbs have special prefixes to express the circumstantial or involuntary nature of these actions. With **um** verbs, use the prefix **maka**. For example: **makabili** *to be able to/to happen to/to come to/to manage to buy*. With **mag** verbs, the prefix is **makapag**. For example: **makapag + laro = makapaglaro** *to be able to/to happen to/to come to/to manage to play*. Look at the guide on how to use the **maka** and **makapag** prefixes in the active **um** and **mag** verbs:

um verbs

Maka = (prefix) + alis (verb stem)

Maka + alis   = makaalis = infinitive

> *to be able to leave*
> *to happen to leave*
> *to manage to leave*
> *to come to leave*

Maka + ka + alis = makakaalis = *will be able* etc. *to leave*   = future

Naka + ka + alis = nakakaalis = *is able* etc. *to leave*   = present

Naka + alis   = nakaalis   = *was able* etc. *to leave*   = past

Some examples:

makakain	=	*to be able* etc. *to eat*
makabili	=	*to be able* etc. *to buy*
makabasa	=	*to be able* etc. *to read*
makasulat	=	*to be able* etc. *to write*
makakanta	=	*to be able* etc. *to sing*
makaalis	=	*to be able* etc. *to leave*

mag verbs

makapag + (prefix)   luto (verb stem)

makapag + luto =   makapagluto =   infinitive (used in requests, commands and suggestions)

to be able to cook
to happen to cook
to manage to cook
to come to cook

maka + ka + pag + luto = makakapagluto = *will be able* etc. *to cook* = future

naka + ka + pag + luto = nakakapagluto = *is able* etc. *to cook* = present

nakapag + luto = nakapagluto = *was able* etc. *to cook* = past

Here are some examples:

makapagsimba	=	*to be able to go to church*
makapagsalita	=	*to be able to talk/speak*
makapagbili	=	*to be able to sell*
makapagluto	=	*to be able to cook*
makapaglakad	=	*to be able to walk*
makapaglinis	=	*to be able to clean*
makapaglaba	=	*to be able to wash clothes*

Some variations of **maka** and **makapag** sentences:

Verb	+ actor	+ object	+ preposition
Nakabili	kami	ng magandang damit	sa palengke

We managed to buy a beautiful dress from the market.

Verb	+ actor	+ particle
Nakapagluto	ka	na ba?

Were you able to cook?/Did you manage to cook?

Verb	+ particle	+ actor	object	preposition
Nakagawa	na raw	ang mga bata	ng saranggola	kahapon.

Apparently, the children [already] managed to make a kite yesterday.

Exercise 13

Look at the following sentences. Can you supply the missing verb form?

1. Araw-araw, _____ kami sa palaruan. (laro)
2. Hindi _____ ang mga turista kanina dahil sa bagyo. (alis)
3. _____ ba tayo ng mga pasalubong bukas? (bili)
4. Sa Sabado, maraming _____ ng masasarap na pagkain. (luto)
5. Sino sa mga babae ang _____ sa bus noong linggo? (tulog)

One-minute phrases

Magmeryenda muna tayo (*mahg-mer-yen-dah moo-nah tah-yaw*) Literally, *to have a snack first let us.* (Please note that 'first' should not be given emphasis here.) An expression of casual but polite invitation meaning *Why don't we have a snack?* or *Could I invite you to have a snack?*

Mag-beer muna tayo/mag-kape muna tayo (*mahg-bber-moo-nah tay-yaw/mahg-kah-pe moo-nah fay-yaw*) *Could I invite you to a beer?*, *Shall we have coffee?* etc. (These expressions have the same connotation as above except that **meryenda** is replaced with beer or coffee) 'Mag +___ muna tayo' has the potential to expand and can be used as a structure for other invitations.

Sa ibang araw na (*sah ee-bahng ah-rao nah*) Literally, *in other days already.* Meaning *Some other day/Next time.* **Sa ibang araw na** is a nice way of turning down an invitation.

Medyo tagilid (*mehd-yaw tah-gee-leed*) Literally, *somewhat tilted.* Similar in meaning to the English expression *The dice are* *loaded.* This phrase pertains to a situation the result of which is not positive. For example: **Sa palagay mo mananalo si Ginoong Santos sa eleksiyon?** *Do you reckon Mr Santos will win the election?* **Hindi yata. Medyo tagilid ang resulta.** *I don't think so. The results are not in his favour/the dice are loaded against him.*

May panahon ka ba? (*migh pah-nah-hawn kah bah?*) Literally, *Do you have time?* Meaning: *Are you available?, Do you have a moment?* etc. Students of the Tagalog language sometimes think that Filipinos are asking about the weather when they hear this question! Be careful not to mix up the two meanings of the word **panahon**.

Insight

Snacks are essential to Filipinos, who tend to eat small amounts of food frequently rather than have 'three meals daily'. If you are travelling long distances with Filipino friends ensure that you bring along plenty snacks. If you don't, the friends won't complain but they will be very hungry indeed.

Summary

1. **Mag** verbs are versatile and can be transitive and intransitive.
2. Add **mag** to cleaning words and cooking words.
3. Add **mag** to games, things to wear, food to eat.
4. The five **ma** verbs are intransitive: **matulog, mahiga, makinig, maligo, maupo.**
5. A further category in Tagalog verbs is the circumstantial mode (to be able to, to manage to, etc.).
6. **Maka** is the prefix used for **um** and **ma** circumstantial.
7. **Makapag** is the prefix used for **mag** circumstantial.
8. You can expand your sentence with **sapagka't/kasi** *because.*
9. **Kailan** is the question marker meaning *when.*
10. Filipinos use Spanish for days of the week and months of the year.

14

Sa tabing-dagat
At the beach

In this unit you will learn how to:

- Hire a boat and prepare for a picnic on the beach
- Use **mang** verbs and particles

Hiring a boat

Dialogue 1

◀) **CD 2, TR 2**

Bill, Louise and Roy Cook are at a beach resort. The surrounding islands look beautiful and so they decide to hire a boat.

Bill	Ma**gan**da na ang pana**hon** nga**yon**, magan**dang** mamang**ka**.
Louise	Oo *nga*. Mamas**yal** *kaya* muna **ta**yo **tap**os magtan**ong** kung sa**an** ma**aa**ring umarki**la** ng *bangka*. Roy, **gus**to mo bang su**ma**ma?
Roy	**Gus**to ko. **Te**na. (Namas**yal** sa tabing-**da**gat ang mag-**an**ak)
Bill	Ma**ra**mi pang *mangingisda* sa **la**ot. Naki**ki**ta ba nin**yo**?
Louise	Oo. O, **he**to na pala ang pa-arki**la**han ng *bangka*.
Bill	Magan**dang a**raw. **Gusto na**ming umarkila ng *bangka* **pa**ra sa tat**lo**. Mag**ka**no ba?
May-ari	Dala**wan**da**ang pi**so *po* sa **ba**wa't **o**ras.
Bill	**Si**no na**man** ang tsuper **na**min?
May-ari	**He**to po si**ya**. Les ang pan**ga**lan ni**ya**. (*Ngumiti si Les*)
Bill	Magba**ba**yad na ba ka**mi** nga**yon**?
May-ari	Pagba**lik** na *po* nin**yo**.
Bill	Ma**ra**ming sa**la**mat.
May-ari	*Wala* pong anu**man**.

para sa tatlo	*for three* (persons)
magkano	*how much*
mamangka	*to go boating*
oo nga	*I agree*
mamasyal	*to take a stroll*
kaya muna tayo	*why don't we first*
tapos	*then*
magtanong	*enquire*
kung saan	*where*
magbabayad	*will pay*
umarkila ng bangka	*to hire a boat*
sumama	*to come/go with*
marami(ng)	*many*
bawa't oras	*each hour*
pa(ng)	*still*
tsuper	*(boat) driver*
mangingisda	*fishing*
laot	*sea*
ang pangalan	*the name*
ngumiti	*smiled*
paarkilahan	*a place to hire*
pagbalik	*when you return*

Translation

Bill	The weather is lovely now, it would be nice to go boating.
Louise	I agree. Why don't we take a stroll first then we can enquire where there are boats for hire. Roy, would you like to join us?
Roy	I'd love to. Let's go. (The family go for a stroll on the beach)
Bill	There are still many fishermen at sea. Can you see (them)?
Louise	Yes. Look, here's the place to hire boats from.
Bill	Good day. We would like to hire a boat for three people. How much will it cost us?
Owner	Two hundred pesos an hour sir.
Bill	(And) who is the captain of our boat?
Owner	Here he is sir. His name is Les. (Les smiles)
Bill	Do we have to pay now?
Owner	When you get back sir.
Bill	Thank you.
Owner	You're welcome.

Exercise 1

Answer the following questions with complete Tagalog sentences:

1. Bakit (why) sabi ni Bill 'magandang mamangka'?
2. Sila ba ay mamamangka muna (first) o mamamasyal muna?
3. Ano ang nakita nila sa dagat habang (while) namamasyal sila?
4. Sa palagay mo (in your opinion), mura ba ang pag-arkila ng bangka?
5. Nagbayad na ba kaagad (immediately) sila sa may-ari ng bangka?

Language skills

1 *Mang* verbs

We have already met the **um** and **mag** active verb forms. The third form of active verbs are known as the **mang** verbs. In Dialogue 1, you will have noticed a few **mang** verbs: **mamangka**, *to go boating*, **mamasyal**, *to go for a walk* and **mangisda**, *to go fishing*. **Mang** verbs form transitive (e.g. **mamili**, *to go shopping*) and intransitive (e.g. **mangawit**, *be tired*) sentences. Broadly speaking, **mang** verbs could be described as **um** verbs where the action has been pluralized. This may sound confusing at first to the native English speaker but it is in fact quite simple.

For example, if we were to say **bumili ako ng sapatos**, then this **um** verb sentence would be translated as *I bought some shoes*. The act of 'buying' shoes is a one-off event. However, if we pluralize the action described by the **um** verb, then we end up with a very different sentence – **namili ako ng sapatos**, *I shopped for shoes*. The **mang** verb form suggests that the action of 'buying' was broader than a one-off event. As such, **namili ako ng sapatos** would be translated as *I shopped for shoes*. As the verb 'to shop' implies the possibility of a process or more than one action (i.e. moving from shop to shop in order to buy more than one pair of shoes), Tagalog would therefore consider it as a plural action. Don't worry if this seems to be confusing. Listen carefully to how native Tagalog speakers use **mang** form verbs. You will soon become accustomed to them.

Apart from the pluralization of actions, a further characteristic of **mang** form verbs is that they can be used to express an action which is either 'deliberately harmful' (e.g. **mangain**, *to devour*) or an 'activity directed towards more than one object' (e.g., **manguha**, *to gather*). Another notable use of **mang** is to indicate an intensive or repeated activity directed towards a single object (e.g. a young man repeatedly dating a young woman = **mangibig**, *to date*).

Formation of *mang* verbs

1. Words that begin with p and b, e.g. mang + pasyal (*take a stroll*), mang + buhay (*life*).
Formula: Change **mang** to **mam**. Drop first letter of word (pasyal becomes asyal), (buhay becomes uhay).

mam + asyal = mamasyal *to go for a stroll* = infinitive
mam + uhay = mamuhay *to live/conduct one's life* = infinitive

2. Words that begin with d = mang + dukot (*put one's hand into a pocket*).
Formula: Change **mang** to **man**. Add the word to **man**.

man + dukot = mandukot *to go pickpocketing* = infinitive
man + daya = mandaya *to go cheating others* = infinitive

3. Words that begin with t and s = mang + takot (*afraid*), mang + saksak (*stab*).
Formula: Change **mang** to **man**. Drop first letter of word (takot becomes akot), (sakit becomes akit).

man + akot = manakot *to frighten* [several people]
man + akit = manakit *to cause pain*

4. Words that begin with k = mang + kuha (*get*).
Formula: Retain **mang**. Drop first letter of word (kuha becomes uha).

mang + uha = manguha *to get* = infinitive

5. Words that begin with a, i (and other vowels) = mang + anak (*child*).
Formula: Merely add **mang** to a word that begins with a vowel.

mang + anak = manganak *to give birth to* = infinitive
mang + isda = mangisda *to go fishing* = infinitive
mang + agaw = mang-agaw *to go grabbing* = infinitive
mang + alok = mang-alok *to offer* = infinitive

Listen to the following verb forms on the CD. Can you see the difference between the underlying verb form and the **mang** verb form?

◀) CD 2, TR 2, 01:26

Underlying verb	Mang verb
bumili *to buy*	mamili *to go shopping*
kumain *to eat*	mangain *to devour*
dumukot *to put hand inside pocket*	mandukot *to go pickpocketing*
sumugat *to wound*	manugat *to wound* (deliberately)
tumaga *to cut*	managa *to slash* (with intent to hurt or destroy)
magwalis *to sweep*	mangwalis *to hit with a broom*
kumuha *to get*	manguha *to gather*
pumitas *to pick*	mamitas *to go a-picking*
tumahi *to sew*	manahi *to sew* (a number of things)
tumakot *to frighten*	manakot *to frighten* (a number of people)
dumikit *to get stuck to*	manikit *to get thoroughly stuck to*
sumuyo *to curry favour with*	manuyo *to curry favour with*
umibig *to love*	mangibig *to pay court to/ to date*
pumasyal *to pay a visit/drop by*	mamasyal *to take a walk/stroll*

Forming *mang* verb tenses

Mang (prefix) + isda (fish) = mang + isda 'to go fishing' infinitive (used for requests, commands and suggestions).

ma + ngi + ngisda = future
na + ngi + ngisda = present
na + ngis + da = past

Mang (prefix) + **buhay** (life) =

mam + uhay = *to live* infinitive
ma + mu + mu + hay = future
na + mu + mu + hay = present
na + mu + hay = past

Variations of a *mang* sentence

Verb	+ actor
Mamimili	si Anne

Anne is going shopping

Verb	+ particle	+ actor
Namamalengke	kaya	+ si Elizabeth?

I wonder if Elizabeth is shopping at the market?

Qualifier	+ verb	+ actor	+ time
Hindi	mangingisda	ang mga lalaki	sa Biyernes.

The men are not going fishing on Friday

Question word	+ actor	+ object	+ place
Sino	ang mamimitas	ng dalanghita	sa bukid?

Who will go picking oranges on the farm?

Qualifier	+ verb	+ place	+ time
Maraming	namamasyal	sa Luneta	tuwing Linggo.

Many (people) go strolling in Luneta every Sunday

Actor	+ verb	+ object	+ beneficiary
Si Edith	ang namili	ng mga aklat	para kay Manny.

It was Edith who shopped for books for Manny

Exercise 2

Can you translate the following?

1. I will go picking fruit tomorrow.
2. They will go fishing on Wednesday.
3. There are many people picking pockets in the market.
4. I will take a stroll tonight.
5. Let us go shopping!

Exercise 3

Can you supply the answer? (Use the explanations in this Unit to help you.)

1. Bukas, _____ sila ng rosas at ibang bulaklak sa hardin. (pitas/pick) (future)
2. Sino ang gustong _____? (isda/fish) (infinitive)

3. Walang _____ ngayon sa palengke kasi may baha. (bili/
   shop) (present)
4. Meron bang _____ sa bayan? (dukot/pickpockets)
   (present)
5. _____ siya ng blusa noong bakasyon (tahi/sew) (past)

Mang verbs and recent action

Remember that when using the recent action with **mang** verbs,
the same rules apply as outlined above except that **mang** changes
to **pang**. For example:

ka +	Future	
ka +	mamalengke (*will go marketing*)	= Recent action
ka +	mamamaril (*will go shooting*)	= kapapamalengke
ka +	mamimili (*will go shopping*)	= kapapamaril
		= kapapamili

(See also Unit 12.)

Language skills

2 Particles

You may remember coming across small words such as **po** (a sign
of respect), **pa** (*still*), **naman** (*on the other hand*) and **na** (*already*) in
previous units. In spite of their small size, these words are important
elements in Tagalog sentence construction. Their function is to
highlight or add impact to a statement, question or exclamation. In
English these small words are known as adverbs, while in Tagalog
they are known as particles. They occur in certain fixed places in
Tagalog sentences.

As a rule, a particle is located 'sandwiched' in-between the comment
on the left and the subject on the right. For example, **Superbisor si
Edith**. *Edith is a supervisor.* (without particle) becomes: **Superbisor**
(comment) **pala si Edith** (subject), *So, Edith is a supervisor,* or
Superbisor na si Edith, *Edith is already a supervisor.* However, it
is possible to use more than one particle. How then do we decide
the correct order of usage? Where two particles are used together,

then the basic rule of thumb is this: the shorter particles (one syllable) go before the longer (two syllable) particles. For example: **Superbisor na pala si Edith.** *So, Edith is already a supervisor!* In some instances, you may find anything up to four or five particles in a single sentence! Due to the many possible combinations, it would be unfair to try to suggest a single rule of usage. In such cases, the trick is to ask one of your Filipino friends how to 'string' the particles together, then memorize a few of the combinations that will be of use to you.

Let's take a closer look at how two of these particles **na** (*already*) and **pa** (*still*) are used:

Explanation of *na* and *pa*
Na denotes immediate performance of an action. It also means *already* or *now*.

Examples:

Bumili ka na	*(You) buy now*
Arkitekto na si Manny	*Manny is already an architect*
Bukas na ang binyag	*The baptism will now be tomorrow*
Ayoko na	*I don't like it anymore*
Malaki na ang anak ni Tessie	*Tessie's child is big now*

Pa is used to mean continuation or resumption of an action.

Examples:

Bumili ka pa	*(You) buy some more*
Hilaw pa ang mga saging	*The bananas are still unripe*
Tulog pa ba si Father Fred?	*Is Father Fred still asleep?*
Bata pa ang bagong meyor	*The new mayor is still young*
Nagluluto pa ako	*I'm still cooking*

Example sentences:

1. Malalaki na ang mga anak ni Ginoong de Leon
   Mr de Leon's children are grown up now
2. Wala pa sila
   They (are not here) haven't arrived yet
3. Bukas na ako mamamalantsa
   I'm going to do my ironing tomorrow

4. Bukas na ang palabas
   The show will be (held) tomorrow
5. Kumain pa po kayo
   Please eat some more sir

Insight

Na and pa indicate the speaker's attitude toward the length of time between the time expressed by the adverb and the moment of speaking. **Pa** extends the psychological distance between the two points of time; **na** reduces it. For example: **Bukas pa ang dating nila.** *Their arrival is tomorrow* (and there is plenty of time between now and then).

Exercise 4

Look at the pictures. Each one is accompanied by two statements (one **na** and one **pa** statement). Can you decide which statement is appropriate to each picture?

1. **a.** Tulog pa si Erwin
   b. Gising na si Erwin

2.
   a. Gising na si Ardin
   b. Tulog pa si Ardin

3. **a.** Nagluluto pa si Fe
   b. Kumakain na si Fe

Exercise 5

Place the following jumbled-up sentences into their correct word order. Be careful to place the particle in the correct position.

1. pasko/malapit/ang/na
2. pa/nakakakain/hindi/ako
3. ba/sa/na/Sabado/ng/binyag/ang/anak mo
4. sa/sagot/na/tanong/alam/ba/ang/mo
5. sila/pa/kumakain/ba

Going swimming

Dialogue 2

◆) CD 2, TR 2, 02:49

The Cook family are back on the beach after their boating trip.

Bill	Ma**bu**ti at naka-arki**la ta**yo ng *bangka*.
Louise	**O**o *nga*. Nakapamasi**yal** tu**loy ta**yo.
Roy	Naka**ki**ta a**ko** ng malala**king** *isda* sa **tu**big.
Louise	Na**ki**ta ba nin**yo** ang mga *mangingisda*?
Bill	**O**o. Nag**ta**taka a**ko** kung **ba**kit na**ka**kapangisda si**la ka**hit may mga na**ma**mangka.
Roy	Nasi**ya**han a**ko** at *nakapamangka* **ta**yo.
Louise	A**ko rin**.
Bill	**Gus**to kong luma**ngoy** na na**man**.
Louise	Masa**rap** ang **tu**big. **Si**ge, luma**ngoy ta**yo.
Roy	**Te**na.

QUICK VOCAB	
tahimik	*calm*
naka-arkila	*was able to hire*
bangka	*boat (canoe)*
nakapamangka	*was able to go boating*
nakapamasyal	*managed to take a stroll*
tuloy	*as a result*
nakakita	*happened to see*
malalaking isda	*big fish*
nakita ba ninyo	*did you see*

212

mangingisda	*fisherman*
nakakapangisda	*are able/manage to catch fish*
masyado(ng)	*so*
namamangka	*boating*
nasiyahan	*was pleased*
kung bakit	*why*
lumangoy	*to swim*
nagtataka	*wondering*
tena	*let's go*

Translation

Bill	It was good that we were able to hire a boat.
Louise	I agree. And the sea was so calm.
Roy	I could see big fish in the water.
Bill	Did you see the fishermen?
Louise	Yes. I was wondering how they are able to fish while there are boats (around them).
Roy	I am pleased that we were able to go boating.
Louise	I am too.
Bill	I'd like to go swimming again.
Louise	The water is nice. Come on let's swim.
Roy	Let's go.

Exercise 6

Answer the following questions in complete Tagalog sentences:

1. Sino ang nasiyahan noong makaarkila sila ng bangka?
2. Ano ang nakita nila noong sila'y namamangka?
3. Ano ang nagagawa ng mga mangingisda kahit maraming bangka sa paligid?
4. Nasiyahan ba ang pamilya Cook sa kanilang pamamangka?
5. Pagkatapos, ano ang ginawa nilang tatlo?

Exercise 7

The following pictures are based on Dialogue 2. Can you find the correct verb to describe each action? Can you make up a simple sentence to describe each picture?

For example:

Verb: mangisda

Sentence: Nangingisda si Roy Cook.

1.

2.

Language skills

3 **_Makapang_** _To be able to, to happen to,_
to manage to, to come to

In Dialogue 2, you will no doubt have noticed some new verb
types: **nakapamasyal** (_managed to go strolling_), **nakapangisda** (_was_
able to go fishing) and **nakapamangka** (_was able to go boating_).
These verb types represent the circumstantial form of the **mang**

verbs. The actions represented by these verb forms are based on 1) circumstances; 2) ability; 3) involuntary actions. For example 1) **makapang + palengke = makapamalengke**, *to be able to go shopping in the market*. **Makakapamalengke na si Jayne kasi dumating na si John.** *Jayne will be able to go to the market because John has arrived.* 2) **makapang + tahi = makapanahi** *to be able to sew*. **Nakakapanahi na si Tina kasi ibinili siya ng makina ni Philip,** *Tina is able to do some sewing now because Philip bought her a sewing machine.* 3) **Makapang + pasyal = makapamasyal,** *to be able to go for a walk/stroll*. **Nakapamasiyal si Bernard at si Gary pagkatapos ng hapunan.** *Bernard and Gary managed to go for a stroll after supper.* Look at some comparisons:

Simple **Mang** Verb	**Makapang** Verb
mangisda *to go fishing*	makapangisda *to be able to go fishing*
mamaril *to go shooting*	makapamaril *to be able to go shooting*
mamili *to go shopping*	makapamili *to be able to go shopping*
mamalengke *to go to the market*	makapamalengke *to manage to go to the market*

How to form the *makapang* tense

Prefix: Makapang, infinitive: mamili, *to go shopping*
Formula: Change **makapang** to **makapa**. Change **mamili** to **mili** = **makapamili**.

= makapamili	= infinitive, *to be able to go shopping*
makakapamili	= future
nakakapamili	= present
nakapamili	= past

Prefix: makapang, infinitive: mangisda *to go fishing*
Formula: Retain **makapang**. Merely add **makapang** to **isda** = **makapangisda**

makapangisda	= infinitive, *to be able to go fishing*
makakapangisda	= future, *will be able to go fishing*
nakakapangisda	= present, *able to go fishing*
nakapangisda	= past *was able to go fishing*

Sentence variation in *makapang*

Verb	+	actor	+ time
Nakakapamalengke		si Rosie	araw-araw

Rosie can go to the market every day.

Qualifier/verb	+	actor	+ place
Hindi nakakapamasyal		ang mga bata	sa tabing-dagat

The children are not able to take a walk on the seashore

Verb	+ particle/s	+ actor	+ time
Nakakapamaril	na ba	ang mga lalaki	kung Linggo?

Are the men [already] able to go shooting on Sundays?

More sentences

1. Ang lalaki ay nakapandukot sa palengke
   The man was able to go pickpocketing in the market

2. Nakakapamalengke ka ba kung Huwebes?
   Are you able to go to the market on Thursdays?

3. Parang makakapangisda ang mga mangingisda ngayon
   It looks like the fishermen can go fishing today

Insight

Manila's busy streets have vendors selling a variety of local delicacies. While many of these items may not appeal to the western palate, Filipino humour shines through in colourful Taglish (Tagalog + English) names: **adidas** (*chicken's feet*), **helmet** (*chicken's head*), **walkman** (*pig's ears*), **IUD** (*barbequed chicken's intestines on a stick*).

Exercise 8

Fill in the blanks with the correct circumstantial verb form **maka** for **um, makapag** for **mag** and **makapang** for **mang**).

1. I wonder if they were able to buy some coke? (bili/past)
   _____ kaya sila ng coke?
2. The children managed to play at night. (laro/past)
   _____ ang mga bata sa gabi.

3. I happened to borrow a book from the library. (hiram/past)

_____ ako ng libro sa silid aklatan.

4. He can leave early. (alis/present)

_____ siya nang maaga.

5. I want to be able to return tomorrow. (balik/infinitive)

Ibig kong _____ bukas.

Exercise 9

The following sentences are wrong because of the verb tense. Can you correct the mistake?

1. Nakapangisda sila bukas.
2. Makabili ako ng pasalubong mamaya.
3. Hindi kami nakakakain sa party kahapon.
4. Sino ang makakabisita sa iyo noong isang linggo?
5. Makakain na po ba kayo?

Exercise 10 Speaking, listening and understanding

Imagine that you have just returned from a boat trip with your Filipino friends. You go to pay the owner who engages you in friendly conversation. Translate your part of the dialogue into Tagalog before practising the conversation with the help of the CD. Use the **Quick vocab** to help you.

◀» **CD 2, TR 2, 03:44**

Owner	Maligayang pagdating! Kumusta ang biyahe mo?
You	_Thank you. It was a very relaxing afternoon. We were able to go fishing too._
Owner	Nangisda? Aba, mabuti naman! May nahuli ba naman kayo?
You	_Yes. We were able to catch a big tuna fish and two lapulapu [red snapper]._
Owner	O, eh di may maluluto kang panghapunan mo.
You	_Yes! I hope we will be able to return here next year and catch more fish._
Owner	Bukas ang bahay namin sa iyo!
You	_Here's my payment for the boat hire._
Owner	Maraming salamat sa iyo.
You	_Thank you very much too._

pagdating	*arrival*
nangisda	*went fishing*
nahuli	*caught*
makahuli	*be able to catch*
maluluto	*able to be cooked*
panghapunan	*for supper*
makabalik	*be able to return*
bukas	*open*
pag-arkila	*hire*

One-minute phrases

Sa madaling salita (*sah mahdah-leeng sah-lee-tah*) Literally, *in quick words*. Similar in meaning to the English expression 'to cut a long story short'. For example: **Marami pa akong ikukuwento sa iyo, pero sa madaling salita, wala na akong panahon,** *I have a lot more to tell you but to cut a long story short, I have run out of time.*

Pagka-alis na pagka-alis (*pahg-kah-ah-lees nah pahg-kah-ah-lees*) Literally, *upon leaving, upon leaving.* Meaning immediately after leaving. For example **Pagka-alis na pagka-alis ng eroplano, umuwi na kami.** *Once the aeroplane left, we went home immediately.*

Mangyari pa (*mahng-yah-ree pah*) Literally, *happening still.* This Tagalog phrase is equivalent in meaning to the English expression 'of course'. For example: **Umalis si Boy nang walang paalam sa magulang niya, mangyari pa, nagalit ang mga ito sa kaniya.** *Boy left without saying goodbye to his parents, of course they were upset with him.*

Masarap maligo (*mah-sah-rahp mah-lee-gaw*). Literally, *delicious to take a bath/to swim.* **Masarap** (*delicious*) is a word we would not ordinarily associate in English with anything other than food. The word has a much broader usage in Tagalog, hence it can be applied to an assortment of pleasurable activities. in this case, the meaning is 'It's nice to take a bath'. For example: **Laging masarap maligo sa dagat,** *It's always nice to take a bath (swim) in the sea.*

218

Lipas na sa moda (*lee-pahs nah sa maw-dah*) Literally, *past the fashion*. Similar to the English phrase 'out of fashion'. For example: **Hindi ba lipas na sa moda ang malaking kuwelyo at bell bottoms?**, *Aren't wide collars and bell bottoms out of fashion now?*

Insight

Bamboo beach houses are always available for short-term rental and boats can be hired for sea trips. Get your Filipino friends to negotiate rental or hire prices in order to get good value.

Summary

1. **Mang** verbs are active verbs; pluralized **um** verbs.
2. **Mang** verbs can also be conjugated in the 'most recent action' aspect using '**kapang**'.
3. **Na** is a particle which means *already* or *now* and denotes immediate performance.
4. **Pa** is a particle which means *yet* or *still* and means continuation or resumption of an action.
5. **Po** is a sign of respect.
6. **Naman** = *on the other hand*.
7. **Pala** = *so*.
8. It is possible to use a string of particles in a sentence but they must be used in the correct order, e.g., Hindi **na po pala** kayo . . .
9. **Mang** verbs also take the circumstantial mode using **makapang**.
10. Formula: **Makapang + infinitive**, e.g., **makapang + isda** = **makapangisda** (*to be able to go fishing*).

15

Sa simbahan
At church

In this unit you will learn:

- More about the passive
- In verbs
- More on particles

Becoming a godparent

Dialogue 1

◄)) CD 2, TR 3

Beth and Edwin have asked Roy to be a godfather at the baptism of their baby.

Beth	Ma**aa**ri bang ga**wi**n ka **na**ming **ni**nong sa bin**yag** ng **a**ming a**nak**?
Roy	Tala**ga**? **A**ba, oo – **i**sang mala**king** karan**ga**lan i**to**.
Edwin	Dala**wa** ka**yong ni**nong at dala**wa** rin ang **ni**nang.
Roy	Kai**lan** ba **ga**ganapin ang bin**yag**?
Beth	Sa **Sa**bado, ika-4 ng Dis**yem**bre sa sim**bah**an sa **bar**yo.
Roy	Anu-**ano** ang **da**pat kong ga**win**?
Edwin	*Madali* lang. Ta**ta**yo lang ka**yo** sa ta**bi** ng ma**gu**lang **ha**bang nagsesere**mon**ya ang **pa**ri.
Roy	Gano**on** lang pa**la**. A**nong or**as sa **Sa**ba**do**?
Beth	A**las** 9:30 nang u**ma**ga. Pagka**ta**pos, may salu-**sa**lo sa **a**ming **ba**hay.
Edwin	O, **si**ge hihinta**yin** ka **na**min ka**sa**ma ni Jobert. Tu**ma**wag ka lang kung **me**ron kang i**ta**tanong.

QUICK VOCAB

maaari	*can*
gawin	*be made*
ninong	*godfather*
ang pari	*the priest*
binyag	*baptism*
aming anak	*our child*
pala	*so*
ninang	*godmother*
kailan	*when*
gaganapin	*will be held*
pagkatapos	*afterwards*
anu-ano	*what are*
dapat	*must/should*
ko(ng)	*I*
hihintayin	*will wait for*
madali lang	*just easy*
tatayo	*will stand*
sa tabi	*next/beside*
kasama	*together with/companion*
habang	*while*
nagseseremonya	*officiating*
ganoon	*like that*
sa baryo	*at the barrio*
salu-salo	*party*
tumawag	*call* (on the telephone)
kung	*if*
itatanong	*something to ask*

Translation

Beth	Would you like to be a godfather to our child? (*at the baptism of our child*)
Roy	Really? Of course - this is a big honour.
Edwin	There will be two godfathers and also two godmothers.
Roy	When will the baptism be held?
Beth	On Saturday December 4 at the barrio chapel.
Roy	What will I have to do?
Edwin	(It's) Easy. You will just stand next to the parents while the priest performs the ceremony.

Roy	So that's it. What time on Saturday?
Beth	9.30 in the morning. Afterwards, a reception follows at our house.
Edwin	All right. We'll be waiting for you with Jobert. Please call if you have anything to ask.

Exercise 1 Mga Tanong: (Questions)

Using Dialogue 1 to help you, answer the following questions in Tagalog:

1. Ano ang paanyaya (*invitation*) ni Beth at Edwin kay Roy?
2. Ilan ang magiging (*become*) ninong at ninang?
3. Saan gaganapin (*will be held*) ang binyag at salu-salo?
4. Tinanggap (*accept*) ba ni Roy ang paanyaya?
5. Sino ang kasama (*companion*) ni Roy papunta (*going to*) sa simbahan?

Language skills

1 *In* passive verbs

In Units 12, 13 and 14 we were introduced to the Tagalog active verb types (**um**, **mag**, **mang**). Dialogue 1 introduces us to a number of passive verbs (**gawin**, *to make*, **gaganapin**, *will be held*, **hihintayin**, *will wait for*). Whereas the active verbs we have looked at lay emphasis on the actor ('doer' of the action), passive verb sentences lay emphasis on the object. With just a glance at the comparison table, you will quickly see that both active and passive verbs use different actors (see table). These different actors are necessary in as far as they inform the listener as to where the emphasis of the sentence lies: on the object or on the actor. In Tagalog, active verbs take the **ang** form actors while passive verbs use **ng** form actors. The basic rule of thumb is this: in passive verb sentences, the actor you use is from the **ng** group (**ni, nina, ko, mo, niya, namin, natin, nila**, etc.), while in active verb sentences the actor is from the **ang** group (**si, sina, ako, ka, ikaw, siya, kami, tayo, kayo, sila**, etc.) Stick to this rule and you won't get lost.

The first of the Tagalog passive verbs is the **in** verb. This verb type is recognized by the suffix 'in' added after the verb root. For example:

kain + in = **kainin** (*be eaten*). Like the active verbs, you can expand passive sentences by adding an adverb, a particle, a preposition, or a time element and so on. It is also important to note that some **in** verbs are directional verbs. For example: **Sasabihin ko sa kanila ang kailangan mo**, *I'll tell them what you need*. This sentence has a verb, an actor, a receiver of the action (the **sa**) and a goal (the object).

Passive and active verb actors: a comparison table

Um/mag/mang	Object	In/i/an	Object
A	Any of B	B	Any of A
Si		Ni	
Sina		Nina	
ako		ko	
ka/ikaw		mo	
siya		niya	
kami		namin	
tayo		natin	
ito		nito	
iyan		niyan	
iyon		noon	
ang		ng	

Don't forget: ko + ka = kita

Look at the following sentences to compare active and passive verbs:

From active verb		to passive verb	
um verb		**in** verb	
Verb	bumili	Verb	binili
Actor	ako	Actor	ko
Object	ng magasin	Object	ang magasin
Time element	kahapon	Time element	kahapon

*I bought **a** magazine yesterday*   *I bought **the** magazine yesterday*

mag verb	to	**in** verb	
Verb	magluto	Verb	lutuin
Actor	tayo	Actor	natin
Object	ng pansit	Object	ang pansit
Time element	para sa party ni Caroline	Time element	para sa party ni Caroline

*Let us cook **some** noodles for Caroline's party*

*Let us cook **the** noodles for Caroline's party*

mang verb	to	**in** verb	
Verb	naninigarilyo	Verb	sinisigarilyo
Actor	si Ambo	Actor	ni Ambo
Object	ng Marlboro	Object	ang Marlboro
Time element	lagi	Time element	lagi

Ambo always smokes Marlboro

*Ambo always smokes **the** Marlboro*

In these sentences you can see that the **in** verbs are followed by a definite article.

> ### Insight
>
> In Tagalog, the adverb of manner is produced by using **nang** (not **ng**) between the verb and the adjective: **maupo nang mabuti** *sit (down) properly*, **matulog nang mahimbing** *sleep soundly*, **isinulat nang malinaw** *written clearly*. **Naupo nang mabuti ang mga bata.** *The children sat (down) properly.* The short **ng** is used to represent an object in active verbs.

Exercise 2

Here are some **um**, **mag** and **mang** sentences. Rewrite them as **in** sentences, using the guide to help you:

Example: Bumasa tayo ng nobela. (Um)
         Basahin natin ang nobela.

1. Bukas ba kayo bibili ng bagong stereo?
2. Gumagawa siya ng bulaklak na papel.
3. Tumatahi ka ba nito?

4. Tumutugtog siya ng kundiman sa piyano.
5. Naglilinis pa ako ng kuwarto ko.
6. Pumili ka ng sariwang gulay.

Attending a baptism

Dialogue 2

◀) **CD 2, TR 3, 01:10**

After the baptism, Roy wants to take a few pictures of the group outside the church.

Roy	Kukunan ko ng retrato ang aking inaanak sa binyag.
Beth	Puwede ba kunan mo rin ng retrato ang mga ninong at ninang?
Roy	Aba oo. Kasama rin ang mga magulang ng sanggol.
Edwin	Eto pala si Father Rex. Isama natin siya.
Beth	Father Rex, sumama po kayo sa amin.
Father Rex	O sige. Salamat. Maganda ang binyagang ito.
Edwin	Salamat po, Father.
Father Rex	Walang anuman.

kukunan	*will take*
retrato	*picture*
aking inaanak	*my godchild*
sumama	*to join*
kunan	*to take*
aba oo	*of course*
sanggol	*baby*
eto pala	*so here is*
isama	*to include*
o sige	*all right*
binyagang ito	*this baptism*

QUICK VOCAB

Translation

Roy	I want to take some pictures of my godchild.
Beth	Can you take a picture of the godparents too?
Roy	Of course. Including the parents of the baby.

Edwin	Here comes Father Rex. Let's ask him to join us.
Beth	Father Rex, please join us.
Father Rex	All right. Thank you. This is a good baptism.
Edwin	Thank you Father.
Father Rex	You're welcome.

Exercise 3

Using complete Tagalog sentences, what do you say when:

1. You want to take a picture of your friends?
2. You are asking your friend to take your picture?
3. You want to make a nice comment about someone's dress?
4. You want to ask someone to join you?

Language skills

2 Changing the tense of *in* verbs

The **in** infinitive is used for requests, commands and suggestions.

kuha	=	stem *get/take*		
kuha + in	=	kuhain (becomes kunin)	=	infinitive
ku + kunin	=	kukunin	=	future
k + in +ukuha	=	kinukuha	=	present
k + in + uha	=	kinuha	=	past

alis = stem *remove*				
alis + in	=	alisin	=	infinitive
a + alis + in	=	aalisin	=	future
in + a + alis	=	inaalis	=	present
in + alis	=	inalis	=	past

Exercise 4

Supply the appropriate tense forms of the following **in** verbs. Use the examples to guide you:

Infinitive			Future	Present	Past
1. ibig	=	stem *love*	=		
2. kain	=	stem *eat*	=		

3. linis = stem *clean* =
4. sulat = stem *write* =
5. tapos = stem *finish* =

More on **in** verbs:

As object, focus **in** verbs typically denote actions 'radically' affecting the goal, such as those causing change in its structure. For example:

Infinitive	Stem	
gawin	gawa	*to make, do*
lutuin	luto	*to cook*
tapusin	tapos	*to finish*
tadtarin	tadtad	*to chop*

Sometimes used with a directional, focus **in** verbs may express motion in relation to a goal (in which case there is usually some element of contact with the goal). For example:

Infinitive	Stem	
panhikin	panhik	*to go up into*
pasukin	pasok	*to enter*
pukulin	pukol	*to throw something at*
salpukin	salpok	*to strike against*
sampalin	sampal	*to slap one's face*

Most cooking terms fall under **in**:

Infinitive	Stem	
saingin	saing	*to cook* (as in rice)
lagain	laga	*to boil*
prituhin	prito	*to fry* (in deep oil)
sangagin	sangag	*to fry* (with very little oil, as in rice)
putulin	putol	*to cut*
hiwain	hiwa	*to slice*
tadtarin	tadtad	*to chop*

Most cleaning terms fall under **in**:

linisin	linis	*to clean*
kuskusin	kuskos	*to scrub*
ayusin	ayos	*to arrange/tidy up*

Most stative actions (actions describing a state of being) are **in**:

gulatin	gulat	*to surprise*
takutin	takot	*to scare*
hiyain	hiya	*to embarrass*
gutumin	gutom	*to make hungry*
biguin	bigo	*to disappoint*

Illnesses can be verbalized under **in**: Here, there is no actor, just a goal:

lagnatin	lagnat	*to have a fever*
sipunin	sipon	*to suffer from cold*
malaryahin	malarya	*to suffer from malaria*

To be infested by insects falls under **in** when verbalized. Here again, there is no actor, just a goal.

anayin	anay	*to be infested with termites*
langgamin	langgam	*to be infested with ants*
lamukin	lamok	*to be swarmed with mosquitoes*
surutin	surot	*to be infested with bedbugs*

For example:

1. Nilalanggam ang cake.
   The cake is swarming with ants.
2. Sinisipon ka ba?
   Are you suffering from cold?
3. Minalarya ang mga sundalo.
   The soldiers suffered from malaria.
4. Nilalagnat si Mario.
   Mario has a fever.

Sentence variations

Verb +	actor +	object:
Hiwain	ninyo	ang sibuyas at kamatis.

You slice the onions and tomatoes

Qualifier +	actor +	verb +	object:
Huwag	ninyong	kainin	ang pagkain nila

Don't you eat their food!

Qualifier +	particle +	actor +	object:
Binabago	talaga	ng araw	ang kulay ng ating balat.

Indeed, the sun changes the colour of our skin

Question marker +		actor +	object (directional):
Sino		ang gumulat	sa kaniya?

Who surprised him/her?

Qualifier +	actor +	object +	verb:
Hindi	ko	siya	pipilitin

I won't force her

Note: There are irregular **in** verbs that change when forming the infinitive. For example: **bili**, *buy* becomes **bilhin**, **sunod**, *follow* becomes **sundin**, **kuha**, *get/take* becomes **kunin**, **dala**, *carry* becomes **dalhin**, **sabi**, *say* becomes **sabihin**.

Exercise 5

Choose the correct verb from the brackets and translate the sentence into English:

1. (Hinuhuli/hulihin/hinuli) ng pulis ang mga sidewalk vendors araw-araw. (present)
2. Alam mo ba kung ilang mangga ang (kinain/kakainin/kainin) ni Bosyo kanina? (past)
3. Kailan mo (tinahi/ tatahiin/ tinatahi) ang aking bestida? (future)
4. Huwag mong (sasabihin/ sinabi/ sinasabi) kay Rex ang sagot mo. (future)
5. Kahapon, (nilinis/ lilinisin/ linisin) na niya ang bagong kotse. (past)

Exercise 6

Look at the three pictures. From the accompanying word box, see if you can match up two appropriate **in** verbs to each picture:

1. 2.

3.

linisin	*to clean*
inumin	*to drink*
bilhin	*to buy*
kainin	*to eat*
sirain	*to destroy*
sipunin	*to have a cold*
gulatin	*to surprise*
lutuin	*to cook*
lagnatin	*to have a fever*
kunin	*to get*
biruin	*to tease/joke*
kilalanin	*to know*
sabihin	*to tell*

Insight

Because of their strong sense of respect, many Filipinos find difficulty in disagreeing with someone they regard as superior. Rather than cause offence or embarrassment, they will provide vague or ambiguous responses. The purpose of such a response is not dishonesty, but rather to avoid confrontation and ensure that nobody loses face.

Dialogue 3

After the baptism the priest is seen speaking to Roy.

Pari	Ku**mus**ta ka Roy.
Roy	Ma**bu**ti *po* na**man**. At ka**yo** *po*?
Pari	Ma**bu**ti rin na**man** sala**mat**. Isa ka pa**la** sa mga **ni**nong ng **ba**gong bin**yag**.
Roy	**Op**o. Ti**nan**ong ni**la** a**ko** kung pu**we**de a**ko** at tinang**gap** ko na**man** ang paan**ya**ya.
Pari	Ma**bu**ti. Ang mga ma**gu**lang mo, **da**rating ba?
Roy	*Hindi po.*
Pari	**Pu**punta ka ba sa salu-**sa**lo?
Roy	Opo.
Pari	O, **si**ge mag-enjoy ka.
Roy	Sa**la**mat *po*.

QUICK VOCAB

isa ka sa mga	*you're one of the*
pupunta	*will go*
salu-salo	*party*
bago(ng) binyag	*newly baptized*
tinanong	*was asked*
puwede ako	*I'm available*
tinanggap	*accepted*
paanyaya	*invitation*
magulang mo	*your parents*
darating	*will arrive*
mag-enjoy	*to enjoy*

Translation

Priest	How are you, Roy.
Roy	I'm fine sir. And you?
Priest	I'm fine too, thank you. So you're one of the godfathers of the newly baptized?
Roy	Yes I am. They asked if I was available and I accepted the invitation.
Priest	Good. Your parents, are they coming?
Roy	No sir.
Priest	Are you going to (attend) the party?
Roy	Yes sir.
Priest	All right. You enjoy yourself.
Roy	Thank you sir.

Exercise 7

Here are the answers, but can you supply the questions?

1. Oo. Ninong din ako.
   Question:
2. Dalawa kaming ninong.
   Question:
3. Wala rito ang mga magulang ko.
   Question:
4. Pupunta siguro ako sa salu-salo.
   Question:

Exercise 8

Look at the following pictures and listen to the CD. You will notice that the pictures are out of sequence with the story. After listening to the story, number the pictures in their correct order:

◀) CD 2, TR 3, 02:48

1.

2.

3.

4.

After replaying the CD and listening to the story several times, why not have fun by retelling the story in Tagalog to some of your Filipino friends.

Language skills

3 More on particles

In Unit 14 we looked at the particles (adverbs) **pa** and **na**. A fuller list of common Tagalog particles and their uses follows. The ability to learn and use particles in your spoken Tagalog will not only add 'polish' to your sentences but will no doubt impress your Filipino friends too! Look at the table and study the examples that follow:

Particle	When and how it is used
naman	*on the other hand* (also used as a form of reply meaning too/as well/in fact)
po	used out of respect in answering or addressing an elder or superior or person of rank
ba	interrogative particle answerable by yes or no
pala	*so!*
nga	*indeed, truly*
raw/daw	*according to them/they say/apparently/she/he said* etc. (raw is used with a word after a final vowel)
kaya	used idiomatically to express doubt *I wonder/do you think*
yata	*I think, maybe, it seems*
rin/din	*also, too, as well* (rin is used with a word after a final vowel)
na naman	*again*

Example sentences

1. Naupo si Phil at tumayo naman si Harry.
   Phil sat down and on the other hand, Harry stood up.
2. Umuulan na naman!
   It's raining again.
3. Kumusta po kayo?
   How are you sir/madam? (very formal)
4. Nagbabakasyon rin kami taun-taon.
   We also go on holiday every year.
5. Mandurukot kaya ang taong ito?
   I wonder if this man is a pickpocket.

6. Ito pala ang istasyon ng pulisya.
So this is the police station.

7. Ginagamit mo ba ito?
Are you using this?

8. Hindi raw niya kailangan ang pasaporte natin.
Apparently he/she doesn't need our passport.

Exercise 9

Here are some sentences. Fill in the blank space with an appropriate particle, then translate the sentence into English. Use the clues to help you:

Example: Kumakain ka ba ng balut?
                      Translation: *Do you eat balut?*

1. Hindi _____ sila Pilipino. (so!)
Translation:

2. Magaganda _____ ang mga bulaklak sa hardin ninyo. (indeed)
Translation:

3. Sino _____ ang mga bagong bisita nila? (I wonder)
Translation:

4. Tinatawag ka _____ ng mga kaibigan mo. (I think)
Translation:

5. Narito _____ ang mga kailangan ko? (?)
Translation:

Use of *ba*

The particle **ba** cannot be translated directly into English. Its purpose is to indicate that a sentence is in fact a question. Use of **ba** is optional, except in question formulas such as **hindi ba**, etc. In the more sophisticated Manila Tagalog, it is often missed out altogether.

As a particle, **ba** is normally found sandwiched between the comment and the subject of a sentence. For example, **Turista** (comment) **ba si Ginoong Abbott** (subject)?, *Is Mr Abbott a tourist?* When more than one particle is used in a sentence, as a permanent rule, **ba** comes after **na** (na ba), **pa** (pa ba), **rin** (rin ba), **raw** (raw ba) and **na naman** (na naman ba). When a long string of particles is used, **ba** can be found at the end of a sentence, thus **Namili ka rin daw ba?**, *Did they say you also went shopping?*

Occasionally the subject is omitted altogether, such as when the speaker raises his / her voice tone clearly indicating that they want to ask a question. For example, **Malinis na ba ang mesa?**, *Is the table clean already?* becomes **Malinis na ba?** (ang mesa), *Is it [the table] clean already?*

An amusing word of warning to the Tagalog learner: Be careful when using the particle **ba** in connection with the second person singular **ka** (informal). In this case, **ka** precedes **ba**, i.e. **ka ba** (instead of **ba ka** which translates into English as *cow*!) For example, **Guro ka ba?** *Are you a teacher?*, not **Guro ba ka?**, which would translate as *teacher cow!*

One-minute phrases

> **Kunan mo ako** (*koo-nahn maw ah-kaw*) Literally, *take/get (something) from me*. Meaning take my picture/photograph!! For example: **Gene, kunan mo naman ako sa camera ko**, *Gene, would you be kind enough to take my picture with my camera?*
>
> **Ikaw ang masusunod** (*ee-kao ahng mah-saw-saw-nawd*) Literally, *you're the one to be followed*. Meaning as you like it/you're the boss! For example: **Kung gusto mong umalis tayo nang maaga, ikaw ang masusunod.** *If you want us to leave early, then you're the boss.*
>
> **Dahan-dahan ang pagsasalita** (*dah-hahn dah-hahn ahng pahg-sah-sah-lee-tah*) Literally, *slow-slow the talking*. Meaning could you speak a little more slowly. For example: **Dahan-dahan lang ang pagsasalita para maintindihan ko ang sinasabi mo**, *Please speak slowly so that I'd be able to understand you.*
>
> **Anuman ang mangyari** (*ah-noo-mahn ahng mahng-yah-ree*) Literally, *whatever the happening*. Similar in meaning to the English expression 'come what may'. For example: **Darating daw sila anuman ang mangyari**, *They said they would arrive come what may.*
>
> **Tumingin-tingin** (*too-mee-ngeen tee-ngeen*) Literally, *to have a look/see*. Meaning to have a look around/to see. For example: **Kapag namalengke ka, tumingin-tingin ka nga kung may sariwang lapulapu**, *If you go to the market, would you have a look if there are fresh lapulapu.*

Insight

Filipinos are deeply loyal to their families and sacrifice their own comfort and personal happiness in order to improve the lot of their loved ones. Relationships need not only be blood ties. The system of 'kumpare' or 'kumare' ('co-father' or 'co-mother') exists whereby a person is invited to be a godparent.

Summary

1. The **in** passive verb takes the **ng** group as doer/actor and the **ang** group as object.
2. **In** verbs are versatile, like the **mag** verbs.
3. Most roots/stems in **um** verbs can be used as **in**.
4. The **ng** group **ko** when used with the **ang** group **ka** always becomes **kita**.
5. The verb stem **kuha** becomes **kunin** in the infinitive.
6. Stative actions are actions that describe a state of being.
7. **Hiyain** is the most commonly used stative verb.
8. Illnesses can be verbalized using the **in** verb.
9. **Raw/Daw** = 'according to/apparently/they say etc. **Rin/Din** = 'also, too, as well' etc.
10. **Ba** = a question marker used to make a statement into a question.

16

Maaari bang gawin mo ito?
Could I ask a favour of you?

In this unit you will learn how to:

- Make requests and suggestions
- Give a command
- Give instructions

Making requests and suggestions

Dialogue 1

◄))) **CD 2, TR 4**

At the Abiva residence, Louise Cook is asking Lily to do something for her.

Louise	Maaari bang ipaki**hu**log mo ang mga **su**lat ko?
Lily	Aba **o**po. Ibi**gay** *po* nin**yo** sa **a**kin at ihu**hu**log ko kaa**gad**.
Louise	**He**to. La**bin**dalawa ang mga i**yan**. *Wala* akong **sel**yo. **I**bili mo na tul**oy a**ko ng **sel**yo at ipakila**gay** mo ang mga **sel**yo sa **su**lat.
Lily	**Si**ge *po*. A**ko** *po* ang ba**ha**la. **Pu**punta a**ko** sa post office.
Louise	Ma**ra**ming sa**la**mat ha? **He**to ang **pe**ra.
Lily	*Wala* pong anu**man**, **Gi**nang Cook.

ipakihulog mo	*could you post*
tuloy	*as well*
aba opo	*of course* (formal)
ibigay	*to give*

QV

sa akin	*to me*
ihuhulog	*will post*
kaagad	*immediately*
ibili	*to buy for*
pakilagay	*please put*
ang bahala	*will look after*

Translation

Louise	Could you kindly post my letters?
Lily	Sure ma'am. If you give them to me I'll post them immediately.
Louise	Here. There are twelve there. I don't have stamps. If you could also buy some stamps for me and put them on the letters.
Lily	All right ma'am. I'll look after them. I'm going to go to the post office.
Louise	Thank you very much indeed. Here is the money.
Lily	You're welcome, Mrs Cook.

Exercise 1

Listen to Dialogue 1 again and then answer the following questions.

🔊 **CD 2, TR 4**

1. Ano ang sinabi ni Louise Cook kay Lily?
   Answer:
2. Ilan ang sulat na ihuhulog ni Lily?
   Answer:
3. Bakit bibili si Lily ng selyo?
   Answer:
4. Saan bibili ng selyo si Lily?
   Answer:

Language skills

1 Passive *i* verbs

A second passive verb form is known as the **i** type verb. Dialogue 1 gives us a few examples: **ibigay**, *to give*, **ihuhulog**, *will post*, ibili, *to buy for*. As with all passive verb forms, it always takes a ng form actor (either ni, nina, ko, mo, niya, namin, natin, ninyo, nila, ninyo, niyan, noon, or ng), while the object or goal is always an ang form word (either si, sina, ako, ka/ikaw, siya, kami, tayo, kayo, sila, ito, iyan, iyon, ang mga ito, ang mga iyan, ang mga iyon, or ang). For example: **Ibinalik ni Elvira** (actor) **ang libro** (object), *Elvira returned the book*. The infinitive of the i verb is easily recognized by the prefix i before the root word. For example: i + hulog = ihulog, *to post* or *to drop*, i + tapon = itapon, *to throw* and so on.

The i verb is unique in that it is object focused, meaning that we lay more emphasis on the object rather than on the doer of the action. For example: **Isinara ko ang bintana**, *The window* (object) *was closed by me* or *I closed the window*. If this same sentence uses an active verb, the focus would then be on the doer of the action: **Nagsara ako ng bintana**, *I closed a window*. Some i verbs are also used as beneficiary words, meaning that an action is performed for the benefit of another person. For example: **ibili**, *to buy for* (someone), **ikuha**, *to get for* (someone), **igawa**, *to make for* (someone), **isama**, *to take someone along* (for someone). In all of these cases, the recipient (or beneficiary) of these verbs is represented with an ang form word.

For example: **Ibinili ko si Eileen ng sapatos**, *I bought (a pair of) shoes for Eileen*. **Igagawa ko si Neneng ng manyika**, *I'll make a doll for Neneng*. The i verb is also directional, that is, it uses sa as a goal. Example: **Ibigay natin ito sa kanila**, *Let us give this to them*. **Ipinasok ni Harry ang mga silya sa loob**, *Harry took the chairs in/ inside/indoors*.

Compare the *um* and *i* beneficiary

Bumili ako ng sorbetes para kay Tess	*I bought some ice cream for Tess*
Ibinili ko ng sorbetes si Tess	*I bought Tess some ice cream*
Gumawa sila ng saranggola para sa akin	*They made a kite for me*
Iginawa nila ako ng saranggola	*They made me a kite*
Sumama ako sa kanila sa sine	*I went to the cinema with them*
Isinama nila ako sa sine	*They took me to the cinema*

Compare the *mag* and *i* forms

Mag-aakyat siya ng panggatong — *He/she will bring/take up some firewood*

Iaakyat niya ang panggatong — *He/she will bring/take up the firewood*

Nagprito ba kayo ng itlog? — *Did you fry some eggs?*

Iprinito ba ninyo ang itlog? — *Did you fry the eggs?*

Naglalabas na sila ng mga silya — *They are taking out some chairs now*

Inilalabas na nila ang mga silya — *They are taking out the chairs now*

Some example sentences:

1. Ibinigay ni Bernie ang bolpen kay Elizabeth
   Bernie gave the pen to Elizabeth
2. Isasama mo ba si Stephen sa sine?
   Are you going to take Stephen to the cinema?
3. Isasampay ko muna ang mga damit
   I'll hang the clothes first
4. Ano ang inilagay mo sa sopas?
   What did you put in the soup?
5. Isasara ko na po ba ang mga bintana?
   Shall I close the windows now?
6. Itinahi ako ni Letty ng magandang blusa
   Letty has sewn a lovely blouse for me
7. Igagawa mo ba siya ng laruan?
   Are you going to make a toy for him/her?

Changing the tense of the *i* verb

Prefix	I		
Stem	tapon *throw*		
Infinitive	I + tapon	=	itapon *to be thrown*
Future	I + ta + tapon	=	itatapon *will be thrown*
Present	I + t + in + a + tapon	=	itinatapon *is being thrown*
Past	I + t + in + a + pon	=	itinapon *was thrown*

Some familiar *i* verbs – Listen and repeat

◄) CD 2, TR 4, 01:00

Listen to the correct pronunciation on the CD. Listen carefully to the slight variations in pronunciation of each tense and then try to repeat without the help of the CD.

Infinitive	Translation	Future	Present	Past
ibigay	*to give*	ibibigay	ibinibigay	ibinigay
ilagay	*to put/place*	ilalagay	inilalagay	inilagay
itapon	*to throw*	itatapon	itinatapon	itinapon
itago	*to keep in a safe place*	itatago	itinatago	itinago
itabi	*to keep aside*	itatabi	itinatabi	itinabi
ibagsak	*to drop with force*	ibabagsak	ibinabagsak	ibinagsak
itaas	*to take up/raise*	itataas	itinataas	itinaas
isabit	*to hang on a hook*	isasabit	isinasabit	isinabit
isampay	*to hang on a line*	isasampay	isinasampay	isinampay
itulak	*to push*	itutulak	itinutulak	itinulak
isukat	*to try something on*	isusukat	isinusukat	isinukat
isara	*to close*	isasara	isinasara	isinara
ipasok	*to take inside*	ipapasok	ipinapasok	ipinasok
ilabas	*to take outside*	ilalabas	inilalabas	inilabas
ipasa	*to pass*	ipapasa	ipinapasa	ipinasa
ibili	*to buy for*	ibibili	ibinibili	ibinili
ikain	*to eat for*	ikakain	ikinakain	ikinain
ikuha	*to get for*	ikukuha	ikinukuha	ikinuha
igawa	*to make for*	igagawa	iginagawa	iginawa
isama	*to take someone with*	isasama	isinasama	isinama
itahi	*to sew for*	itatahi	itinatahi	itinahi
isakay	*to take aboard*	isasakay	isinasakay	isinakay

Some **i** verbs are used in connection with activities of a social nature (beneficiary):

	Stem	Meaning
ikumusta	kumusta	*to say hello for*
idalo	dalo	*to attend for*
ihalik	halik	*to kiss for*
iyakap	yakap	*to embrace for*
ibalita	balita	*to send news for*

Ikumusta mo kami sa kanila	*Say hello to them from us*
Ihalik mo ako sa nanay	*Kiss Mother for me*

Some **i** verbs denote actions affecting the position of the **ang**, without causing a change in its structure. They often correspond to **mag** verbs.

	Stem	**Meaning**
iakyat	akyat	*to bring/take up*
ialok	alok	*to offer*
itapon	tapon	*to throw*
iuwi	uwi	*to take home*

Inialok ni Peter ang kotse niya sa akin	*Peter offered his car to me*
Bakit mo iuuwi iyan?	*Why are you taking that home?*

In their passive form, **mag** verbs denoting ways of preparing food are represented as **i** verbs:

	luto	*to cook*
iluto	luto	*to cook*
iihaw	ihaw	*to broil/grill*
iprito	prito	*to fry*
ipaksiw	paksiw	*to make paksiw*

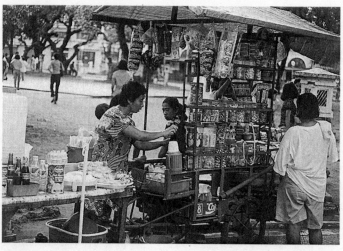

Ipinirito mo ba ang isda?	*Did you fry the fish?*
Iniluto ko na ang bangus	*I have cooked the milkfish already*

Exercise 2
Look at the cartoons. Can you say what actions are being performed? Write your answer in the space provided. A noun has been provided to help you.

Example: Itinatapon ang basura (ang basura)

aklat

bestida   bola

Sentence variations using **i** form verbs:

Verb	+	actor	+	beneficiar	+	object	+	adverb
Ikukuha		ko		siya		ng tubig		

I will get him/her (a glass of) water.

Igagawa   namin   sila   ng laruan
We will make a toy for them.

Isinasama   nila   ako   sa parke   lagi.
They always take me along with them to the park

Ibili   mo   kami   ng sandwich
Buy some sandwiches for us

Pseudo-Verb + particle +verb + actor + receiver of the action + object

Maaari   bang   ibili   mo   kami   ng sandwich?
Could you buy some sandwiches for us?/ Could you buy us some sandwiches?

verb   actor   object
Ilalabas   ni Tessie   ang mga panindang gulay
Tessie will take the vegetable goods outside/outdoors

adverb   particle   actor   verb   object
Mamaya   na   namin   itatapon   ang basura
We will throw out the rubbish later on

Question word + object   +   actor + place   +   time
Ano   ang itinulak nila   sa kalsada kahapon?
What was it that they pushed on the street yesterday?

Exercise 3 Listening and speaking
Listen to the CD. You will hear the speaker mention different times of the day. Each time of day is accompanied by a verb in the infinitive form. Using your skill and knowledge of **i** verbs, provide the correct tense to accompany the time element.

◄) **CD 2, TR 4, 06:11**

Dialogue 2
Jobert has been a great help to the Cook family. Bill is speaking to him.

Bill	Jobert, masyado yatang pinapagod ka namin. *Nahihiya kami sa ginagawa mo para sa amin.*
Jobert	*Hindi naman.* Konting bagay lang ito. Noong nasa London ako tinulungan ninyo ako. Malaki ang utang na loob ko sa inyo.
Bill	Ikaw naman. Bale *wala iyon.* Kalimutan mo na *iyon.*
Jobert	Aba, isinama ninyo ako sa mga lugar na *hindi* ko maaabot kung *hindi* sa inyo. Ibinili ninyo ako ng mga kailangan ko. Inihatid ninyo ako sa paliparan.
Bill	Maraming salamat Jobert sa pag-alaala mo pero *hindi* ka dapat mag-isip ng ganiyan.
Jobert	Walang anuman. Maraming salamat na *muli.*

isinama	*accompanied*
pinapagod ka	*tiring you*
nahihiya	*embarrassed*
ginagawa	*doing*
para sa amin	*for us*
hindi naman	*not so*
bagay	*thing*
noong	*when*
tinulungan	*helped*
muli	*again*
utang na loob	*debt of gratitude*
bale wala	*means nothing*
kalimutan	*forget*
maaabot	*won't be able to reach*
kung hindi	*had not been*
ibinili	*bought for*
kailangan	*needs*
inihatid	*took to*
pag-alaala	*concern*
mag-isip	*to worry*
ganiyan	*like that*

QUICK VOCAB

Translation

Bill	Jobert, I think we are tiring you a lot. We are feeling (a little) embarrassed by what you're doing for us.
Jobert	Not at all. This is only a small thing. When I was in London you helped me. I owe you a lot.
Bill	Oh, you. That's nothing. Please forget about that.
Jobert	Well, you took me to places that I would not have reached had it not been for you. You bought me things I needed. You took me to the airport.
Bill	Thank you Jobert for your concern but you shouldn't think like that.
Jobert	Don't mention it. Thank you very much again.

Exercise 4

Can you answer the following questions?

1. Bakit nahihiya si Bill kay Jobert?
2. Bakit nag-aalaala si Jobert?
3. Magbigay ng dalawang bagay na ginawa nina Bill para kay Jobert sa London.
4. Kung ikaw, mag-aalaala ka rin ba katulad ni Jobert?

Insight

Where a Filipino makes insufficient progress in communicating an important point, they may choose to engage a go-between. Go-betweens are often chosen because they are close to or respected by the other party. The purpose is to minimize embarrassment.

Language skills

2 *May* + verb
Walang + verb

May + active verb *or* **mayroong** + active verb = *someone, somebody*
May + passive verb *or* **mayroong** + passive verb = *something*
Walang + active verb = *no one, nobody*

Walang + passive verb   = *nothing*
Marami + active or passive   = *a lot of/lots of*

We have already met the words **may**, **mayroon** *has/have*, **mayroon** *there is/there are* and **marami** *many*.

These words are used not only to express possession but may also be used as **may** phrases expressing 1) presence; 2) something indefinite. Simply speaking, a **may** phrase expresses presence when there is no subject in the sentence and **may** (or **mayroon**) is followed by a noun. This is in fact less complicated than it sounds. Look at this example: **May pagkain sa mesa.** *There is food on the table (food is present on the table).*

In indefinite phrases, **may** (or **mayroon**) is followed by a verb. For example: **May bibili ba ng Coke bukas?**, *Will someone buy Coke tomorrow?*, **May bumibili ng coke**, *Someone is buying Coke.* **May naglilinis dito araw-araw**, *Someone cleans here everyday.* **Mayroong* kumatok kagabi**, *Someone knocked on the door last night.* **Maraming* namimili sa palengke kung Sabado**, *Many (people) go to the market on Saturdays.* (* **Note**: as a general rule, **mayroon** and **marami** become **mayroong** and **maraming** when followed by a noun). No doubt you will have noticed that each of these sentences has no subject. When the verb in an indefinite **may** phrase is an active verb (**um, mag, mang**), then the sentence has no subject. However, if the verb in an indefinite **may** phrase is a passive verb (**in, i, an**) then there is a subject. For example: **May kinuha ako sa kaniya**, *I took something from him/her.* **Mayroong itinapon si Stephen sa sahig**, *Stephen threw something on the floor.* **Maraming inalis sa trabaho noong bago mag-pasko**, *Many (employees) were made redundant before Christmas.*

You will remember that the opposite to **may** is **wala**. **Wala** + **ng** not only expresses absence or non-possession of something, but like **may**, **mayroon** and **marami**, it can be used to express the indefinite. As with **may**, **mayroon** and **marami**, if the verb used with **wala** is an active verb (**um, mag, mang**), then there is no subject. For example: **Walang kumakain ng luto ko**, *No one is eating what I've cooked*, **Walang naglalaro ng tennis ngayon**, *Nobody is playing tennis today.* **Wala bang mamimili bukas?** *Isn't anyone going shopping* *tomorrow?* Again, if the verb used with **wala** is a passive verb (**in**, **i** or **an**) then there is a subject. For example: **Walang binili si Roy sa duty free,** *Roy didn't buy anything from the duty free.* **Wala ka bang ibibigay kay Sophie?** *Aren't you giving anything to Sophie?* **Walang tinawagan si Amy kagabi,** *Amy didn't call anyone* (on the telephone) *last night.*

Reference table			
Active verb (**um, mag, mang**)		No Subject +	Time etc.
may	kumakain		kagabi
mayroong	kumakain		kagabi
maraming	kumakain		kagabi
walang	kumakain		kagabi
Passive verb (**in, i, an**)		Subject +	Time etc.
may	kinain	si Patricia	kanina
mayroong	kinain	si Patricia	kanina
maraming	kinain	si Patricia	kanina
walang	kinain	si Patricia	kanina

Sample sentences:

May sumigaw sa klase kanina
Someone shouted in class a while ago

Maraming nagbabasketball sa kalye hapon-hapon
Many play basketball in the street every afternoon

May tumawag raw sa akin kagabi
Apparently someone called me (on the telephone) *last night*

Walang kumain ng luto ni Bennie
Nobody ate Bennie's cooking

May nagdarasal sa simbahan sa umaga
Someone prays in church in the morning

May nangyari sa kaniya
Something happened to her/him

May kumakatok yata
I think someone is knocking on the door

May sinabi ka ba sa kaniya?
Did you tell him/her anything?

Walang ginagawa ang mga empleyado dito
The employees here are not doing anything

Maraming binili si Ginang de los Reyes sa tindahan
Mrs. de los Reyes bought a lot of things from the store

Exercise 5
The following sentences are jumbled up. Can you put them back into their correct order?

1. dito marami(ng) araw-araw bumibili ng libro.
2. sa pinto may kumakatok yata.
3. ako kahapon may kinuha sa kaniya.
4. walang noong Linggo sa akin sa ospital sumama.
5. sa kabila ng tennis na naman may naglalaro.

··

Insight
The infinitive form of the verb (a form of a verb that does not indicate a particular tense or number or person, in English used with or without *to*) is used in commands, suggestions and requests both in the active and passive verbs. **Kumain ka!** *(You) Eat!* **Kainin mo ito!** *(You) eat this!*

··

Language Skills

3 Requests, commands and suggestions

To make a simple request in Tagalog, just use **maaari bang/puwede bang** followed by the infinitive form of an active or a passive verb! What could be simpler? Look at these examples:

Maaari bang maupo kayo?   *Would you mind sitting down?*
Puwede po bang huwag   *Would you mind not smoking?*
  tayong manigarilyo.

Exercise 6
Try making your own command, request or suggestion:

Example: **pumirma**. (Request): Maaari bang pumirma kayo dito? *Sir/madam, could you please sign here?*

1. Command: tumayo (*to stand up*)
   Sentence:
2. Request: maupo (*to sit down*)
   Sentence:
3. Suggestion: matulog (*to sleep*)
   Sentence:
4. Request: manigarilyo (*to smoke*)
   Sentence:
5. Suggestion: mamasiyal (*to go for a walk*)
   Sentence:

Exercise 7

You are on the telephone to your local hardware store. You have decided to help your Filipino friend make some improvements to her house but first of all, you will need a few supplies. Complete the following dialogue, using the vocabulary box to help you:

Ikaw	*Say good morning*
Store	Magandang umaga. Ano po ang maipaglilingkod ko sa inyo?
Ikaw	*Ask if they have any cement*
Store	Marami po kami niyan.
Ikaw	*Say you would like to reserve ten bags*
Store	Aba opo. Mayroon pa po ba kayong nais (bilhin)?
Ikaw	*Ask if they have any marine plywood*
Store	Wala po. Ordinaryong plywood lamang.
Ikaw	*Ask if they have any aluminium roofing sheets*
Store	Opo. Mayroon po. Kararating lang po ng bagong delivery ngayong umaga.
Ikaw	*Good. Ask him to reserve twelve sheets for you*
Store	O, eh iyon pong pampako sa pambubong na aluminum?
Ikaw	*Yes. Two kilos please*
Store	Mayroon pa po ba kayong kailangan?
Ikaw	*No, that's all thank you. I will drop by at midday*
Store	Ayos lang po, sir. Paalam na po.
Ikaw	*Goodbye*

Ask one of your Filipino friends to help you practise this dialogue aloud.

250

One-minute phrases

Ikumusta mo ako (*ee-koo-moos-tah maw ah-kaw*) Literally, *Say hello you me*. Similar to its English equivalent ('say hello for me'), this Tagalog expression is used when sending greetings to a third person.

Ipagpaumanhin po ninyo (*ee-pahg-pah-oo-mahn-heen paw neen-yaw*) Literally, *Please bear with/excuse* (formal) *you*. Meaning 'to make something appear less serious/to excuse'. This is a very polite and commonly used expression acknowledging any form of inconvenience caused to another person. For example: **Ipagpaumahin po ninyo ang sagabal na ito sa inyong kalsada**, *We apologize for this obstruction on your street*.

Unti-untiin (*oon-tee oon-tee-een*) Meaning 'to do something little by little/slowly'. A useful phrase used in the same way as its English equivalent. For example, **Sabi ni Nanay, unti-untiin daw natin ang pagkain ng sorbetes**, *Mother said that we have to eat the ice-cream little by little*.

Labag sa batas (*lah-bahg sah bah-tahs*) Meaning 'against the law'. For example: **Labag sa batas ang magpasok sa ating bansa ng anumang drugs**, *It is against the law to bring into our country any drugs*.

Pagdating na pagdating (*pag-dah-ting nah pag-dah-ting*) Literally, *upon arrival, upon arrival*. Meaning 'immediately upon arrival'. For example: **Sabihin mo kay Pedro na pumunta sa opisina ko pagdating na pagdating niya**, *Tell Pedro to come straight to my office the moment he arrives*.

Insight

Filipinos have developed a way of engendering good standing with one another. This is the 'utang na loob' or 'debt of gratitude' system by which any favours received or granted must be returned. Local politicians have been known to use this cultural value to their benefit, particularly around election time.

Summary

1. The **i** passive verb takes the **ng** group as doer/actor.
2. **I** verbs are mobile object verbs.
3. **Um** and **mag** verbs can be recycled as **i** verbs.
4. **May/Mayroong** added to an active verb = *someone/somebody*.
5. **May/Mayroong** added to a passive verb = *something*.
6. **Walang** added to an active verb = *no one, nobody*.
7. **Walang** added to a passive verb = *nothing*.
8. **Marami** added to an active or passive verb = *a lot of/lots of*.
9. Use **puwede bang/maaari bang** + **infinitive verb** to make a simple request.
10. To give a command, make a request or suggestion, use the **infinitive** form of the active/passive verb.

17

Isang kasalan
A wedding

In this unit you will learn how to:

- Understand Filipino customs and traditions: a wedding
- Use reflexive verbs

Understanding Filipino customs and traditions: a wedding

◆) CD 2, TR 5

Dialogue 1

It is Pinky Abiva's wedding day. The bride and groom are talking to their guests.

Louise	Kay gan**da** ng da**mit**-pangka**sal** mo Pinky.
Pinky	Sal**a**mat Louise. Ma**hu**say ang mo**dis**ta **na**min.
Roy	Mali**gay**ang **ba**ti, Pinky. **Na**rito na pa**la** ang mga **ni**nong, **ni**nang sa ka**sal**, mga **a**bay sa ka**sal**, mga cord sponsors at mga tagapagda**la** ng sing**sing**.
Pinky	Oo, tinu**lu**ngan ni**la** a**kong** *maghanda* **pa**ra sa **a**raw ng ka**sal** ko.
Louise	Ma**ra**ming mata**ta**pos na ga**wa**in kung ma**ra**mi ang *gagawa*, *hindi* ba?
Roy	Na**a**yos na rin ba ang pro**ble**ma tung**kol** sa retra**tis**ta?
Pinky	A**ba**, oo. I**na**yos na ni Jobert.
Louise	Ang tung**kol** sa pulot-*gata*?
Pinky	*Hindi* pa **na**min naiisip, ka**si** ma**ra**mi ka**ming in**asikaso. *Sandali* lang ha? Ma**ra**ming du**mar**ating na mga **bi**sita.
Louise	**O**kay lang.

kay ganda	*how beautiful*
damit-pangkasal	*wedding dress*
modista	*dressmaker*
narito na	*here now*
mga ninong at ninang	*witnesses*
sa kasal	*wedding*
mga abay sa kasal	*wedding assistants*
tagapagdala ng singsing	*ring bearer*
tinulungan ako	*helped me*
maghanda	*to prepare*
para sa araw ng kasal ko	*for my wedding day*
matatapos na gawain	*jobs will be finished*
dumarating	*arriving*
ang gagawa	*will do*
naayos	*managed to arrange*
problema	*problem*
tungkol sa	*about*
retratista	*photographer*
inayos	*fixed/arranged*
pulot-gata	*honeymoon*
hindi pa	*not yet*
naiisip	*able to think about*
inasikaso	*dealt with*
sandali lang	*wait a moment*

Translation

Louise	Your wedding dress is so beautiful, Pinky.
Pinky	Thank you Louise. Our dressmaker is very good.
Roy	Congratulations, Pinky. So the witnesses are here now, the cord sponsors and the ring bearers.
Pinky	Yes, they (all) helped me prepare for my wedding day.
Louise	Things can be done if there are many (hands) to help, isn't that so?
Roy	Was the problem concerning the photographer solved?
Pinky	Oh, yes, thanks to Jobert. (Jobert helped fix it)
Louise	How about your honeymoon?

Exercise 1

True or false? If the answer is false, try to give the correct one:

Example: Kasama sa mga abay sa kasal ang pari.

Answer: Mali. Hindi isa sa mga abay sa kasal ang pari. Ang pari ang nagbibigay ng seremonya.

1. Maaaring walang ninong at ninang ang ikinakasal.
   Sagot:
2. Kailangang maghanda maraming buwan bago ikasal.
   Sagot:
3. Laging puti ang damit-pangkasal ng babaeng ikinakasal.
   Sagot:
4. Sa Pilipinas, laging may handaan kung may kasalan.
   Sagot:

Exercise 2

Improving your vocabulary. Look at the puzzle. Find as many wedding-related words as you can:

N	I	N	O	N	G	S	O	L	S
P	A	I	L	I	R	O	K	O	I
A	M	N	O	R	I	F	I	B	M
G	P	A	R	I	L	M	B	I	B
K	A	N	A	N	G	D	U	S	A
A	R	G	A	L	U	M	L	I	H
I	P	U	L	O	T	G	A	T	A
N	O	S	O	T	I	M	K	A	N
S	I	N	G	S	I	N	G	R	O
R	E	T	R	A	T	I	S	T	A
T	R	A	C	O	R	D	M	H	M

Language skills

1 Passive *an* verbs

Dialogue 1 introduced us to a third type of passive verb known as
the **an** verb. Like the **in** and the **i** passive verb forms, the 'doer' of
the action (actor) in the **an** verb form is identified by a **ng** word (**ni,
nina, ko, mo, niya, namin, natin, ninyo, nila** etc.). The **an** verb is
easily recognized by the addition of **an** (as a suffix) to the root verb.
For example: hugas + an = **hugasan**, *to be washed*. In a passive **an**
verb sentence, the **ang** form (**si, sina, ako, ka, siya** etc.) indicates the
goal of the sentence while another **ng** word indicates the object. For
example: **Bigyan natin ng pagkain ang bata**, *Let's give the child some
food*.

The **an** form verb differs from other verb forms in that: 1) the goal
(or **ang**) is the receiver of the action. For example, if we were to
say: **Binigyan ko si Alan ng mainit na kape**, *I gave Alan* (a cup of)
hot coffee, then Alan is clearly identified as the receiver of the act
binigyan because he has received the coffee. Any action therefore
that the **an** verb suggests is received by the goal. In English, we
would express this by using the words from, at, with, to, etc. For
example: **Tinapunan ko si Lewis ng bola**, *I threw a ball at Lewis*.

2) The goal (or **ang**) is treated as a 'space'. For example: **Winawalisan
ni Patricia ang balkonahe**, *Patricia is sweeping the porch*. For the
'info-holics' among us, it is interesting to note that most **an** verbs
are derived from transitive **um** or **mag** verbs. For example, the **um**
verb **Bumili siya ng saging sa matandang babae**, *He/she bought
some bananas from the old woman* becomes **binilhan niya ng saging**

256

ang matandang babae, *from the old woman he bought bananas*, when expressed in the **an** form. Here, the emphasis is on the goal or **matandang babae**. In the same way, **Nagbigay kami ng damit sa pulubi**, *We gave some clothes to the beggar*, becomes **Binigyan namin ng damit ang pulubi**, *the beggar was given some clothes by us*, with emphasis on **pulubi** as the goal. When **in** and **i** verb roots are used as **an** verbs, the meaning of the verb changes. Look at the examples.

How to form *an* verb tenses

Verb root: punas + suffix: an = punasan = *to wipe (to be wiped)* infinitive (can be used in requests, commands and suggestions)

pu + punas + an = pupunasan = *will be wiped* = future
p + in + u + punas + an = pinupunasan = *being wiped* = present
p + in + u + nas + an = pinunasan = *was wiped* = past

In some instances, **an** verbs change to **han** when forming the infinitive. This depends on whether the accent on the second syllable is hard or soft:

For example:

Verb root: sama + suffix: han = samahan = *to be accompanied* infinitive

sa + sama + han = sasamahan = *will be accompanied* = future

s + in + a + sama + han = sinasamahan = *being accompanied* = present

s + in + a + ma + han = sinamahan = *was accompanied* = past

Listen carefully to native Tagalog speakers and you will soon pick up the difference between hard and soft accented words. Here are a few examples:

tira +	an	= tirahan/tirhan
pila +	an	= pilahan
para +	an	= parahan
sara +	an	= sarahan/sarhan
asa +	an	= asahan
bili +	an	= bilihan
basa +	an	= basahan
ganda +	an	= gandahan

dami +	an	= damihan
dumi +	an	= dumihan
pinta +	an	= pintahan
punta +	an	= puntahan

A brief comparison between **in**, **i** and **an** verbs.

in	**an**
kain (*eat*)	
Kakainin nila iyan	Kakainan nila iyan
They will eat that	*They will eat from that*
alis (*remove*)	
Inalis ni Joe ang plato sa mesa	Inalisan ni Joe ng plato ang mesa
Joe removed the plate from the table	*A plate was removed by Joe from the table*
punit (*tear off*)	
Pinupunit ni Sarah ang papel	Pinupunitan ni Sarah ang papel
Sarah is tearing the paper (into pieces)	*Sarah is tearing off from the paper*

You will remember that the receiver of the action in **i** verbs is always indicated by **sa**. In the **an** verb form, the receiver of the action is indicated by an **ang** form word. Compare the following examples:

i	**an**
Ibibigay ni Alan kay Lina ang pera	Bibigyan ni Alan si Lina ng pera
Alan will give Lina the money	*Alan will give Lina some money*
Itatapon ko ang sirang silya sa basurahan	Tatapunan ko ng sirang silya ang basurahan
I will throw the broken chair into the bin	*I will throw a broken chair in the bin*
Isinara ni Mario ang pinto	Sinarhan ni Mario ang pintuan
Mario shut the door	*Mario closed the door*

An verb sentence variations:

Verb +	actor +	object/goal
Dinumihan	ni Charlotte	ang kaniyang damit.
Charlotte soiled her clothes		

258

Verb +   particle +   actor +   receiver of the action/goal
Sinulatan   ba   ni Louisa   ang kaibigan niya?
Did Louisa write to his/her friend?

Qualifier + actor + particle + verb +   object +   goal
Hindi   mo   raw   binigyan   ng pera   si Viv
Apparently, you didn't give Viv (any) money.

Question word +   receiver of the action +   actor +   time
Sino   ang nginitian   ni Tim   kanina?
Who did Tim smile at a while ago?

Pseudo-verb +   verb +   actor +   object +   receiver/goal
Gustong   bigyan   ni Lucy   ng bibingka   ang bata.
Lucy would like to give the child some rice cakes.

Exercise 3

Using the examples to guide you, change the following sentences into an **form** sentences:

1. Kakainin ko ang pansit sa plato.
   Answer:
2. Tumutulong ako sa kaniya.
   Answer:
3. Maglalagay kami ng rosas na halaman dito.
   Answer:
4. Gusto kong ibigay kay Harry ito.
   Answer:
5. Ilalagay ba natin ito doon?
   Answer:
6. Huwag mong aalisin ang libro sa mesa.
   Answer:

Exercise 4

Fill in the blank spaces with the correct verb form:

1. Bukas _____ (tulong) namin sila. (future)
2. Kailan ninyo _____ (laki) ang inyong kusina? (past)
3. _____ (sukli) ka na ba ng tsuper? (past)
4. Si Wills at si Ruth ang _____ (sama) niya bukas. (future)
5. Mahusay sumayaw ang _____ (bigay) nila ng premyo sa disco. (past)

6. _____ (halik) ng bata ang lolo niya. (present)

7. _____ (sarap) ng tagapagluto ang handa sa parti. (future)

8. Ayokong _____ (palit) ang aking maleta. (infinitive)

Exercise 5

When arranged in the correct sequence, the following sentences will tell a story. Arrange the sentences into the correct order and then translate the story into English. Use the **Quick vocab** to help you.

Sa kasalan

Napagod sa pagsayaw ng Tinikling ang pamilya Cook subali't nasiyahan sila.

Habang kumakain ang ilan sa mga bisita, tumugtog ang maliit na banda.

Isa sa mga tugtugin ay Tinikling.

Tumulong sa paghahain at pagsisilbi ang mga kaibigan ni Pinky.

May tugtugin at ang mga panauhin ay sumayaw.

Tuwang-tuwa ang lahat dahil sa marunong mag-Tinikling si Bill at si Louise.

Maraming kumuha ng retrato sa bagong kasal paglabas nila ng simbahan.

Dumating ang bagong kasal kasunod ang mga panauhin.

Isa-isang nagpaalam ang mga panauhin.

Nagbigay din ng speech ang 'best man'.

Inihanda ng mga tagapagluto ang pagkain at inumin dahil sa darating na ang mga panauhin.

Maraming sasakyan ang umalis sa simbahan papunta sa bahay ng bagong kasal.

Ang mga nagluluto sa kusina ay abala.

Paglabas nila sa simbahan, sinabugan ng bigas ang bagong kasal.

Inanyayahan ng mga panauhin na sumayaw ng Tinikling si Bill, Louise at Roy. Maraming pagkain at marami ring inumin.

Sa dulang, nagbigay ng maikling speech ang mga bagong kasal.

napagod	got tired
pagsayaw	dancing
subali't	but
bagong-kasal	newly wed

260

paglabas	*upon leaving*
tumugtog	*played* (a musical instrument)
banda	*band*
inihanda	*prepared*
tugtugin	*music*
tumulong	*helped*
paghahain	*offering*
pagsisilbi	*serving*
panauhin	*guests*
sumayaw	*danced*
tuwang-tuwa	*happy*
lahat	*everybody*
sinabugan	*sprinkled with/showered with*
marunong	*know*
kumuha	*took*
nagpaalam	*said goodbye*
nagbigay	*gave*
tagapagluto	*cook*
sasakyan	*cars etc.*
nagluluto	*cooking*
inanyayahan	*invited*
dulang	*table*

Exercise 6 Listening

Here are some commonly used **an** verbs. Listen to the correct pronunciation on the CD.

After listening to the pronunciation a few times, try to repeat what you heard without the help of the CD:

🔊 **CD 2, TR 5, 01:19**

Infinitive	Meaning	Verb root
awitan	*to sing*	awit
ayusan	*to arrange*	ayos
asahan	*to rely upon*	asa
alalayan	*to assist/guide*	alalay
basahan	*to read to*	basa
bigyan	*to give to*	bigay

bihisan	*to clothe*	bihis
damitan	*to clothe*	damit
damihan	*to make many*	dami
dumihan	*to soil/dirty*	dumi
gandahan	*to make beautiful*	ganda
halikan	*to kiss*	halik
habaan	*to lengthen*	haba
sundan	*to follow*	sunod
tularan	*to copy/imitate*	tulad
puntahan	*to go to*	punta
pintahan	*to paint*	pinta

Language skills

2 Expressing the circumstantial in passive verbs

Ma, Mai, Ma-an *To be able to, to happen to, to come to, to manage to*

The three passive verbs **in**, **i** and **an** form the circumstantial as follows:

- by adding the prefix **ma** to **in** verb roots. For example: **ma + kain = makain** (*to be able to be eaten*)
- by adding the prefix **mai** to **i** verb roots. For example: **mai + tapon = maitapon** (*to be able to be thrown*)
- by adding the prefix **ma** and suffix **an** to **an** verb roots. For example: **ma + hugas + an = mahugasan** (*to be able to be washed*).

As in active verbs, some actions are brought about purely by circumstance, by accident or by occurrences beyond the actor's control.

Here is a guide on how to use the **ma**, **mai** and **ma-an** prefixes with the passive **in**, **i** and **an** verbs.

In **verbs**

Ma = (prefix) + **kain** (verb root)
ma + kain =   makain   =   infinitive
                to be able to be eaten
                to happen to be eaten

> to manage to be eaten
> to come to be eaten

ma + ka + kain = makakain = *will be able* etc. *to be eaten* = future

na + ka + kain = nakakain = *able* etc. *to be eaten* = present

na + kain = nakain = *was able* etc. *to be eaten* = past

I verbs

Mai = (prefix) + **bigay** (verb root)

Mai + bigay =   maibigay   =   infinitive

> to be able to be given
> to happen to be given
> to manage to be given
> to come to be given

mai + bi + bigay = maibibigay = *will be able* etc. *to be given* = future

nai + bi + bigay = naibibigay = *able* etc. *to be given* = present

nai + bigay = naibigay = *was able* etc. *to be given* = past

An verbs

Ma (prefix) + **hugas** (verb root) + **an** (suffix)

Ma + hugas + an =   mahugasan   =   infinitive

> to be able to be washed
> to happen to be washed
> to manage to be washed
> to come to be washed

ma + hu + hugas + an = mahuhugasan = *will be able* etc. *to be washed* = future

na + hu + hugas + an = nahuhugasan = *able* etc. *to be washed* = present

na + hugas + an = nahugasan = *was able* etc. *to be washed* = past

Some examples of the circumstantial in passive verbs

In verbs

mabili	*to be able* etc. *to be bought*
makain	*to be able* etc. *to be eaten*
madala	*to be able* etc. *to be brought*
malinis	*to be able* etc. *to be cleaned*
maluto	*to be able* etc. *to be cooked*
masulat	*to be able* etc. *to be written*

I verbs

maitapon	*to be able* etc. *to be thrown*
maibigay	*to be able* etc. *to be given*
maisama	*to be able* etc. *to be taken with*
maituro	*to be able* etc. *to be taught*
maigawa	*to be able* etc. *to be bought for*
maisakay	*to be able* etc. *to be given a lift*

An verbs

mahugasan	*to be able* etc. *to be washed*
malinisan	*to be able* etc. *to be cleaned*
mahalikan	*to be able* etc. *to be kissed*
masulatan	*to be able* etc. *to be written to*
masamahan	*to be able* etc. *to be accompanied*
mabayaran	*to be able* etc. *to be paid*

Insight

English uses direct and indirect objects. In Tagalog the direct object is the object of the verb whether active or passive, e.g., **Bumili ako ng bolpen!** (direct object). *I bought a ballpen.* The indirect object is the receiver of the action, e.g., **Binigyan ko ng lapis si Boy** translates as: *I gave Boy a pencil.* **Boy** receives the action so **Boy** is the indirect object of the verb *gave.*

Exercise 7

Read each of the following sentences carefully. Using the alternative tense given in the brackets, rewrite each sentence. Don't forget to adjust the time-element, if any is given.

Example: Gusto kong malinisan ang mesa. (present)
Answer: Nalilinisan ko ang mesa.

1. Nasulatan mo na ba si Sophie? (present)
   Answer:
2. Naitatapon ni Harry ang basura lagi. (future)
   Answer:
3. May nabuksan siyang kabinet kanina. (present)
   Answer:

4. Hindi nasamahan ni Caroline si Phil sa bayan kagabi. (future)
Answer:

5. Sino ang naisasakay mo sa kotse araw-araw? (past)
Answer:

Talking about customs

Dialogue 2

🔊 **CD 2, TR 5, 02:32**

At the party following the marriage ceremony, Bill Cook witnesses some traditional Filipino wedding customs for the first time. He strikes up a conversation with Peter, Pinky's uncle.

Peter	Kumusta kayo, si Peter ako. Tiyo ni Pinky. Sana nagustuhan ninyo ang aming handaan.
Bill	Aba oo. Masaya ang kasalang ito. Ngayon lang ako nakakita ng pera na ikinakabit sa damit ng bagong kasal.
Peter	Isa iyan sa mga tradisyong Pilipino.
Bill	Napansin ko rin na nagmamano ang bagong kasal sa mga lolo at lola at ang lola ay bumubulong sa babae at ang lolo naman ay bumubulong sa lalaki.
Peter	Oo nga. Hindi lang iyon. Mamaya, may ibibigay ang matatanda sa kanila. Nakabalot ito sa panyo. Kadalasan ito'y pera upang gawing puhunan ng bagong mag-asawa.
Bill	Magandang kaugalian iyan. Bakit naman tumatakbo ang bagong kasal na parang nag-uunahan sila?
Peter	Ah kasi, may kasabihan ang mga Pilipino na kung sino sa dalawang bagong kasal ang unang umakyat sa bahay, siya ang masusunod.
Bill	Ganoon ba?

tiyo	*uncle*
sana	*I hope*
nagustuhan	*liked*
handaan	*reception*
ibibigay	*will be given*
ngayon lang	*just now*
nakakita	*was able to see*

QUICK VOCAB

ikinasal	*married*
kinakabitan	*being attached*
tradisyon(g)	*tradition*
napansin	*noticed*
nagmamano	*kissing the hand*
bagong kasal	*newly wed*
masusunod	*will be followed*
lolo at lola	*grandpa and grandma*
bumubulong	*whispering*
babae at lalaki	*man and woman*
oo nga	*indeed*
matatanda	*the old ones*
nakabalot	*wrapped*
kadalasan	*often times*
puhunan	*capital*
tumatakbo	*running*
nag-uunahan	*beating each other*
kasabihan	*saying*
umakyat	*climb up*

Translation

Peter	How are you, I'm Peter, Pinky's uncle. I hope you like our party.
Bill	Oh, yes. This wedding celebration is good. This was my first time to see (paper) money being pinned to the clothes of the newly weds.
Peter	That's a Filipino tradition.
Bill	I also noticed that the newly weds kissed the hands of the (their) grandparents and that the grandmother whispered (something) to the girl (while) the grandfather whispered (something) to the boy.
Pete	Indeed. That's not all. Later on, the old people will give (something) to them wrapped in a handkerchief. Usually this is money to be used by the newly weds as capital.
Bill	That's an interesting custom. Why are the newly weds chasing one another?
Peter	Oh, that's because we have a Filipino saying that whoever (between them) manages to climb up (the stairs) to the house first will be the 'boss'.
Bill	Really?

Exercise 8

Answer in complete Tagalog sentences:

1. Ano ang unang tradisyon na binanggit (mentioned) ng tiyo ni Pinky?
2. Sino ang humahalik sa bagong kasal na babae?
3. Bakit binibigyan ng nakabalot na pera ang bagong kasal?
4. Ano ang dahilan (reason) kung bakit tumatakbo ang mag-asawa?

Language skills

3 *Sarili ko/aking sarili* etc. Reflexive *Mismo* Intensive

'I myself will do the painting.' 'Letty will feed herself.' 'Liam overworks himself.' All of these examples indicate an action done to or on behalf of the self. The subject is the beneficiary of the action. These are reflexive expressions. The Tagalog word used to express the reflexive is **sarili** (*self, own*). The Tagalog reflexive is used either in connection with a **ng** form personal pronoun (**ko, mo, niya, namin, natin, ninyo** and **nila**) or a **sa** form personal pronoun (**akin, iyo, kaniya, amin, atin, inyo** or **kanila**) plus a **ng** ending. The **sa** form personal pronouns then become: **aking, iyong, kaniyang, aming, ating, inyong** and **kanilang**. Both **ng** and **sa** form personal pronouns can be used interchangeably. There is no hard and fast rule suggesting when **sa** or **ng** can or cannot be used. Look at the following examples given in both forms: **sarili ko/aking sarili** = *myself*, **sarili mo/iyong sarili**, *yourself* etc. Here are some example sentences: **Sinaktan niya ang sarili niya**, *He hurt himself.* **Huwag mong saktan ang sarili mo**, *Don't hurt yourself.* However, the word **sarili** may also be used on its own. For example: **Sarili ko ito.** *This is my own.* **Sarili ni Steve ang bahay na ito**, *This house is Steve's own.* When a reflexive phrase is used as a describing word, a **ng** word may be used. For example: **Tumitingin si Mamerta ng sarili niyang retrato**, *Mamerta is looking at a picture of herself.*

Another way of expressing the reflexive in Tagalog is through the word **mismo**. **Mismo** is a stronger word than **sarili** and so serves to further stress the personal pronoun that accompanies it. **Mismo** takes a **ng** ending when following a pronoun. For example:

Mismong ako, *I myself*, mismong sila, *they themselves*, mismong kami, *we ourselves* and so on. When a personal pronoun precedes mismo, then ng is not used. For example: Ako mismo, *I myself*, Siya mismo, *he himself*, Sila mismo, *they themselves* and so on. Mismo can also be used with a sa form word. For example: Mismong sa Cubao siya nakatira, *It's in Cubao itself that he/she lives.*

Some example sentences:

1. Kinuha niya mismo ang pera sa bangko
   He took the money himself from the bank
2. Ako mismo ang sumalubong kay Paul sa paliparan
   I myself went to meet Paul at the airport
   (or *I went to meet Paul at the airport myself*)
3. Sinaktan niya ang sarili niya
   He hurt himself
4. Siya mismo ang tumingin sa akin
   It was he himself who examined me

Exercise 9

Supply mismong + noun/pronoun or a pronoun + mismo in the blank space: Don't forget the linker ng if one is necessary.

1. Sumulat _____ sa akin. (he/she)
2. _____ ang bumili ng pagkain para sa party. (we)
3. Nilinisan _____ ang kotse namin. (they)
4. _____ ba _____ ang nagdala ng mga maleta? (you)
5. _____ ang pumunta sa kasal ni Pinky. (Fred and friends)

Exercise 10

Look at the pictures below while listening to your CD. Can you match the verb with the correct picture?

◀) CD 2, TR 5, 04:11

3.

4.

5.

6.

One-minute phrases

Saan ang punta mo? (*sah-ahn ahng poon-tah moo?*) Meaning *where are you going?* A very common question in Tagalog. It is not meant to be taken literally, requiring an explanation of where you are going. Rather, it is just another way of saying 'hello' or acknowledging you. It is just another way of making small talk.

Diyan lang (*dyan lahng*) Literally, *just there*. This phrase is usually used as a polite answer to the question: **Saan ang punta mo?**, *Where are you going?* As **Saan ang punta mo?** it is only a form of saying 'hello' it commonly elicits a simple reply such as **D'yan lang**, *just there*.

Wala nang oras (*wah-lah nahng aw-rahs*) Literally, *no more time*. Meaning we've run out of time/time is short. This short phrase can also mean: **Wala nang panahon**, *time has run out*. For example: **Wala nang oras ang mga bisita upang matulog**, *The guests have no time left to go to sleep*.

Maghintayan tayo (*mahg-heen-tah-yahn tah-yaw*) Meaning let's wait for one another. Used when two people agree to meet one another at an agreed location. For example: **Maghintayan tayo sa harap**

ng McDonald's sa Kalye Lorenzo, *Let's wait for one another in front of* [the] *McDonald's in Lorenzo Street.*

Nag-uurong-sulong (*nahg-oo-oo-rawng soo-lawng*) Literally, *moving backward, moving forward.* Meaning 'hesitating'/'cannot make one's mind up'. For example: **Nag-uurong-sulong si Maria kung pupunta siya sa Palawan bukas,** *Maria cannot make her mind up/is hesitating as to whether she will go to Palawan tomorrow.*

Insight

Although Filipino weddings are formal, they are also very festive occasions steeped in many fascinating traditions. Formal dress is obligatory. Sponsors of the bride and groom are required to be dependable and available to give advice and support to the couple throughout their married lives.

Summary

1. The **an** passive verb takes the **ng** form as doer/actor.
2. **An** is different from the **in** and **i** verbs in that only a part of the subject is acted upon. e.g., **sigawan** *shout at.*
3. Adjectives can be used with **an**, meaning: to make the subject what the adjective implies.
4. The **in**, **i** and **an** verbs have a circumstantial mode too.
5. Add **ma** prefix to an **in** stem to form the circumstantial.
6. Add **mai** prefix to an **i** stem to form the circumstantial.
7. Add **ma** prefix + stem + **an** suffix to form the circumstantial.
8. **Sarili** + **ng** group is reflexive (on behalf of the self).
9. **Mismo** is stronger than **sarili**.
10. Pronouns of the **ng** or **ang** group can be used with **sarili** or **mismo**.

18

Sa isang pistang bayan
At a town fiesta

In this unit you will learn how to:

* Celebrate the Filipino fiesta
* Use the gerund
* Handle a water buffalo!

Celebrating the Filipino fiesta

Dialogue 1

◄) CD 2, TR 6

Bill, Louise and Roy have been invited to a barrio fiesta.

Bill	Na**pa**kara**ra**ming **ta**o sa pis**tang** i**to**. Mara**ming** dekoras**yong** pala**wit** sa **kal**ye, sari**sa**ring ban**de**ra at tala**gan**g ma**ku**lay ang bu**ong** lu**gar**.
Louise	O**o** nga. A**pat** raw ang **band**a at mara**ming** pap**u**tok **ma**mayang ga**bi** ka**pag** nag**ko**ronas**yon** ng **rey**na ng pistang **bay**an.
Roy	Nagpun**ta** a**ko** sa kabaya**nan** at mara**ming** mga may pu**west**o. Kara**mi**han ay mga tin**dang** da**mit** at laru**an**.
Louise	Sang-a**yon** sa **me**yor **may**roon daw **rey**na ng pis**tang bay**an. Si**ya** ang na**na**lo sa 'popularity contest.' Ma**ya**man si**gu**ro.
Roy	Sa **par**ke ay may tsu**bi**bo at mga laba**nan** sa basketbol. **Me**ron ding iba't i**ban**g *palaro* **pa**ra sa mga **ba**ta katu**lad** ng pag-ak**yat** sa ka**way**an, pagsung**kit** ng **las**o, pagsa**kay** sa kala**baw**, pagtak**bo** sa **sak**o, pag**ka**in ng **mu**rang ni**yog** at i**ba** pa. **Gus**to kong mano**od**.

napakarami(ng)	*so many*
pista(ng)	*feast day*
dekorasyon(g)	*decoration*
palawit	*bunting*
sarisari(ng)	*assorted*
talagang makulay	*really colourful*
buong lugar	*whole place*
kawayan	*bamboo*
pagsungkit	*hooking with a pole*
paputok	*fireworks*
mamayang gabi	*tonight*
kapag	*when/during*
nagkoronasyon	*crowned*
nagpunta	*went*
kabayanan	*town*
puwesto	*stalls*
karamihan	*many of*
tinda(ng) damit	*clothes for sale*
ililigid	*will be driven around*
sang-ayon	*according to*
reyna	*queen*
nanalo	*won*
mayaman	*rich*
para sa atin	*for us*
pistang bayan	*town fiesta*
parke	*park*
tsubibo	*ferris wheel*
labanan	*contest*
palaro	*games*
katulad ng	*like*
pag-akyat	*climbing*

QUICK VOCAB

pagsakay	*riding*
pagtakbo	*running*
sako	*sack*
pagkain	*eating*
murang niyog	*young coconut*
manood	*watch*
parada	*parade*
karosa	*procession cart*
kaniya(ng)	*her*
mga abay	*consorts*
kumbidado	*invited*
kapitan	*captain*
naghanda	*prepared food*
pumunta	*go*

Translation

Bill	The (town) fiesta is packed with people. The streets are decorated with different kinds of flags and the whole place is really colourful.
Louise	I agree. I heard that there are four bands and there will be plenty of fireworks tonight during the coronation (of the fiesta queen).
Roy	I went to the town centre and there are many stalls. Most (of them) are of clothes and toys.
Louise	According to the mayor there will be a fiesta 'queen'. So she won the popularity contest! Perhaps she's rich.
Roy	There is a ferris wheel at the park and a basketball contest. There are also children's games like bamboo climbing, hooking the ribbon, riding the water buffalo, sack racing and eating young coconut. I'd like to go and watch.
Louise	Let's also watch the parade. There is a decorated cart and the 'queen' and her consorts will be driven around (the town). I'd like to see their costumes.
Bill	We have been invited to the Barrio Captain's house. They have made some preparations (for us). Apparently they are preparing *lechon*.*
Roy	Okay, let's go. I'd like to be able to see how to cook *lechon*.
Bill	I agree.

*Lechon: a traditional Filipino delicacy

Exercise 1 Mga tanong: (Questions)

1. Anong uri ng pagdiriwang ang pinuntahan nina Bill?
2. Kailan kokoronahan ang 'reyna'?
3. Anu-ano ang mga tinda sa kabayanan?
4. Sa palagay mo, ano ang mahalaga sa isang popularity contest?
5. Magbigay ng tatlong palaro para sa mga bata.
6. Bakit isasakay sa karosa ang reyna at mga abay?
7. Sino ang nag-imbita sa pamilyang Cook?

Language skills

1 ***Pag*** + **verb root**
   Ka + **verb root** + ***an***
   Ang + **verb**

No doubt you are familiar with stories from your childhood
where frogs were transformed into handsome princes (or was it
the other way round?) at the wave of a magic wand. The Tagalog
language cannot endow you with magical powers but it too has
its own form of magic wand with the ability of transforming
verbs into nouns. This process is known as nominalization, and
the resulting word a gerund. This process of transforming verbs
into nouns may at first sound rather complex, but is in fact quite
simple. Notwithstanding a few exceptions in English, a gerund is
basically a nominalized verb ending in 'ing' (i.e. cooking, singing,
dancing etc.). In Tagalog, the prefix **pag** is added to a verb stem to
produce a gerund. The gerund is commonly used in response to the
question word 'how', expressing the manner in which a word is
performed. For example: **pag** + **kanta** = **pagkanta** (*singing*). **Gusto
ko ang pagkanta mo,** *I like your singing,* **pag** + **sayaw** = **pagsayaw**

274

(*dancing*). **Ang pagsayaw ang paborito kong libangan,** *Dancing is my favourite pastime.*

Another method of forming a noun from a verb stem is by using the prefix **ka** together with the suffix **an**. **Ka** and **an** sandwich the verb resulting in a nominalized verb. For example: **Ka + galing + an = kagalingan,** *goodness,* **ka + ibig + an = kaibigan,** 'friend' etc. Occasionally, the suffix **an** may become **han** if this makes the word easier to pronounce. For example: **ka + ligaya + han = kaligayahan,** *happiness.* **Ka + ganda + han = kagandahan,** *beauty.* When a verb stem ends with the letter 'd', this letter becomes an 'r' when forming a gerund with **ka + an**. For example: **tamad,** *lazy* = **ka + tamad + an = katamaran,** *laziness.* More examples follow.

Another way of transforming a verb into a noun in Tagalog is simply by placing the word **ang** before the verb (in any tense)! For example: 1) **ang nagsasalita** (the person talking) or *speaker.* **Sino ang nagsasalita?,** *Who is the speaker?*; **ang maglalaba ko,** (the person washing clothes for me) *my laundry person,* **Narito na ang maglalaba ko,** *My laundry person is already here.*

Further example sentences:

1. Kami ang mag-aayos ng mga gamit mo
   We will be the ones to tidy up your things
2. Maraming kaibigan si Harry
   Harry has many friends
3. Kumusta ang pagtulog mo?
   How's your sleeping? [how did you sleep?]
4. Gusto ng mga guro ang pagtula ni Doming
   The teachers liked Doming's poem recitation
5. Kilala mo ba ang nagsasalita?
   Do you know the person talking?
6. Ayaw ni Nanay ang pagsama ni Stephen sa barkada niya
   Mother doesn't like Stephen going out [with his gang]
7. Gabi na ang kaniyang pagsimba
   His/her churchgoing is/was quite late already
8. Ano ang ipinagbili mo?
   What (goods) did you sell?

Exercise 2
Give the **ka + an** form of the following words (remember the rule about verb stems ending with the letter 'd'):

1. palad (*palm*)
   Answer:
2. tamad (*lazy*)
   Answer:
3. wala (*none*)
   Answer:
4. yaman (*rich*)
   Answer:
5. bahay (*house*)
   Answer:
6. mali (*wrong*)
   Answer:

Some commonly nominalized verbs
Pag prefix:

pagkain	*eating*
pag-alis	*leaving*
pagtawa	*laughing*
pagsalita	*talking/speaking*
paglapit	*coming nearer*
paglayo	*going away*
pag-ibig	*love*

Ka prefix + **an** suffix:

kahinaan	*weakness*
kabaitan	*kindness*
kabutihan	*goodness*
karapatan	*right*
karunungan	*knowledge*
kasinungalingan	*lies*
katindihan	*intensity*
kalimitan	*frequency*
kalalakihan	*menfolk*
kababaihan	*womanhood*
katauhan	*personality*
katarungan	*justice*
kakayahan	*ability*

Exercise 3

Fill in the blanks with an appropriate noun from the two preceding lists.

1. _____ ay lakas.
2. Puro _____ daw ang sinasabi ng mga politiko.
3. Dalawa ang pila. Isa sa mga _____ at isa sa mga _____.
4. Lahat tayo ay may _____ sa mundong ito.
5. Ano ang _____ mo sa trabahong ito?

Exercise 4 Listening and recognizing

Listen to the conversation on the CD. You will hear a number of nominalized **pag** and **ka** + **an** words used. Can you pick out the words used from those listed here?

◀) **CD 2, TR 6, 02:06**

karapatan	pagngiti
kaligayahan	kasabihan
paglabas	kasunduan
pagpunta	kalimitan
pag-alis	kasalanan
pagsama	pagtawa
kaayusan	pagsulat
kasamaan	pagtalima
pagkain	pagpasok

Dialogue 2

The Cook family continue to enjoy their day out at the barrio fiesta. Bill is in conversation with one of the guests at the Barrio Captain's house.

◀) **CD 2, TR 6, 03:54**

Rudy	Kumusta *po* ka**yo**? Si Rudy *po* a**ko**. **Sa**na nag-e**e**njoy ka**yo** sa a**m**ing pis**tang bay**an.
Bill	**O**o. Nag**ta**taka lang a**ko**. **Pa**rang guma**ga**stos ang mga **ta**o kapag may pis**tang ba**yan. **Kah**it sa**an ak**o tumin**gin**, may pag**ka**in at may **in**u**min**.
Rudy	Gano**on** *nga po*. Nag-i**ip**on ng **pe**ra ang mga **ta**o sa lo**ob** ng i**sang** ta**on up**ang *makapaghanda* sa pis**ta**.

Bill	*Hindi* **ya**ta **ta**ma iyan ka**si** mag**pap**agod ka sa tra**ba**ho sa lo**ob** ng i**sa**ng ta**on** pagka**ta**pos **ga**gastusin mo ng min**sa**nan. Big-**lang** ma**wa**wala ang **ini**pon mong **pe**ra **da**hil lang sa pis**ta**.
Rudy	Toto**o** iyan su**ba**li't kauga**li**an na ng mga Pili**pi**no iyan. Ka**pag** na**u**bos na ang **pe**ra, ba**ha**la na!
Bill	Gan**oo**n ba?
Rudy	**O**po. Kadala**sa**n pa *nga* ang iba nangu**ngu**tang **pa**ra *makapaghanda* lang.
Bill	Ma**hi**rap din pa**la** ang kauga**li**ang it**o**, an**o**?
Rudy	Tala**ga** – **pe**ro sina**sa**bi lang **na**min – 'ba**ha**la na!'

pagkatapos	*afterwards*
gagastusin	*will be spent*
nag-eenjoy	*enjoying*
bigla(ng)	*suddenly*
pistang bayan	*town fiesta*
kahit saan	*anywhere*
tumingin	*look*
may pagkain	*there is food*
totoo	*true*
ganoon nga	*really like that*
nag-iipon ng pera	*saving money*
kapag	*if/when*
sa loob ng	*in(side)*
isang taon	*one year*
upang	*in order to*
makapaghanda	*be able to prepare*
magpapagod	*become tired*
sa trabaho	*at work*
minsanan	*in one go*
mawawala	*will disappear*
ang inipon	*the savings*
dahil lang	*just because of*
subali't	*but*
kaugalian	*custom*
naubos	*finished*
bahala na	*come what may*
kung minsan	*sometime*
nangungutang	*borrow money*
sinasabi lang	*just say*

Translation

Rudy	How are you sir? I'm Rudy. I hope you're enjoying our town fiesta.
Bill	Yes (I am). I'm just wondering. It looks as though people like to spend money when there is a fiesta. Everywhere I look there is food and drink.
Rudy	It's really like that. People save money all year in order to enjoy the fiesta.
Bill	I'm not sure that's a good idea because people work very hard at work all year just to spend (their earnings) in one go. Their savings suddenly disappear just because of the fiesta.
Rudy	That's true but that's already a Filipino custom. When the money happens to run out, leave it to destiny!
Bill	Is that so?
Rudy	Yes. Often times others even borrow money just to prepare.
Bill	This custom is rather difficult, isn't it?
Rudy	Indeed – but we just say 'bahala na'. (See Insight an the end of this unit.)

Insight

Moderative expressions in Tagalog are represented by **medyo** or **nang kaunti**. For example: **Medyo sanay na ako.** *I'm somewhat used to it now.* **Sanay na ako nang kaunti.** *I'm somewhat used to it now.* Moderative adjectives are made by reduplicating the stem of an adjective: thus: **Mabuti-buti ito.** *This is rather good.*

Exercise 5

Which of the following statements are true? If the statement is false, can you give the correct answer in Tagalog?

1. Ayaw gumastos ng mga tao kapag may pistang bayan.
2. Nag-iipon ang mga tao ng pera upang bumili ng kalabaw.
3. Unti-unti nilang ginagastos ang perang inipon nila.
4. Mabuting kaugalian ang magdiwang ng pista.
5. Mabuti para sa lahat ng tao ang pista.

Exercise 6 Listening and speaking

On your way to a fiesta, you meet some friends on the road. You stop to have a chat before continuing. Use the suggestions to help you fill out your part of the dialogue. Use the CD to practise the dialogue:

Nonoy	Kaibigan, kumusta ba? Dadalo ka ba sa pista?
Ikaw	(Say yes, we are going to the fiesta)
Nonoy	Marami nang tao doon. Mahilig ka bang sumayaw?
Ikaw	(Tell him you like dancing very much)
Nonoy	Mabuti!! Maganda ang tugtog at may pagkain din.
Ikaw	(Ask him where the food and drinks are being sold)
Nonoy	Doon, malapit sa Munisipyo.
Ikaw	(Thank him and invite him to join you)
Nonoy	Hindi na, salamat. Busog na ako.
	Magkita na lang tayo mamaya, sa sayawan.
Ikaw	(Tell him that you will look for him)
Nonoy	O, sige. Paalam na kaibigan!
Ikaw	(Goodbye)

Language skills

2 Maki, Makipag, Makipang
Participational verb forms in active verbs

Tagalog reserves a special group of verb forms to express actions done collectively or requiring the participation of others. These verb forms are known as participational or social verbs. Social verbs are characterized by the prefix **maki** for **um** and **ma** verbs, by **makipag** for **mag** verbs, and finally by **makipang** for **mang** verbs. Since participational verbs are actor focused (i.e., with the emphasis on the 'doer' of the action), it follows logically that they only take active verbs. For example: **Makiupo tayo doon**, *Let's share the seat over there*. **Nakikipaglaro ka ba sa mga bagong kapitbahay?**, *Do you play with the new neighbours?*. Kahapon, **nakipamaril sina John**, *Yesterday, John went shooting* (with others). In some cases, when the 'doer' of the action takes part in an activity previously initiated by another person, this is expressed by means of the **sa** form. For example: **Nag-swimming sila sa ilog;** (prior action) **nakipagswimming ako sa kanila**, *They went swimming in the river; I went swimming with them.* **Kumakain sila ng pansit; nakikain ako sa kanila.** *They were eating noodles; I ate with them.*

280

How to form participational verbs

Maki (source *um* verbs)

Maki (prefix) + bili (verb root) *buy*
maki + bili = makibili *to buy with* = infinitive
maki + ki + bili = makikibili *will buy with* = future
naki + ki + bili = nakikibili *buying with* = present
naki + bili = nakibili *bought with* = past

Makipag (source *mag* verbs)

Makipag (prefix) + laro (verb root) *to play with* = infinitive
maki + ki + pag + laro = makikipaglaro *will play with* = future
naki + ki + pag + laro = nakikipaglaro *playing with* = present
naki + pag + laro = nakipaglaro *played with* = past

Makipang (source *mang* verbs)

Makipang becomes makipam (prefix) + balita (drop b) = alita
makipam + alita = makipamalita *to share news with* = infinitive
makiki + pa + ma + lita = makikipamalita *will share news with* =
future
nakiki + pa + ma + lita = nakikipamalita *sharing news with* = present
naki + pa + ma + lita = nakipamalita *shared news with* = past

Sentence variations
Verb +   actor +   social counterpart
Nakikipag-away   si Joselito   kay Toto
Joselito is quarrelling/fighting with Toto.

Pseudo-verb +   verb +   actor   +   social counterpart
Ayaw   makipag-usap   ni Will   kay Gladys.
Will doesn't want to talk to Gladys.

Question word + verb + social counterpart + time
Sino   ang makikipagsayaw   sa akin   mamaya?
Who will dance with me later on?

Exercise 7
Translate the following into Tagalog:

1. Auntie Marge will be eating with them tonight. (kumain)
2. Where did you ask for a seat? (maupo)

3. Are you going shopping with Auntie Dot? (mamili)
4. Jose is getting into a fight again. (mag-away)
5. I'm still talking with Janet. (mag-usap)

A few participational verbs indicate a request to use other people's facilities:

makikain	*to ask to share some food with*
makiinom	*to request a drink*
makisindi	*to request a light*
makitulog	*to request to share sleeping facilities of*
makihiga	*to request to share resting facilities of*
makisuyo	*to request to do something for*
makipagluto	*to request to use cooking facilities of*
makitawag	*to request to use the telephone of*
makisakay	*to request to use other people's transport*
makiangkas	*to request a lift*

Sentences in **maki** form (remember that requests and suggestions use the infinitive form):

1. Maaari po ba kaming makiinom?
Could we ask for a drink?
2. Puwede bang makiupo si Kim dito?
Could Kim sit here?
3. Puwede bang makipamasyal kami sa inyo?
Could we take a stroll with you?
4. Maaari bang makisakay kami hanggang sa bayan?
Could we kindly have a lift to the town?
5. Puwede bang huwag kang manigarilyo dito?
Could you not smoke here?
6. Makisindi ka sa lalaking iyon.
Ask for a light from that man.

Some reciprocal social verbs:

makipag-away	*to fight with*
makipagtalo	*to argue with*
makipaglaban	*to fight with*
makipag-usap	*to converse with*
makipagkamay	*to shake hands with*
makipaghiwalay	*to separate from*

Example sentences:

1. Nakikipag-away na naman si Matthew
   Matthew is fighting again
2. Nakipagtalo si Sue sa opisyal
   Sue argued with the official
3. Gusto kong makipag-usap sa iyo nang masinsinan
   I want to talk to you seriously
4. Nakipagkamay si Lennard sa kaniyang kalaban
   Lennard shook hands with his opponent
5. Ayaw makipaghiwalay ni Anto sa asawa niya
   Anto doesn't like to separate from his wife

Exercise 8
Change the following sentences into either a request or suggestion (remember to change the actor or the time element):

Example: Makikitawag ako sa telepono bukas.
Request form: Maaari bang makitawag ako sa telepono bukas?

1. Nakipag-usap kami kay Ginoong Reyes.
2. Nakitulog ako sa kanila.
3. Nakikipag-away kayo sa mga bata.
4. Makikisakay kami kina Baby.
5. Nakikipagluto ang mga bisita dito.

Insight
To understand the modern Filipino, it is essential to understand the influence of kinship on Filipino thought and behaviour. Loyalty to family and clan runs deep. The individual is always perceived as a part of the whole; never as separate, independent or autonomous. Such values are viewed as alien and western.

Handling a water buffalo!

Dialogue 3

◀) CD 2, TR 6, 07:17

Bill, Louise and Roy are visiting a farm in the barrio. Roy is learning how to handle the carabao (water buffalo).

Roy	Gani**to** ba ang pag**ha**wak sa **ren**da ng kalab**aw**? *Baka* suwa**gin** a**ko** ni**to**.
Kiko	Puwe**de** na sa **un**ang **be**ses. *Hindi*, maba**it** iyan. Hindi ka **su**suwa**gin** ni**yan**. Hawa**kan** mo nang malu**wag**. Gani**yan** *nga*. **Tap**os **med**yo kau**sa**pin mo si**ya**. Sa**bi**hin mo rin sa kani**ya** 'Tsk. . .Tsk. . .Tsk' kung **gus**to mo siyang luma**kad**.
Roy	Gano**on** lang pala. U**u**litin ko. Gani**to** ba? 'Tsk. . .Tsk. . .Tsk. . .'
Kiko	Oo, gani**yan**. Maga**ling** ka pa**lang** hu**ma**wak ng kala**baw**. Kung **gus**to mo, suma**kay** ka.
Roy	May ka**un**ti a**kong** karana**san** no**ong** nagtra**ba**ho a**ko** sa i**sang** sabsa**ban** ng ka**ba**yo sa Ingla**ter**ra.
Kiko	Gano**on** ba, ka**ya** pa**la** *madali* kang ma**tu**to!
Roy	*Hindi* ba hi**git** na ma**hir**ap ang hu**ma**wak ng ka**ba**yo.
Kiko	*Hindi* na**man**.
Roy	**Sa**sabihin ko sa mga kai**bi**gan ko na naka**ha**wak a**ko** ng kalab**aw**. Puwe**de** mo ba a**kong** **ku**nan ng re**tra**to?
Kiko	**Ba**kit *hindi*?
Roy	Sa**la**mat. **Te**ka, ku**ku**nin ko lang ang **ka**mera ko sa **ba**hay.
Kiko	O, **si**ge.

QUICK VOCAB	
ganito	*like this*
ang paghawak	*how to hold*
renda	*reins*
baka	*might*
suwagin	*gore* (bull)
nito	*this* (ng form)
higit	*more*
sa unang beses	*for the first time*
ang paghawak	*handling*
hawakan	*hold*
niyan	*that* (ng form)
karanasan	*experience*
nagtrabaho	*worked*
sabsaban	*stable*
kabayo	*horse*
kaya pala	*no wonder*
madali(ng)	*easily*
matuto	*to learn*
mahirap	*difficult*
sasabihin	*will tell*

nang maluwag	*loosely*
ganiyan	*like that*
medyo	*sort of*
kung gusto mo(ng)	*if you want*
lumakad	*to walk/move*
kausapin	*talk to*
sabihin	*tell/say*
sa kaniya	*to him/her*
uulitin	*will repeat*
magaling	*good at/clever*
nakahawak	*managed to handle*
kunan	*take*
bakit hindi	*why not*
teka	*just a moment*
kukunin	*will get/fetch*
sumakay	*ride*

Translation

Roy	Kiko, is this how to hold the reins of the carabao? He won't try to swipe me, will he?
Kiko	Not bad for a first timer. No, he's a good-natured carabao. He won't charge you. (Just) Hold him loosely. Yes, just like that. Talk to him too. Just say 'Tsk. . .Tsk. . .Tsk' if you want him to move.
Roy	Ah! So it's that easy. Let me try: Like this? 'Tsk. . .Tsk. . .Tsk. . .'
Kiko	Yes! Just like that. You're very good at handling a carabao. If you like, you can even ride him.
Roy	I've got a little bit of experience from when I used to work at a stable back in England.
Kiko	Is that so? No wonder you are learning so quickly!

Exercise 9

Answer the following questions:

1. Ano ang ginagawa ni Roy?
2. Ano ang dapat (should) niyang gawin (do) upang (so that) hindi siya suwagin ng kalabaw?
3. Maari bang sumakay si Roy sa kalabaw?
4. Ano ang dahilan (reason) at magaling si Roy sumakay ng kalabaw?

Language skills

3 *Ganito* Like this
Ganiyan Like that
Ganoon Like that (over there)

In our dialogue, Roy Cook was learning how to handle a water buffalo or carabao. He asked Kiko to comment on how well he was doing. You may have noticed the words: **ganito**, *like this*, **ganiyan**, *like that*, **ganoon**, *like that* (over there). These words are commonly used in Tagalog in connection with the demonstration of an action. On most occasions, **ganito**, **ganiyan** and **ganoon** are used together with a gerund. For example: **Ganito ba ang paghiwa ng sibuyas?**, *Is this how onions are cut?* **Ganiyan ang pagpinta ng dingding**, *That's (the way) to paint the wall.* **Ganoon ang sinabi ni Dave**, *Dave said something like that.* The words **ganito**, **ganiyan** and **ganoon** may also be used in situations where two objects are compared. When this happens, then the stem of the adjective is prefixed by the letters **ka**. For example: ka + layo (from **malayo** *far* = **kalayo**) **Ganito ba kahaba ang tali ng kahon?**, *Is the string of the box as long as this?* **Ganiyan kaganda ang bulaklak na rosas.** *The rose is as beautiful as that.* **Ganoon kalaki ang mapa ng Cebu**, *The map of Cebu is as big as that.*

Sentence variations in the use of *ganito*, *ganiyan*, and *ganoon*

Qualifier	+	ganiyan	+	gerund	+	object
Hindi		ganiyan		ang pagsulat		ng abakada

That's not how to write the ABC/Writing the ABC is not like that

Ganito	+	particle	+	comparison	+	subject/topic
Ganito		pala		kalayo		ang baryo ninyo

So your barrio is as far as this

Qualifier	ganoon	comparison	subject/topic
Walang	ganoon	kasarap	ang luto ni Aling Puring

Nothing like that is as tasty as Aling Puring's cooking

Exercise 10
Reorganize the following into coherent Tagalog sentences:

1. sa amin kabait ganoon si Ginoong Cruz.
2. ba ng silyang rattan ganito ang paggawa?

286

3. ang pagsara paano ng kahong ito?
4. ang pagluto hindi ng adobo ba ganito?
5. sa akin mo ang pagtugtog sabihin ng himig (*piece*) na ito.

Exercise 11

Look at the picture. Which of the words best describes the articles listed beneath it? Use **ganito**, **ganiyan** or **ganoon** as your answer.

1. apoy	_____;	7. aso	_____;
2. bata	_____;	8. kaldero	_____;
3. barko	_____;	9. kutsara	_____;
4. bola	_____;	10. ulap	_____;
5. tinidor	_____;	11. punong niyog	_____;
6. bahay	_____;	12. pinggan	_____

One-minute phrases

> **Saka na lang** (*sah-kah nah lahng*) Literally, *later already just.* Meaning 'later on'. This phrase is commonly used to indicate that something has been postponed. For example: **Saka na lang tayo mamasyal**, *Why don't we just take* [our] *stroll later on.*
>
> **Baka sakali** (*bah-kah sah-kah-lee*) Literally, *might perhaps.* This Tagalog phrase is similar in meaning to the English expression 'just in case'. It denotes the need to be prepared. For example,

Maghanda tayo at baka sakaling dumating ang mga bisita, *Let us make some preparations in case the visitors arrive.*

At sa wakas (*aht sah wah-kahs*) Literally, *and at the end.* Similar to the English exclamation 'At last!'. For example: **At sa wakas, dumating din ang lolo at lola,** *At last, grandfather and grandmother* [have finally] *arrived!*

Ako ang bahala (*ah-kaw ahng bah-hah-lah*) Meaning, *I will take responsibility.* This Tagalog phrase is similar in meaning to the English expression 'Don't worry, leave it all to me'.

Masyadong magulo (*mahs-yah-dawng mah-goo-law*) Meaning, 'very messy/entangled'. This expression is used to express lack of clarity in another person's words or explanations. Sometimes it is used in connection with a troublemaker. For example: **Masyadong magulo ang usapan ng mga politiko sa Congress,** *The conversation of the politicians in Congress is rather messy.*

Insight

Filipino society is an intricate web of interdependent relationships which carry mutual obligations. Within these relationships, when expectations are not fulfilled or realized, the frustration experienced may result in the **bahala na** attitude surfacing. **Bahala na** (*it's up to God*) could be understood as fatalism or resignation in difficulties or decisions. Rather than confront the source of the frustration, the Filipino shrugs his or her shoulders and says 'just let it be'. Avoidance may seem to be a wiser move than open or direct confrontation of circumstances beyond his or her control. (*Bathala is an ancient Filipino name for *god*, pre-dating the Christian era.)

Summary

1. A **nominalized** verb (verb becoming a noun) is called a '**gerund**'.
2. A Tagalog gerund is made by adding the prefix **pag** to a stem. E.g., **pag** + **alis** = **pagalis** – *leaving*.

3. Another form of nominalization is constructed by using **ka + adjective + an**.
4. It is also possible to nominalize by using the word **ang** + a verb of any tense.
5. Participational mode in **um** verbs is formed by adding **maki** to the stem.
6. Some **maki** stems are used to make a request.
7. Participational mode in **mag** verbs is formed by adding **makipag** to the stem.
8. Participational mode in **mang** verbs is formed by adding **makipang** to stem.
9. Follow the phonological variations of the **mang** verb and apply to **makipang**.
10. *'like this', 'like that', 'like that'* (over there)' = **ganito, ganiyan, ganoon**.

19

Ang buhay sa baryo
Life in the barrio

In this unit you will learn how to:

- Live in the barrio
- Help on the farm
- Use causative verbs

Living in the barrio

Dialogue 1

◀) CD 2, TR 7

Bill, Louise and Roy Cook are enjoying their stay with Kiko and his family.

Louise	**Ting**nan mo ang mga **pu**nong-**ka**hoy. Nag**pa**paganda ang mga **i**to sa pa**li**gid ng **ba**hay.
Bill	Oo nga. Gano**on** din ang mga iba't i**bang** hal**a**man. **Me**ron si**lang** sampagi**ta**, ro**sal** at mala**king pu**no ng ilang**gi**lang. Nag**pa**pabango ang mga i**to** sa kapaligi**ran**.
Roy	A**lam** ba ni**nyo** na may mali**it** na palais**da**an si **Ki**ko? Nag**pa**palaki si**ya** ng **ba**ngus. Sumu**nod** ka**yo** sa **a**kin, itu**tu**ro ko sa in**yo**.
Louise	*Madali* lang **ta**yo ka**si** nagpa**lu**to ng mga kaka**nin** si **Ki**ko at ang a**sa**wa ni**ya**. Nagpa-ak**yat** din si**la** ng **mu**rang ni**yog pa**ra sa i**nu**min.
Bill	Anu-a**nong** mga kaka**nin**?
Louise	Bibobi**lo**, bibing**ka**, *kutsinta* at dila**di**la.
Roy	Masa**rap** ang bilobi**lo** *lalo* na kung may pan**sit**.
Bill	Tala**ga**! **I**to ang **bu**hay.

tingnan	*look*
mga punong-kahoy	*fruit trees*
nagpapaganda	*making* (something) *pretty*
paligid	*around*
nagpapa-akyat	*asking someone to climb*
mura(ng) niyog	*young coconut*
iba't iba(ng)	*different kinds*
halaman	*plants*
sampagita	*sampagita* (the national flower)
rosal	*gardenia*
ilangilang	*ylang-ylang*
nagpapabango	*making* (something) *fragrant*
kapaligiran	*surroundings*
alam	*know*
palaisdaan	*fish pond*
nagpapalaki	*making* (something) *grow*
bangus	*milkfish*
sumunod sa akin	*follow me*
ituturo	*will show/point*
madali	*easy*
lang	*only*
nagpaluto	*caused someone to cook*
anu-ano(ng)	*what* (plural)
kakanin	*rice cakes* (local delicacies)
bilobilo	*a delicacy* (marble-shaped)
bibingka	*a delicacy* (see page 112)
kutsinta	*a delicacy*
dila-dila	*a delicacy* (tongue-shaped)

QUICK VOCAB

Translation

Louise	Look at the fruit trees. They make a beautiful sight around the house.
Bill	Oh yes. It's the same with the different types of plants. They even have sampagita, gardenia and a very large ylang-ylang tree. They make the surrounding (area) smell fragrant.
Roy	Did you know that Kiko also has a small fish pond? He is trying to raise milkfish. Why not come along with me and I'll show you (the fishpond).

Louise	We have to be quick because Kiko and his wife have cooked some delicacies (for us). He's also asked someone to pick some young coconuts for us to drink.
Bill	What kind of rice cakes are they?
Louise	Bilobilo, bibingka, kutsinta and dila-dila.
Roy	Bilobilo is delicious, especially with noodles.
Bill	I agree! This is the life!

Exercise 1

Using Dialogue 1, answer the following questions in Tagalog:

1. Ano ang nagpapaganda sa paligid ng bahay?
2. Magbigay ng mababangong halaman na alam mo.
3. Ano ang ginawa ni Kiko upang magpalaki ng isda?
4. Bakit kailangang magmadali ang pamilya Cook?
5. Ipaliwanag kung bakit sinabi ni Bill 'Ito ang buhay'!

Language skills

1 *Magpa* + **Active** *To cause, to let, to have, to permit to ask, to make* **etc.**

'Tessie is *letting* the corn dry.' 'I will *allow* Elvira to cook tonight.' 'Bob will *let* the tomatoes grow in his garden.' ' I'll *ask* Lagring to sew

292

a dress for me.' 'Why don't you *make* Erwin clean your car?' 'Amado *permitted* me to walk.' All of the italicized words in these sentences are examples of indirect action verbs, also known as causatives. Tagalog uses causative verbs to point to an action performed by another person. In active verb sentences the causative is preceded by an **ang** form word. For example, **Nagpadala si Samantha ng regalo sa akin**, *Samantha sent some gifts to me*. **Nagpagawa sina Kim at Sue ng garahe**, *Kim and Sue had a garage built*. **Magpapasama ako kina Rosie at Aida sa ospital**, *I'll ask Rosie and Aida to accompany me to the hospital*. Notice that the **ang** form does not indicate the identity of the person actually performing the action, but rather, it indicates the identity of the one causing, letting, having, asking, making or permitting the action to be performed. The action is therefore said to be indirect or 'caused' by the other.

Dialogue 1 offers us a few examples: **nagpapaganda** (from **ganda**, *beautiful*) meaning 'making something beautiful', **nagpapabango** (from **bango**, *fragrant*) meaning 'making something fragrant', **nagpaluto** (from **luto**, *cook*) 'had someone cook something', **nagpapa-akyat** (from **akyat**, *climb*) 'having someone climb' (in this case, a tree). With active verbs, the causative is easily recognized by the prefix **magpa** followed by the verb. In **magpa** causatives, the causer is identified in the **ang** form (**si, sina, ako, ka, siya, kami, tayo, kayo, sila** etc.) while the caused (i.e., the person caused/asked/ led to perform the action) is identified in the **sa** form (**kay, kina, sa akin, sa iyo, sa kaniya, sa amin, sa atin, sa inyo, sa kanila** etc.) The object (which may be optional) is the **ng** form.

In order to avoid confusion, it is worth noting that some **mag** form verbs beginning with the letters **pa** may be mistakenly identified as causatives, even though they don't carry a causative meaning. These verbs are commonly known as dead **pa** verbs. For example: **paalam** (*goodbye*), **magpaalam**, *to say goodbye*. **Nagpaalam ka ba kay Jayne?**; *Did you say goodbye to Jayne?*, **parusa** (*punishment*) **magparusa**, *to punish*. **Sino ang nagparusa sa magnanakaw?**, *Who punished the burglar?*, **palabas** (*show*) **magpalabas**, *to give a show*. **Nagpapalabas na sila sa oras na ito**, *They have already started the show at this time*, **pakana** (*plan*) **magpakana**, *to plan*. **Nagpapakana na ang meyor ng programa para sa pista**, *The mayor is already planning the programme for the fiesta*.

Three important rules in the **magpa** causative form:

1. The causer is in the **ang** form.
2. The caused is in the **sa** form.
3. The object (optional) is in the **ng** form.

Some example sentences

Nagpapabili ako (causer) kay Stewart (caused) ng kamatis at sibuyas (object) sa palengke (place) *I had Stewart buy some tomatoes and onions for me.*

Changing the tense of the *magpa* verb

magpa (prefix) + **um** verb root:
Magpa + bili = magpabili *to have* etc. *someone buy* = infinitive
Magpa + pa + bili = magpapabili *will have* etc. *someone buy* = future
Nagpa + pa + bili = *nagpapabili having* etc. *someone to buy* = present
Nagpa + bili = nagpabili *had* etc. *someone to buy* = past

magpa (prefix) + **mag** verb root:
Magpa + luto = magpaluto *to cause* etc. *to cook* = infinitive
Magpa + pa + luto = magpapaluto *will cause* etc. *to cook* = future
Nagpa + pa + luto = nagpapaluto *causing* etc. *to cook* = present
Nagpa + luto = nagpaluto *caused* etc. *to cook* = past

Some sentence variations in *magpa* causative

Verb + causer + caused + object + time etc.
Magpapaluto ako kay Jamie ng pansit bukas.
I will ask Jamie to cook Filipino noodles tomorrow

Verb + particle + causer + caused
Nagpapaganda raw ang make-up sa mukha ng babae.
It is said that make-up makes a woman's face beautiful

Question word causer + verb + object + caused
Bakit kayo nagpapabili ng pagkain sa kanila?
Why are you asking them to buy food?

Verb + actor + time
Nagpalabas sila kagabi
They put on a show last night

Exercise 2

Can you change the following into **magpa** sentences?

1. Kumukuha ako ng libro sa kanila.
2. Maglalabas ba tayo ng silya?
3. Nagpasok ba si Henry ng mga maleta kanina?
4. Saan ka bumibili ng gulay at prutas?
5. Bumasa siya ng aklat sa klase.

Exercise 3 Listening, speaking and understanding

Your friend Edgar has invited you to attend his birthday party. It is the first time you have attended a Filipino birthday party and you are keen to watch and see what happens. Listen to the CD. Imagine that it is you who is speaking.

🔊 **CD 2, TR 7, 01:36**

1. How many **magpa** causative verbs can you recognize?
2. Your friend arrives late and wants to know what has been happening. Listen again to the CD and respond to each of your friend's questions.

Insight

From infancy, the Filipino child is trained to pick out the nuances of another person's body language and tone of voice, and to anticipate reactions. Little is left to explicit verbal expression. This intuitive sense, known as **pakiramdam**, is a sophisticated skill which characterizes relationships throughout the entire lifespan of the Filipino.

Helping on the farm

Dialogue 2

🔊 **CD 2, TR 7, 04:40**

The Cook family are giving their hosts a hand on the farm.

Bill	**A**nong **o**ras sa **u**ma**ga** ni**nyo** pinaka**ka**in ang in**yong ba**boy? **A**ko na lang ang mag**pa**pakain, **Ki**ko.
Kiko	O **si**ge, ba**ha**la ka. Pinaka**ka**in ko si**la** sa mga **a**las si**ye**te nang **u**ma**ga**. Kasa**bay** ng **a**ming almu**sal**. **A**ko kada**la**san ang nag**pa**pakain sa kani**la**.

Bill	**Gus**to mo bang paka**in**in ko rin ang mga ma**nok**?
Roy	A**ko** na lang ang mag**pa**pa**ka**in sa mga ma**nok**.
Kiko	Ku**ma**in **mu**na **ta**yo ng almu**sal**. Pinag**lu**to ko na si **Mi**sis ng **at**ing **a**almusa**lin**.
Bill	Okey lang.

ang mga manok	*the chickens*
sa umaga	*in the morning*
pinakakain	*give food/feed*
magpapakain	*will feed*
pinagluto	*asked to cook*
aalmusalin	*what someone's having for breakfast*
kasabay	*at the same time*
aming almusal	*our breakfast*
kadalasan	*often*
nagpapakain	*give them food*
gusto mo ba(ng)	*would you like*
pakainin	*to serve/feed*
magpapakain	*will cause to eat*

Translation

Bill	What time in the morning do you have to feed your pigs? Could I feed them?
Kiko	Well all right, it's up to you. I feed them at around 7.00 in the morning, at [about] the same time [as] we have our breakfast. Usually I feed them myself.
Bill	Would you like me to feed the chickens too?
Roy	Could I feed the chickens?
Kiko	Let's eat our breakfast first. I've already asked my wife to prepare our breakfast.
Bill	That's OK by me.

Exercise 4

Answer the following questions:

1. Ano ang gustong gawin ni Bill?
2. Sino ang madalas nagpapakain sa mga baboy?
3. Ano ang gustong pakainin ni Roy?
4. Bakit kailangan muna nilang kumain ng almusal?

Exercise 5
Following the English as closely as possible, translate the following into Tagalog:

1. . . . will have someone write a letter . . .
2. . . . had someone clean the car . . .
3. . . . asking someone to sew a dress . . .
4. . . . having someone to cut [my] hair . . .
5. . . . making yourself beautiful . . .

Exercise 6
Look at the picture of a typical rural Filipino. Using **magpa** and **pa-in**, **pag-in** and **pang-in** words, create a present tense sentence to describe each of the actions you can see. For example: **Nagpapaligo si Mang Kiko ng kalabaw sa ilog.** 'Mang Kiko is washing the carabao in the river.' Use the word stems provided to help you.

| ligo | lipad | kain | alis | tuyo |

Language skills

2 *Pa-in (ma/um* verb roots), *papag-in (mag* verb roots), *papang-in (mang* verb roots)

Having managed to digest the basics of **magpa** causative verbs (causer = **ang** form, caused = **sa** form), you will be delighted to hear that there are other variations and forms of causative verbs, too! Look at the simple explanation that follows. You will soon notice that in these causative variations, the person permitting or causing the action is identified in the **ng** form (**ni, nina, ko, mo, niya, namin, natin, ninyo, nila**) while the person caused to act (the 'doer' of the action) is in the **ang** form (**si sina, ako, ka/ikaw, siya, kami, tayo, kayo, sila**). Note also that these variations are used in connection with active verbs.

Other causative forms
Ma and *um* verbs

Prefix pa + verb root + suffix in.
For example **pa** + **tulug** + **in** = **patulugin,** *to cause someone to sleep*
Patutulugin (verb) ni Tessie (causer) ang bata (caused)
Tessie will put the child to sleep

Mag verbs

Prefix papag + verb root + suffix in.
For example **papag** + **lutu** + **in** = **papaglutuin** *to have someone cook*
Pinapagluto (verb) kami (caused) ng guro (causer) sa klase namin
Our teacher had us cook in our class

Mang verbs

Prefix papang + verb root + suffix in.
For example **papang** + **ibig** + **in** = papangibigin *to cause/permit to pay court to*
Pinapangibig (verb) ng Lola (causer) si Ian (caused) kay Karen
Lola is permitting Ian to pay court to Karen

Four important rules to remember in the **pa-in, papag-in, papang-in** causative form:

1. The causer is the **ng** form.
2. The caused is the **ang** form.
3. The object (which can be optional) is another **ng** form.
4. There may be a receiver of the action which is a **sa** form.

Example sentences

pa-in   Pinabili (verb) ng guro (causer) ang mga estudyante (caused) ng aklat (object) *The teacher asked/caused the student to buy a book.*

papag-in	Papaglabahin (verb) natin (causer) sila (caused) mamaya (time). *We will have/make them wash clothes later.*
papang-in	Papamamalantsahin (verb) mo (causer) ba (particle) si Dorothy (caused)? *Will you ask Dorothy to iron clothes?*

Changing the tense of the *pa-in, papag-in, papang-in* verb

Pa (prefix) + verb root + **in** (suffix) Origin: **ma/um** verbs

pa + higa + in = pahigain *to make* etc. *someone lie down* = infinitive

pa + hi + higa + in = pahihigain *will make* etc. *someone lie down* = future

p + in + a + hi + higa pinahihiga *making* etc. *someone lie down* = present

p + in + a + higa = pinahiga *made* etc. *someone lie down* = past

Papag (prefix) + verb root + **in** (suffix) Origin: **mag** verbs

Papag + linis + in = papaglinisin *to make* etc. *someone clean* = infinitive

Papag + li + linis + in = papaglilinisin *will make* etc. *someone clean* = future

P + in + a + pa + pag + linis = pinapapaglinis *making* etc. *someone clean* = present

P + in + a + pag + linis = pinapaglinis *made* etc. *someone clean* = past

Papang (prefix) + verb root + **in** (suffix) Origin: **mang** verbs

Papang+isda+in = papangisdain *to permit* etc. *someone to fish* = infinitive

Papangi+ngisda+in = papangingisdain *will permit* etc. *someone to fish* = future

P+in+a+pa+pang+isda = pinapapangisda *permitting* etc. *someone to fish* = present

P+in+a+pang+isda = pinapapangisda *permitted* etc. *someone to fish* = past

Some sentence variations in *pa-in, papag-in, papang-in* causative

Verb	+	causer	+	caused	+	object
Pabibilhin		ni Tony		si Mario		ng aklat

Tony will ask Mario to buy a book

| Question marker | + | caused | + | causer + | object + | time |
| Sino | | ang pinaglaba | | ni Rene | ng kumot | kahapon? |

Whom did Rene ask to wash the bedsheets yesterday?

| Verb | + | causer | + | caused | + | place |
| Pinapapangisda | | ng gobyerno | | ang mga mangingisda | | sa lugar na ito. |

The government allows the fishermen to fish in this area

Exercise 7 Listening, speaking and understanding

Listen to the CD. You will hear a number of statements, each read out three times. Two of the statements use the incorrect verb form while one of the statements uses the correct verb form (**pa-in, papag-in, papang-in**). Which of the statements is correct? Repeat the correct verb form aloud, then translate into English.

◀) CD 2, TR 7, 05:32

Insight

Baon refers to the provisions or necessities carried by a person when travelling or away from home. **Baon** may take the form of food, clothing or money. Thus, if one has lunch at the office, a person may use the office canteen or bring his own **baon**, i.e., his *lunch*. Verbalized, **magbaon** means *to take/bring provisions*.

Dialogue 3

Roy and Bill are giving Kiko more help on the farm.

◀) CD 2, TR 7, 08:34

Bill	Kiko, tutulungan ka namin sa pagtatanim. Narito rin si Roy.
Kiko	Salamat. Ipalalagay ko kay Roy ang damo sa sako.
Bill	Gusto mo bang ipatapon ko ang mga damo?
Kiko	Mabuti. Ipapipitas ko rin sa kaniya ang mga hinog na guyabano. At saka, maaari bang palagyan ko kay Roy ng tubig ang mga banga? Kailangan ang tubig para sa inumin ng mga hayop.
Bill	Sige lang. Mabuti at makatutulong siya dito. Pinagamasan mo ba ang iyong palayan? Mukhang malinis ito.
Kiko	Oo. Oo nga pala, uminom muna tayo ng sabaw ng murang niyog.
Bill	Mabuting ideya. O, heto na si Roy.

tutulungan	*will help*
pagtatanim	*planting*
narito	*here*
ipalalagay	*will cause to put*
makatutulong	*will be able to help*
ipatapon	*to cause to throw*
damo	*grass*
mukhang malinis	*looks quite clean*
ipapipitas	*will have something picked*
hinog	*ripe*
guyabano	*sour sap*
at saka	*and*
maaari	*can/possible*
palagyan	*to ask to be put*
banga	*earthen pot*
hayop	*animal*
pinagamasan	*had it cleaned*
palayan	*rice field*
oo nga pala	*by the way*
sabaw	*thin soup*
mura(ng)	*young*
niyog	*coconut*
ideya	*idea*

Translation

Bill	Kiko, we're going to help you with the planting. Roy is coming as well.
Kiko	Thank you. I'm going to ask Roy to put the grass in the sacks.
Bill	Shall I get Roy to throw the grass away?
Kiko	Yes, that's a good idea. I will have him pick the ripe guyabanos too. Can I ask Roy to put some water into the earthen pots? The animals need water to drink.
Bill	All right. (It's) Good that he'll be able to help here. Did you have the field cleaned up? It looks quite clean.
Kiko	Yes. By the way, let's have some coconut juice to drink.
Bill	Good idea. Thank you. Here comes Roy.

Exercise 8 Sagutin

1. Ano ang ipalalagay ni Kiko sa sako?
2. Sino ang magtatapon ng damo?
3. Bakit kailangang pitasin na ang guyabano?
4. Bakit sila naglalagay ng tubig sa banga?
5. Saan kinukuha ang sabaw ng niyog?

Exercise 9

Here are some familiar daily activities. Can you identify the causative verb?

Languages skills

3 *Ipa* (*in* and *i* verbs), *pa-an* (*an* verbs) *To cause, to let, to make, to allow to have, to permit*

The causative in passive verb sentences is easily recognized by the prefix **ipa** for **in** and **i** verbs, and the prefix/suffix **pa-an** for **an** verbs. The **ipa** and **pa-an** causatives both take the **ng** form when identifying the causer while using the **sa** form to identify the person caused to perform the action. In **ipa** and **pa-an** sentences, the object is identified by the **ang** form. Let's look at some example sentences:

ipa + **tapon** = **ipatapon**, *to cause to be thrown*
Ipatatapon ni Ginang Cruz kay Henry ang mga lumang kahon
Mrs Cruz will have Henry throw out the old boxes

ipa + **bili** = **ipabili**, *to cause to be bought*
Ipabibili ko kay Abner ang mga kailangan ko sa pagtuturo
I will have Abner buy my teaching materials

Three important rules to remember in the **ipa** and **pa-an** causatives forms:

1. The causer is the **ng** form.
2. The caused is the **sa** form.
3. The object (optional) is the **ang** form.

Some example sentences:

Ipasasara (verb) namin (causer) kina Bebot (caused) ang mga bintana (object) dito (place). *We will have Bebot and her friends shut the windows here.*

Ipinalalagay (verb) po (particle) ito (object) ni Ginoong Castillo (causer) sa mesa (place). *Sir/madam, Mr. Castillo wants this placed on the table.*

Ipapabuhat (verb) na lang (particles) namin (causer) ang mga maleta (object) sa kargador (caused) mamaya (time). *We will just have the porter carry the suitcases later on.*

Pinasasarhan (verb) ng gobyerno (causer) ang tambakan ng basura (object). *The Government is having the rubbish dump closed.*

Gusto (pseudo-verb) mo (causer) ba[ng] (particle) palagyan (verb) ng asukal (object) ang kape (receiver of the action)? *Would you like some sugar (to be put) in the coffee?*

*Note: The **an** verb takes a **ng** object as well as actor.

Changing the tense of the **Ipa** and **Pa-an** causatives:

Ipa (prefix) + (**in** and **i** verb root)
ipa + tapon ipatapon *to cause* etc. *to be thrown* = infinitive
ipa + ta + tapon ipatatapon *will cause* etc. *to be thrown* = future

ipi + na + ta + tapon ipinatatapon *causing* etc. *to be thrown* = present
ipi + na + tapon inpinatapon *was caused* etc. *to be thrown* = past

Pa (prefix) + (verb root) + **an** (suffix)
pa + hugas + an pahugasan *to cause* etc. *to be washed* = infinitive
pa+hu + hugas + an pahuhugasan *will cause* etc. *to be washed* = future
pina + hu + hugas + an pinahuhugasan *causing* etc. *to be washed* = present
pina + hugas + an pinahugasan *caused* etc. *to be washed* = past

Some sentence variations in the *ipa* and *pa-an* causative forms

Verb +	causer +	caused +	object
Pinapalitan	ko	kay Citta	ang binili kong pantalon

I had Citta exchange the (pair of) trousers I bought

Qualifier +	causer +	verb +	object
Hindi	nila	ipinatapos	ang bakod

They didn't have the fence finished

Question word +	verb +	causer +	place
Sino	ang ipinadala	ng eskuwelahan	sa paligsahan?

Who did the school send to the contest?

Question word +	causer +	verb +	object
Kailan	mo	pinaputulan	ang buhok mo?

When did you have a haircut?

Example sentences:

1. Pinalakihan ni Ely ang kanyang kusina
   Ely had her kitchen made bigger
2. Pasasamahan kita kay Manny
   I'll ask Manny to accompany you
3. Pinatawagan niya sa akin si Citta
   He/she had me call Citta
4. Ipatutulak namin sa mga lalaki ang malaking mesa
   We'll have the men push the big table
5. Ipinasara ng Ate ang mga bintana kay Al
   Ate had the windows closed by Al

Exercise 10

Choose the appropriate causative verb form from the brackets, then translate the sentence:

1. Bukas, (ipinalagay, ipalalagay, ipinalalagay) ko kay Sarah ang mga halaman sa paso. (future)
2. Kailangan bang (ipapasok, ipasok, ipinasok) na ngayon ang mga damit sa sampayan? (infinitive)
3. Kailan natin (ipamimigay, ipamigay, ipinamimigay) ang mga lumang damit? (future)
4. Noong isang taon (ipinaaayos, ipaaayos, ipinaayos) ni Binibining Zapanta ang kaniyang bahay. (past)
5. Ayaw nilang (papintahan, pinapintahan, papipintahan) ang kanilang bahay. (infinitive)

One-minute phrases

> **Hindi na bale** (*heen-dee nah bah-leh*) Meaning 'It doesn't matter/never mind'. For example: **Hindi na bale kung hindi sila dumating sa miting,** *It doesn't matter if they don't/didn't arrive at the meeting.*
>
> **Pang-araw-araw** (*pahng ah-rao ah-rao*) Meaning 'For daily use'. For example: **Pang-araw-araw ko ang lumang jeans na ito,** *I wear this old pair of jeans daily.*
>
> **Tamang-tama lang** (*tah-mahng tah-mah lahng*) Literally, just enough only. Meaning something fits perfectly (like a glove). For example: **Tamang-tama lang sa iyo ang bagong sapatos mo,** *Your new pair of shoes fits you perfectly well.*
>
> **Mahirap na lang magsalita** (*mah-hee-rahp nah lahng mahg-sah-lee-tah*) Literally, (it's) difficult already just to speak/talk. This is a common Tagalog phrase used to suggest that it may be difficult or inappropriate to offer comment. For example: **Mahirap na lang magsalita pero kailangang pagsabihan mo ang anak mo,** *It's rather difficult to make any comments but you should talk to your child.*
>
> **Gawan ng paraan** (*gah-wahn nahng pah-rah-ahn*) Similar in meaning to the English expression 'I'll do anything I can to make sure it works'. For example: **Gagawan ko ng paraan upang makabili ka ng uniporme mo,** *I'll do everything I can to make sure you can buy your uniform.*

Insight

The **barrio** or **barangay** is the traditional Filipino village or settlement and lies at the very heart of the cultural, political and religious life of the Philippines. A quick glance around almost every **barrio** will reveal the existence of a small chapel and a meeting hall. There is a strong sense of 'togetherness' (**pakikisama**) among **barrio** folk. The people draw much of their identity from this sense of 'togetherness'. This attitude becomes a pattern of living wherever the Filipino finds him/herself.

Summary

1. *To make, to let, to allow, to ask, to permit* etc. are **causatives**.
2. The Active verb causatives are made by using the prefix **magpa** + an **um** stem. The causer is from the **ang** group.
3. The **pa** + stem + **in** takes the **ma** and **um** stems.
4. Three important rules in the **ipa** and **pa-an** forms are: the causer is the **ng** form, the caused is the **sa** form and the object is the **ang** form.
5. The **i** Passive verb causative is made by using the prefix **ipa** + stem.
6. The **an** Passive verb causative is made by using the prefix **pa** + stem + **an**.
7. Important rules in the **magpa** causative form: the causer is in the **ang** form; the caused is in the **sa** form; and the object (optional) is in the **ng** form.
8. By using the base, most adjectives can be used in **pa-in**, e.g., **pa** + **liit** + **in** '*to make small*'.
9. Also, by using the base, most adjectives can be used in **pa-an**, e.g., **pa** + **ganda** + **han** '*to make pretty*'.
10. In the **ipa** and **pa-an** form, the object is optional.

20

Paalam
Goodbye

In this unit you will learn how to:

- Make comparisons
- Express embarrassment
- Do last-minute shopping
- Say your last goodbyes

Expressing embarrassment

Dialogue 1

◄) **CD 2, TR 8**

Bill, Louise and Roy Cook have enjoyed their stay with Kiko and his family in the barrio. They are preparing to leave.

Roy	Ting**nan** ni**nyo**! Binig**yan ako** ni **Ki**ko ng re**ga**lo.
Louise	A**non**g ibini**gay** ni**ya** sa iyo? Ga**a**no kala**ki**?
Roy	**Isang** kala**baw** na i**nu**kit sa **ka**hoy. Hu**wag** kay**ong mag**-ala**la**. *Hindi* i**to** mas mala**ki** sa ma**le**ta ko.
Bill	**Na**pakagan**da** ni**to**. *Mahiya* ka naman. *Wala* **ta**yong ibini**gay** na pasa**lu**bong sa kan**ila** *kundi* mga pag**ka**in lang. Malak-**ing** aba**la** rin ang naibi**gay na**tin sa kani**la**.
Louise	Na**ka**kahiya nam**an**. **Nag**pasalamat ka ba?
Roy	**O**po. *Nahihiya* nga ako nang ibi**gay** ni**ya** i**to** sa akin **pe**ro mag**dar**amdam daw si**la** ka**pag** *hindi* ko tinang**gap** ang re**ga**lo.
Bill	Gano**on** ba?

binigyan	*was given*
abala	*disturbance*
ibinigay	*handed/gave*
gaano kalaki	*how big*
huwag	*don't*
mag-alala	*worry*
hindi mas malaki	*not as big as*
ng maleta ko	*of my suitcase*
magdaramdam	*will feel bad*
inukit	*carved*
kahoy	*wood/wooden*
napakaganda	*how beautiful*
mahiya ka naman	*are you without shame, don't you feel a little ashamed?*
ibinigay	*gave*
nakakahiya	*embarrassing*
nagpasalamat	*gave thanks*
nang ibigay	*when (it) was given*
kundi	*instead*
tinanggap	*received*

Translation

Roy	Look! Kiko gave me a (parting) gift.
Louise	What did he give you? How big is it?
Roy	A wooden carving of a water buffalo. Don't worry. It's not too big for my suitcase.
Bill	It's really beautiful. Don't you feel a little ashamed? We didn't bring any gifts for them other than a little foodstuff. We were a bit of a disturbance to them, too.
Louise	Shame on you. Did you at least thank them?
Roy	Yes, I did. Actually I was embarrassed when (the gift) was handed to me but (he) said he'd feel bad if I declined it.
Bill	Is that so?

Exercise 1

Answer the following questions in complete Tagalog sentences:

1. Ano ang regalo ni Kiko sa pamilya Cook?
2. Ano ang mangyayari kapag hindi tinanggap ni Roy ang regalo?

3. Anong uri ng regalo ang ibinigay ng mga Cook kina Kiko?

4. Bakit nag-alala ang mga Cook?

Language skills

1 *Kasing/sing* As . . . as

'As old as the hills', 'as white as snow', 'as sweet as honey', 'as strong as an ox'. These short sentences are examples of comparatives, expressed in English by means of an as . . . as construction. Tagalog expresses comparatives by the prefix (**ka**)**sing** before the root of a **ma**-adjective. The actor is expressed by a **ng** phrase (**ni, nina, ko, mo, niya, namin, natin, nila** etc.) and the complement (to which the comparison is being made) is in the **ang** form (namely **si, sina, ako, ka, siya, kami, tayo, kayo, sila** etc.). For example: **Kasinghaba/singhaba ng kalye namin ang kalye ninyo**, *Your street is as long as our street*. **Kasinlaki ng Pilipinas ang Inglaterra**, *England is as big as the Philippines*. Some speakers use **kasing** only and other speakers use both **sing** and **kasing** interchangeably in ordinary conversation. Both are correct.

It is worth remembering that certain adjectives can stand alone and are known as unaffixed adjectives. Any unaffixed adjective that corresponds to a noun (i.e. **tulog** (noun) *sleep*, **tulog** (adjective) *asleep*) do not occur with (**ka**)**sing**; whereas most other unaffixed adjectives (i.e. **pula**, *red*, **tanga**, *dumb*) do occur with (**ka**)**sing**. Here are some examples of the (**ka**)**sing** construction: (**Ka**)**singtangkad ni Samantha si Sally**, *Sally is as tall as Samantha*. **Kasingyaman ni Ginoong Ramos si Ginoong Cruz**. *Mr Cruz is as rich as Mr Ramos*. The prefix (**ka**)**sing** changes to (**ka**)**sim** when the preceeding adjective root begins with b and p. However, when (**ka**)**sing** is followed by an adjective beginning with the letters d or t, then it becomes **kasin**. For example: (**ka**)**singbait** to **kasimbait**, *as kind as*; (**ka**)**singpula** to (**ka**)**simpula**, *as red as*; (**ka**)**singdami**, *as many as*; to (**ka**)**sindami**, (**ka**)**singtamad** to (**ka**)**sintamad** and so on.

Comparison of inequality is expressed in English by simply using the negative of the 'as . . . as' formula. For example: Bobby is not as noisy as Fred. This is not as sweet as that (one). In Tagalog, the same basic rules used in comparison of equality apply to comparison of inequality. For example: **Hindi kasingganda ng sampagita ang gumamela,** *(The) gumamela (flower) is not as beautiful as sampagita.* **Hindi kasinsariwa nito iyan,** *That is not as fresh as this (one).*

It is also possible to verbalize both the comparison of equality and the comparison of inequality through the simple addition of the prefix **mag**. If this happens, then the prefix **mag** is understood to mean 'equally' or 'equal in'. For example: **mag + (ka)sing.** The resulting formation expresses a quality shared equally by exactly two people, things, places, etc. For example: **Mag(ka)singtalino sina Jonathan at Manny,** *Jonathan and Manny are equal in intelligence.* **Magkasintaas si Joe at si Anne,** *Anne and Joe are equally tall.* Look at the example sentences that follow. Practise reading them aloud in order to familiarize yourself with the word order.

Example sentences:

1. Kasimbango ng rosal ang camia
   (The) camia (flower) is as fragrant as gardenia
2. Kasimbaho ng bagoong ang tuyong isda
   Dried fish is as smelly as fish sauce
3. Kasinlinis ng mesa ang silya
   The chair is as clean as the table
4. Magkasintangkad sina Erwin at Ardin
   Erwin and Ardin are equally tall
5. Magkasinlayo ang Australia at New Zealand buhat sa Inglaterra
   Australia and New Zealand are equally far from England
6. Hindi magkasinlapit ang Maynila at Makati buhat sa Paliparang Ninoy Aquino
   Manila and Makati are not equally close to Ninoy Aquino airport

Exercise 2
Look at the following adjectives together with their **(ka)sing** prefixes. Build a Tagalog sentence around each adjective ((**ka)sing** + adjective) and then translate into English.

Example: (ka)sintanda: as old as
                   Kasintanda ni Joanna si Amy *Amy is as old as Joanna*

1. (ka) simbait: as kind as
2. (ka) simputi: as white as
3. (ka) sintaas: as high as (as tall as)

4. (ka) sinluwang: as wide as
5. (ka) singkipot: as narrow as
6. hindi (ka) singganda: not as pretty as
7. mag(ka)simbuti: equally good

Doing last minute shopping

Dialogue 2

◄)) CD 1, TR 8, 01:17

Bill, Louise and Roy Cook have to do some last minute shopping for their **pasalubong** (*gifts*).

Louise	Kailangan kong bumili pa ng mga **pam**pasalubong. Alam kong nakabili na ako noon pero may nakalimutan yata ako.
Bill	Naiintindihan ko. Heto na ang Priscilla's Gift Shop. Kung mga pamigay lang ang bibilhin natin, napakarami nating mapagpipilian dito.
Roy	O, sige gusto ko ring humanap ng laruang jeepney. Ibibigay ko ito kay Stewart.
Louise	Aba, maganda ito – kawayang tumutunog sa hangin para kina Viv at Tim. Ito namang mga nilalang handbag ay pangshopping nina Consuelo at Clarita.
Bill	Marami yata tayong pamimilihin *kaya* credit card na lang ang ipambayad natin sa halip na cash.
Louise	Sang-ayon ako.
Roy	Kung gayon bibili ako ng barong Tagalog na **pang**-okasyon ko.
Bill	Ako rin!
Louise	Kayo lang ba? Bibili ako ng ternong saya na yari sa jusi. *Wala* akong ganitong uri ng terno.
Bill	Sige, walang problema. Dalian lang natin ang pamimili kasi mag-iimpake pa tayo.
Roy	Oo *nga* pala!

tumutunog	*making a musical sound*
nakabili	*was able to buy*
noon	*then/before*
may nakalimutan	*forgot something*

QV

naiintindihan	*understand*
pamimilihin	*things to buy*
kaya	*that's why*
pamigay	*to give around*
sa halip na	*instead of*
bibilhin	*will buy*
napakarami	*so many*
mapagpipilian	*to choose from*
pang-okasyon	*for certain occasions*
humanap	*to find*
ibibigay	*will be given*
yari sa	*made of*
daliin	*be quick*
terno	*evening gown*
nilala(ng)	*woven*
pangshopping	*for shopping*
ipambayad	*to pay with*
sang-ayon	*agree*
kung gayon	*if that is so*
oo nga pala	*oh that reminds me*
mag-iimpake	*will get packing*
ternong saya	*a lady's terno*
pamimili	*shopping*
ganito(ng) uri	*this kind*
jusi	*pineapple fibre cloth*

Translation

Louise	I need to buy some more gifts to give away. I know that I've already bought (some), but I think I've forgotten a few things.
Bill	I understand. Look, here's Priscilla's Gift Shop. If we want to buy a few things to hand out, (then) there's an enormous choice here.
Roy	All right. I also want to look for a toy Jeepney. I'm giving it to my friend Stewart.
Louise	This is nice – a bamboo wind chime for Viv and Tim. These woven handbags are for Consuelo and Clarita.

Bill	I think we'll be buying a lot of things so why don't we pay by credit card instead of cash.
Louise	That's a good idea.
Roy	In that case, then I'm going to buy myself a *barong Tagalog* to wear on special occasions.
Bill	I will too.
Louise	And you think it's only for you (two). I think I'll buy a long evening gown made of *jusi* for myself. I haven't got anything like this yet.
Bill	OK. That's not a problem, but we'll have to hurry up with our shopping because we still have the rest of the packing to do.
Roy	Oh, that reminds me . . . (good that you reminded me)

Exercise 3

Mga tanong: Sagutin sa Tagalog na pangungusap. Answer in Tagalog sentences. Use the glossary to help you.

1. Ano ang kailangang gawin ni Louise?
2. Saan sila pumunta upang mamili ng pampasalubong?
3. Para kanino ang tumutunog na hangin?
4. Ano ang maaaring ibigay ni Louise kina Consuelo?
5. Sabihin kung paano sila magbabayad ng kanilang pinamili.
6. Bakit kailangan nilang magmadali?

Language skills

2 Making nouns *pang*

By now you will have begun to grasp something of the versatility of the Tagalog language. One further 'trick' Tagalog has up its sleeve is the ability to form nouns from verbs, simply by adding the prefix **pang** to the verb root. For example **ligo, lakad, tulog, pasok, pasyal** etc. can be made into nouns meaning 'used for' simply by adding the prefix **pang**: pang + ligo = panligo, 'used for bathing', pang + lakad = panlakad, 'used for going out'. You will notice that words that begin with l, d and t turn the **pang** into **pan**, for example pang + tulog = pantulog 'used for going to sleep'; while words beginning with p make **pang** into **pam**. Example: pang + pasok = pampasok, 'used for going to work or school', pang + pasyal = pamasyal, 'used to go out in'. Look at these example sentences: **Pantulog ba ang damit na iyan?**, *Is that clothing used for sleeping in?*. **Pamputol ng kahoy ito**, *This is for cutting firewood with*. **May pandagdag ka ba sa pera ko?**, *Do you have anything to add to my money?*

By adding the letter **i** to the **pang** prefix, the resulting word is transformed back into a verb, but it is different in meaning from the original verb. The new verb then carries the meaning 'to use for' and is consequently known as an instrumental verb. Here are some examples: I + pang + laba, 'wash clothes' = ipanlaba, 'to use for washing clothes'. **Ipanlaba natin ang sabong ito sa blusa mo**, *Let's use this soap to wash your blouse with*. I + pang + tali 'string' = ipantali. **Ipinantali ni Divin ang lubid sa malaking kahon**, *Divin used the string/rope to tie around the big box*.

Changing the tense of an **ipang** verb:

ipang + linis *clean* =	ipanlinis	*to clean with*	infinitive
ipan+li+linis =	ipanlilinis	*will clean with*	future
ip+inan+li+linis =	ipinanlilinis	*cleaning with*	present
ip+inan+linis =	ipinanlinis	*used to clean with*	past

Some commonly used nominalized words:

1. pantulak = *to push with*
2. pangkain = *to eat with*
3. pantulog = *to sleep with*

4. panlakad = *to walk with*
5. panlaro = *to play with*
6. pananggalang = *for protection*
7. panlaban = *to fight against/with*
8. panulat = *a writing instrument*
9. panigarilyo = *money to buy cigarettes with*
10. panlasa = *taste*

Exercise 4

Here are some everyday things we might see around the house. What are they used for? Use the glossary to help you to find the correct **pang** noun for each:

1.

2.

3.

Exercise 5

Give the Tagalog 'pang' nouns for the following (the italicized word will give you a clue).

Example: a hammer to *break* with
　　　　　　Answer: *pandurog*

1. a *scratch*er
2. something you *cut* with
3. to *wash clothes* with
4. to *write* with
5. to use *to go strolling* in

Exercise 6

Having found the correct **pang** words for Exercise 5, can you make a sentence out of them?

Example: **Pambiyak ng niyog ang malaking kutsilyo,** The big knife is for cutting the coconut with

1. _____
2. _____
3. _____
4. _____
5. _____

Insight

Some critics have suggested that Filipinos are insincere; saying one thing and meaning another. This is a common misreading of the Filipino cultural dislike of directness. Filipinos typically use indirect speech to communicate a need or desire. A helpful question for any non-Filipino to ask themselves is: What is the statement behind the statement?

Saying last goodbyes

Dialogue 3

◄) CD 2, TR 8, 03:21

The Cook family are saying goodbye to the Abiva family at the airport.

| Bill | Ma**ra**ming, ma**ra**ming sa**la**mat sa pagtang**gap** ni**nyo** sa **a**min. Pa**sen**siya na ka**yo** sa *nagawa* **na**ming pang-aa**ba**la sa in**yong** taha**nan** at sa **inyong** katahi**mi**kan **la**lo na kay Jobert. |

Tita Abiva	**A**ba, hu**wag** ka**yong** mag-alaa**la**. Na**si**siyahan nga ka**mi** at **di**to ka**yo** tu**mi**gil. Hi**git sa**na kay**ong** magpa**sen**siya sa **a**ming pagku**ku**lang. Mas **la**lo ka**ming** hu**mi**hingi ng pa**sen**siya.
Louise	Lu**bu**san ka**ming** nasiya**han** at **sa**na ay hu**wag** kay**ong** ma**da**dala sa **a**min. Nagbi**gay** ka**mi** sa **in**yo ng kagu**lu**han.
Tita	Ka**mi** nga ang mas nag-**a**alala na *baka hindi* ka**yo** naka**tu**log nang ma**bu**ti. A**lam** kong mas ta**hi**mik sa Ingla**te**ra **kay**sa **di**to. O, tina**ta**wag na **ya**ta ang flight ni**nyo**.
Mr Abiva	Hu**wag** kay**ong** mag-**a**atubiling bu**ma**lik sa **a**min sa **su**sunod ni**nyong** pagbabakas**yon**. Su**mu**lat lang ka**yo**.
Bill	**Ga**gawin **na**min i**yon**. Pa**sen**siya na ka**yo** sa **a**ming mun**ting** rega**long** i**to**.
Tita	Aba, **nag**-abala pa ka**yo**. Ma**raming** sa**la**mat. I**sang na**pakagandang ku**wa**dro **pa**ra sa la**ra**wan ng **a**king pa**mil**ya!
Mr Abiva	Kay gan**da**! O, **si**ge ma**raming** sa**la**mat na *muli*.
Jobert	Su**su**lat ka**yong la**gi at kung ma**aari** tu**ma**wag ka**yo** sa **a**kin.
Roy	Ma**raming** sa**la**mat po sa in**yo** Gi**noo** at **Gi**nang Abiva, nag-enjoy a**ko di**to at ma**raming** sa**la**mat Jobert, **o**key ka tala**ga**.
Jobert	Hu**wag** kang **mag**-alala, Roy. Ka**tu**lad mo, nag-enjoy ako.
Louise and Bill	Ma**raming** sa**la**mat. **A**alis na ka**mi**.
Tita	Wa**lang** anu**man**. O **si**ge. Pa**alam**.
(*The Cooks and the Abivas kiss*)

pagtanggap	*receiving*
pasensiya na	*accept our apologies*
nagawa	*what's been done*
pang-aabala	*disturbance*
tahanan	*home*
katahimikan	*peace*
lalo na kay	*especially*
sa susunod	*next time*
pagbabakasyon	*vacationing*
nasisiyahan	*pleased*
tumigil	*stopped*
higit	*more*

QUICK VOCAB

magpasensiya	*to accept our*
pagkukulang	*shortcomings*
mas lalo	*more*
humihingi	*asking*
lubusan	*earnestly*
kay ganda	*how pretty*
huwag	*don't*
madadala	*be turned off*
nagbigay	*gave*
kaguluhan	*chaos*
mas nag-aalala	*more bothered*
baka hindi	*might not*
nakatulog	*managed to sleep*
mag-aalaala	*be worried*
paalam	*goodbye*
tahimik	*quiet*
kaysa	*than*
tinatawag	*calling*
mag-aatubili(ng)	*hestitate*
bumalik	*return*
munti(ng) regalo	*small gift*
nag-abala	*bothered*
napakaganda(ng)	*very pretty*
kuwadro	*frame*
larawan ng	*picture of*
muli	*again*
susulat	*will write*
lagi	*always*
kung maaari	*if possible*
tumawag	*call*
nag-enjoy	*enjoyed*
nang mabuti	*soundly*
alam mo ba	*do you know*

Translation

Bill	Thank you so much for letting us stay. We apologize if we have been an intrusion in your home and to your peace, especially Jobert's.

Tita Abiva	Please don't worry. In fact we were very pleased that you stayed with us. We hope you have been able to bear with our shortcomings. We're the ones who have to apologize.
Louise	We are really happy and hope that we didn't put you off coming again. We must have caused you a lot of inconvenience.
Tita Abiva	In fact, we're more worried that you might not have been able to sleep properly. I know that it's much quieter in England than it is here. Listen, I think they are calling your flight number.
Mr Abiva	Please don't hesitate to come back to our home the next time you come for your holidays. Please write.
Bill	We most certainly will. Please accept our small (parting) gift.
Tita	You should not have bothered. Thank you so much. What a lovely frame for my family's picture.
Mr Abiva	How beautiful! OK, thank you so much again.
Jobert	Please write regularly and if possible, give me a call.
Roy	Thank you so much, Mr & Mrs Abiva. I enjoyed myself here and thank you very much Jobert, you're really OK!
Jobert	Don't worry Roy. I enjoyed it as much as you did.
Louise and Bill	Thank you so much. We've got to go now.
Tita	Don't mention it. OK. Goodbye.
	(*The Cooks and the Abivas kiss*)

Exercise 7 Bigyan ng tamang sagot:

1. Nang humingi ng paumanhin si Bill, ano ang sagot ni Tita Abiva?
2. Bakit nag-aalala si Tita Abiva na hindi nakatulog ang mag-anak?
3. Anong regalo ang tinanggap ni Tita Abiva buhat sa mag-anak?
4. Ano ang hiniling ni Jobert kay Roy?

Exercise 8

The Cook family don't want to miss their flight back to London and so are carefully monitoring the flight announcements. Listen to the announcements on the CD and write down the correct flight numbers and departure times over the page. What are the correct gate numbers for each flight? Are there any delays?

Ninoy Aquino International Airport Manila			Departures board		
Destination	Flight No.	Arrivals	Departures	Delays	Gate No.
Hong Kong					
Singapore					
Los Angeles					
Sydney					
Tokyo					
London					
Dubai					
Kuala Lumpur					

Language skills

3 *Mas, lalong, kaysa sa*

Richard is tall, Justin is taller, but Chris is the tallest. You will notice from this example that there are three levels or degrees of comparison in English adjectives: tall, taller, tallest. These different levels are known as the positive, comparative and superlative degrees. Take for example the adjective good. The word good is in its positive degree. When comparing two adjectives, the adjective 'good' (positive degree) becomes the word 'better' in the comparative degree, and finally 'best' in the superlative degree. In Tagalog, **mas, lalong** or **kaysa** + the **sa** form are used in the comparative degree, while in the superlative degree, the prefix **pinaka** is used. Look at the examples that follow:

malaki	*big =*	positive degree
mas/lalong malaki kaysa sa	*bigger =*	comparative degree
pinakamalaki	*biggest =*	superlative degree

Mas malaki ang problema ni John kaysa kay Tony
John's problem is bigger than Tony's

maliit	*small =*	positive degree
higit na maliit	*smaller =*	comparative degree
pinakamaliit	*smallest =*	superlative degree

Pinakamaliit si Louella sa magkakapatid
Louella is the smallest among the siblings

Further examples:

1. Higit na malaki ang sombrero ko kaysa sa sombrero mo
   My hat is bigger than your hat
2. Mas mahaba ang nilakad namin kaysa sa nilakad ninyo
   Our walk was longer that your walk
3. Maganda ang hardin mo pero mas maganda ang hardin ni Patricia
   Your garden is pretty but Patricia's garden is prettier
4. Higit na malayo ang Pilipinas kaysa sa India buhat sa Inglaterra
   The Philippines is farther than India from England
5. Masarap ang luto mo pero mas masarap ang luto ko kaysa sa luto mo
   Your cooking is good but my cooking is better than yours

> ## Insight
> Tagalog makes a lot of use of contractions. This is familiar to us in English when we say *don't* instead of *do not*, *I'll* for *I shall* or *I will*, *they've* instead of *they have* etc. Common Tagalog contractions are: **siya'y** for **siya ay**, **ito'y** for **ito ay**, **subali't** for **subali at**, **sapagka't** for **sapagka at**, etc. The most commonly heard is: **Hindi ba't** for **Hindi ba at** meaning *isn't/wasn't it?*

Exercise 9
Look at the pictures and use the adjectives provided to produce a statement about each picture using the comparative degree:

Tom is taller than Benny   _____

1. matangkad

2. masipag

322

3. mataba

4. masaya

Exercise 10

Imagine that you are Bill or Louise Cook and have just returned from your wonderful holiday in the Philippines. Email your friends the Abivas to thank the family for their kindness. This is your chance to impress them by writing your thank you letter in Tagalog. Don't forget to use polite words and as many different types of Tagalog verbs as you can remember. Close your email by inviting them to England to stay with you.

One-minute phrases

Alis d'yan (*ah-lees jahn*) Literally, **alis** means *leave* and **d'yan/diyan**, *there*, hence: *go away from there* or, more colloquially, *get lost!!!, beat it!!!*

Buwena mano (*bwehnah mah-naw*) Literally, **buwena** means *good* from the Spanish word *buena* and **mano**, *hand*. It is believed that the first shopper cannot be turned down by the storekeeper as he/she will bring luck for the rest of the day.

Labas-masok (*lah-bahs mah-sawk*) Literally, **labas** means *out/outside* and **masok** or **pasok** means *enter*. A person who comes and goes. **Labas-masok ang mga tao sa opisina ng meyor**, *The people come and go into the mayor's office.*

Walang tawad (*wah-lahng tah-wahd*) Literally, *no discount, no bargain/last price*. This is usually what vendors say to you when you start to haggle in the markets. You can still try to ask for a discount but they usually get annoyed if you insist. If the price can be haggled they usually encourage you otherwise.

Hindi kasya (*heen-dee kahs-yah*) Meaning it doesn't fit. An expression commonly used when you are trying something on. **Hindi kasya sa akin ang sombrero mo kasi maliit ito sa akin,** *Your hat doesn't fit me because it's too small for me.*

Insight

The high value Filipinos place on harmonious relationships may at first seem rather quaint to the visiting westerner. This is hardly surprising when on closer inspection, the westerner tends to value having 'a mind of his/her own' and a strong sense of autonomy. Filipino social behaviour on the other hand is expected to promote the sense of community and togetherness (**pakikisama**). One of the principal means of ensuring socially acceptable behaviour is through **hiya** or 'shame'. **Hiya** is a key form of social control, determining how people feel about themselves (self-esteem) as well as their social standing. A person with a strong sense of his or her own **hiya** learns how to negotiate a way through potentially sensitive or embarrassing situations. Compromise is always a key factor, ensuring that others involved do not lose face and feel **mahiya**. The Filipino will avoid at all costs making another person feel **mahiya**. To do so not only damages that person's social standing but also gains them a potential enemy. It is extremely important for the foreigner to understand this. The golden rule is very simple: Never put anyone to shame in public, even in a joking way. Others may laugh, but only out of politeness. Filipinos often laugh and smile in order to cover their sense of discomfort or embarrassment. If you have a problem with someone, look for an appropriate time and place to speak to the person alone and in private. Even if you are upset, always make sure you speak in a low voice. Be prepared to compromise in order to help the other person save face and minimize their sense of **hiya**, even if they are clearly in the wrong. This will always act in your favour, indicating to others a sensitivity on your part to the intricacies of the Filipino social relationship system. If you are ever in doubt, smile, keep your mouth shut and ask your Filipino friends for advice.

Summary

1. **Kasing** or **sing** is a prefix added to the stem of an adjective in order to make a comparison.
2. The **ng** group is used to compare against the **ang** group.
3. **Pang** is a prefix used to nominalize verbs.
4. Use **pam** when the word begins with **p** or **b**.
5. By adding **i** to **pang** the result means 'to use for' what the attached word suggests.
6. **ipang** can be conjugated. Ex: Ipinantali. Used to tie with.
7. The degrees of comparison in English are: positive, comparative and superlative.
8. **Mas** or **mas lalong** is used to compare between two adjectives.
9. **Lalong** can be used on its own to compare.
10. **Pinaka + adjective** is used for the superlative degree.

Key to the exercises

Unit 1

Exercise 2 1. siya 2. kami 3. ako 4. ka 5. sila 6. kayo 7. tayo 8. kayo 9. sila 10. siya. **Exercise 3** 1. hapon 2. umaga 3. tanghali 4. gabi **Exercise 4** 1. umaga 2. gabi 3. tanghali 4. hapon **Exercise 5** a3/5, b6, c2/4, d1, e3/5, f2/4 **Exercise 6** a. kayo b. ka c. ka d. ka

Unit 2

Exercise 1 May tuwalya ba kayo? May sabon ba kayo? May telepono ba kayo? May menu ba kayo? May telebisyon ba kayo? **Exercise 3** 1. Doktor sila 2. Turista ako 3. Matatangkad/matangkad sila 4. Maganda siya 5. Amerikano ka/kayo **Exercise 5** 1. May payong ba kayo? May payong ka ba? Oo. Mayroon 2. May sasakyan ba? Oo. Mayroon 3. May pinggan ba sa mesa? Oo. Mayroon 4. May kutsilyo ba? Oo. Mayroon 5. May baso ba kayo? Oo. Mayroon **Exercise 6** 1. May libro 2. May barko 3. May mesa 4. Walang pera 5. May basura 6. May sombrero 7. Wala (ng) pasahero 8. May sanggol **Exercise 7** 1. Sino ang pagod? 2. Sino ang Reyna? 3. Anong oras na? 4. Anong kulay ng bandila/bandera?

Unit 3

Exercise 1 a. Magandang hapon sa inyong lahat b. Ito ang lola ko c. Ito ang tatay ko, _____ d. At si _____, ang kapatid ko e. Ito ang lolo ko f. Ito si _____, ang kapatid ko g. At katapusan, ang nanay ko **Exercise 2** a. Tatay b. Hipag c. Lola at Lolo d. Pamangkin e. Nanay f. Bayaw g. Kuya at Ate **Exercise 3** 1. mapa 2. payong 3. posporo 4. shampoo **Exercise 4** 1. Kailangan ko ng tee-shirt 2. Gusto kong bumili ng tiket 3. May 'street guide' ba kayo? 4. Nagtitinda ba kayo ng tinapay? **Exercise 5** 1. Mainit ang panahon 2. Marumi ang kalye 3. Malinis ang kotse 4. Maganda ang bahay 5. Doktor ang lalaki **Exercise 6** a. Maraming salamat b. Maraming salamat po or Maraming salamat sa inyo c. Maraming Salamat or Salamat d. Maraming salamat po or Maraming salamat sa inyo e. Maraming salamat **Exercise 7** 1. Hindi ito barko 2. Hindi malinis ang mesa 3. Hindi estudyante si Amy 4. Hindi tumatakbo ang Jeepney. **Exercise 8** 1. Wala. Walang sasakyan sa bus stop 2. Wala. Wala kaming yelo. 3. Wala. Walang katulong si Ginoong Reyes.

Unit 4

Exercise 1 1. kumaliwa 2. kumanan 3. diretso 4. kanan 5. tumawid kayo 6. kaliwa **Exercise 3** 1. Nasaan ang simbahan? Reply: Nasa Sto. Domingo ang simbahan 2. Nasaan ang Jeepney stop? Reply: Nasa Guzman Street ang paradahan ng Jeepney. 3. Nasaan ang palengke? Reply: Nasa Cubao ang palengke 4. Nasaan ang bangko? Reply: Nasa Makati ang bangko **Exercise 4** 1. Gusto kong bumili ng selyo para sa pakete ko 2. Gusto kong bumili ng selyo papunta sa Amerika 3. Magkakano ang Air Letter? 4. Nasaan ang timbangan? 5. Pakitimbang mo nga ang pakete ko or Maaari bang timbangin mo ang pakete ko? **Exercise 6** Listening: kahon, bolpen, sulat, selyo, pakete, timbangan **Exercise 7** 1. bata, payat, puti ang blusa, mahabang itim na buhok, nakasalamin, nakapantalon 2. babaeng hindi masyadong matanda, itim ang palda at jacket, itim ang sapatos at handbag 3. matabang babae, pandak, hindi itim ang blusa, itim ang palda, nakarelos at singsing 4. matandang babae, putting buhok, mahabang itim na bestida, nakakuwintas **Exercise 8** 1. malaking masipag na hayop 2. magandang matalinong dalagita 3. malaking puting simbahan 4. makulay na mabilis na Jeepney.

Unit 5

Exercise 1 1. Disinuwebe 2. Animnapu't apat 3. Nubenta y nuwebe 4. Dalawampu't pito 5. Siyento kinse 6. Apat na raan at walumpu **Exercise 3** 1. Labinlimang piso 2. Sampung piso

3. Pitumpung piso 4. Isandaang piso 5. Isanlibong piso; total = 1195 (isanlibo isandaa't siyamnapu't lima) **Exercise 4** 1. Alas dose beinte 2. Menos kinse para alas tres 3. Alas siyete 4 Ala-una diyes 5. Alas kuwatro medya 6. Alas sais **Exercise 5** Examples: Magkakano ang mangga, magkano ang lanzones? Magkano ang bayabas? **Exercise 6** 1. True 2. True 3. True 4. False 5. True **Exercise 7** 1. Gusto kong magpapalit ng dolyar 2. Magkano ang palit? 3. Ang palit ay 40 pesos 4. Nagpapalit din ba kayo ng Australian dollars? **Exercise 8** 1. Limandaan 2. Mil singko sientos

---

Unit 6

Exercise 2 1. Saan sila nakatira 2. Saan kayo matutulog 3. Saan nag-aaral sina Lucy? 4. Saan po kayo bumibili ng sorbetes? 5. Saan kakain ng almusal si Adam? **Exercise 3** 1. ka 2. bahay 3. mapa 4. Nakikita 5. kasama **Exercise 4** 1. Hindi. Masyadong malapit ito 2. Sa Sikatuna Village 3. Sa Kalye Roxas 4. Walang kasama si Roy 5. Nasa Kalye Vito ito. **Exercise 5** Magbabakasyon, masyadong mainit, masyadong malayo, buhat sa, masyadong mataas. Kapitan ng eroplano, ang dating **Exercise 6** 1. Dadaan ba ito sa Sikatuna Village? 2. sa Kalye Maningning 3. Magkano + Sikatuna? Heto ang bayad. May sukli ka ba?

Unit 7

Exercise 1 1. Nasa likuran 2. Nasa harapan 3. Nasa harapan katabi ni Toto 4. Nasa likuran 5. Nasa harapan 6. Nasa harapan katabi ni Tita **Exercise 2** 1. Kaibigan ko si Margaret 2. Kapatid niya siya John 3. Bisita nila si Ann 4. Kaklase ko sila. **Exercise 4** 1. ng 2. namin 3. ni 4. ng 5. ko 6. ng 7. niya. **Exercise 5** 1. Bahay ni Pedro ito 2. Pagkain ng aso ito. 3. Kampana ng simbahan ito. **Exercise 6** 1. kaibigan 2. Matangkad 3. magkakapatid 4. pinakamatanda 5. pinakabunso 6. anak ninyo 7. anak ko. 8. ilan 9. ang may-asawa. Ang anak niya. 10. apo **Exercise 7** 1.d 2.e 3.b 4.a 5.c **Exercise 8** 1. ang piknik natin 2. mas matanda sa dalawa 3. tatlong taon 4. mas bata 5. hindi mo ba alam 6. kapatid siya ng aking nanay 7. ng malamig na inumin 8. ang piknik na ito **Exercise 9** 1. Siya ay anak mo 2. Ako ay may

tiket 3. Ang tubig ay malamig 4. Ngayon ay mainit 5. Ang handa
mo ay masarap.

Unit 8

Exercise 1 1. Apat kami. 2. May mesa ba kayo para sa apat (na tao)?
3. Gusto ko ng malamig na tubig. 4. Gusto ko ng San Miguel beer.
5. May malaking mesa ba kayo? **Exercise 2** 1. False 2. True 3. True
4. False 5. False 6. True **Exercise 3** 1. mga aklat 2. mga babae 3. mga
bahay **Exercise 4** 1. May mga bisita na sa bahay 2. Mga estudyante
ba kayo? 3. Hindi sila mga Pilipino 4. Kailangan ko ang mga silya
at mesa. 5. Mga sariwang prutas ang mga ito **Exercise 5** 1. Oo.
Suka nga para sa bangus 2. Oo. Maaari bang bigyan mo ako ng
asin? 3. Gusto ko ng sarsa 4. May toyo ba kayo? **Exercise 6** 1. mga
dalawang kilong 2. mga tatlong yarda. 3. Mga alas-dos 4. Mga siyam
5. mga walong tao **Exercise 7** Customer 1. adobong manok sa gata,
kanin at malamig na guyabano 2. pansit, guinataan, malamig na
buko juice 3. lechon, kanin, pansit at malamig na Coke.

Unit 9

Exercise 1 1.f 2.d 3.e 4.a 5.c 6.b **Exercise 2** 1. Para sa kape ang gatas
2. Para sa bintana ang kurtina 3. Para sa sulat 4. Para sa ulan 5. Para
sa pagtulog ang kama 6. Para sa biyahe ang maleta 7. Para sa tubig.
Exercise 3 1. Magandang umaga 2. ngipin ko 3. gamot 4 Okey
lang. Maraming salamat 5. Magkano iyan 6. ang bayad 7. Walang
anuman **Exercise 4** 1. buhok 2. ulo 3. mata 4. panga 5. tiyan
6. kamay 7. daliri 8. binti 9. paa 10. talampakan **Exercise 5** Tama.
2. Mali. Nasa harapan ang dibdib. 3. Tama. 4. Mali. Nasa paa ang
talampakan. 5. Mali. Nasa bibig ang labi. 6. Tama **Exercise 6** 1. Ang
sakit ng ulo ko. 2. Hatsing! May sipon ako. 3. Masakit ang paa ko.

Unit 10

Exercise 1 1.b 2.c 3.c 4.b **Exercise 2** 1. Sa akin ang maletang ito
2. Sa bata ba ang bisikleta 3. Sa kanila ang bagong Jeepney 4. Hindi

sa iyo iyan 5. Kay Beth ang tsinelas. 6. Kina Philip ba ito? **Exercise 3** 1. dilaw 2. puti 3. pula 4. asul 5. kulay pilak 6. biyoleta 7. itim 8. berde 9. ginto **Exercise 4** 1. Hindi. Kay Amy ang itim na tote bag 2. Hindi. Kay Paul ang itim na tote bag 3. Hindi. Kay Stephen ang duffel bag 4. Kay Dad ang denim tote bag 5. Oo. Kay Lucy ang dilaw na plastic bag. **Exercise 5** 1. Kanino ang mga iyon? 2. Kaninong bahay ito? 3. Kaninong guro si Cora? 4. Kanino iyan? 5. Kanino ang mga gulay na ito? 6. Kanino ang mga berdeng mangga? 7. Kanino ang maleta? 8. Kaninong anak si Joanna? 9. Kaninong maleta ito? 10. Kaninong kamera iyan? **Exercise 6** 1. bata, 2. beach, 3. turista, 4. bata, 5. turista, 6. beach, 7. bata, 8. turista, 9. beach, 10. bata, 11. beach, 12. turista, 13. bata, 14. beach, 15. bata, 16. turista, 17. beach, 18. turista **Exercise 7** 1. sa tindahan 2. sa paliparan 3. sa dagat 4. sa tindahan ng laruan 5. sa palengke 6. sa palaruan 7. sa kalye **Exercise 8** 1. sa hapon 2. Sa Linggo 3. sa gabi 4. sa tanghali 5. sa hapon 6. sa umaga 7. sa isang lingo

---

Unit 11

Exercise 2 1. gusto 2. kailangan 3. ayaw 4. dapat 5. ibig **Exercise 3** 1. Hindi masyadong mahaba 2. Hindi 3. Sa tabi 4. Huhugasan muna ng barbero ang buhok ni Bill 5. Gusto rin ni Bill ng masahe **Exercise 4** 1. ang bagong kotse 2. ng katulong 3. ng aking tulong 4. magpagupit 5. ng malamig na kape **Exercise 5** 1. Kailangan (Do you want a pencil?) 2. Ibig (Baby wants to buy some bananas from the market) 3. kailangan (Why do you need a blackboard?) 4. gusto (Who do you want to go with you to the cinema?) 5. Ibig (Do you like a cold Pepsi?) **Exercise 6** 1. Mahaba ang inyong buhok 2. Bagay sa inyo ang mahabang buhok 3. Kailangan kong hugasan ang inyong buhok. **Exercise 7** 1. Maikli sa harapan, medyo mahaba sa likuran 2. Putulin nang kaunti ang tagiliran, medyo kulot, medyo kingki 3. Pakiputulan ang hulihan, huwag masyadong maikli, hanggang batok lang. **Exercise 8** 1. Magandang umaga naman 2. Gusto kong magpagupit 3. Maaari bang ngayon na ako magpagupit? 4. Hindi na salamat. Gupit lang 5. Gusto ko maikli ang gupit 6. Gupit na lang muna 7. Maraming salamat **Exercise 9** 1. sa matatanda 2. sa iyo 3. sa kaniya 4. sa akin 5. sa atin 6. sa kaniya

Unit 12

Exercise 1 1. kailangan 2. pantalon at kamisadentro 3. maluwag 4. sarisaring kulay 5. maganda 6. pumili 7. sombrero **Exercise 2** 1. Bibili ako ng laruan bukas 2. Kumakain kami ng gulay araw-araw 3. Gumawa tayo ng laruan 4. Humihiram si Ely ng libro sa akin 5. Iinom kami ng malamig na beer sa kantina ngayon. **Exercise 4** 1. Gusto ko ng berdeng palda 2. Ayaw ko ng mahabang palda 3. Kailangan ko ito sa Lunes 4. Nasa bahay ang palda ko. **Exercise 5** 1. lumalaki 2. gumaganda 3. luminis 4. lumayo **Exercise 6** lumalaki, lumiwanag, luminaw, sumarap **Exercise 7** 1. kanina sumikat ang araw 2. sa amin noong isang linggo 3. tag-init 4. umuulan 5. madilim ang langit. **Exercise 8** 1. Bumabaha sa Maynila. 2. Hindi. Sa Kanluran ito lumulubog 3. Sumisikat ang araw sa Pilipinas mga alas 6:00 nang umaga 4. May ingay kung kumukulog at kumikidlat 5. Hindi. Sumisikat ang buwan sa gabi. **Exercise 9** 1. kumikidlat 2. umulan 3. bumaha **Exercise 10** 1. Maulap, maaaring umulan sa Hilagang Luzon 2. Mainit 3. Mainit ang araw

Unit 13

Exercise 1 1. False 2.True 3. False 4. True 5. True 6. False 7. False 8. True 9. True 10. False **Exercise 2** 1. Hindi ko gustong bumili ng tiket 2. Hindi puwede bukas nang umaga. 3. Hindi humihinto ang bus nang mga alas 7:30 4. Malayo ang Banaue buhat sa Maynila 5. Hindi mabuti ang alas 4.30 nang umaga. **Exercise 3** 1. Huwebes 2. Septyembre 3. Nobyembre 4. Linggo 5. Miyerkoles 6. Hunyo 7. Sabado **Exercise 4** 1. Sa ika-30 ng Agosto ang kaarawan niya 2. Sa Lunes ang simula ng pasukan 3. Dadalaw kami sa iyo sa Sabado, ika-sampu ng Mayo. 4. Noong Martes, ika-14 ng Hunyo ang komperensiya 5. Pupunta kami sa zoo sa Linggo, ika-3 ng Septyembre 6. Sa Sabado ka ba aalis? 7. Sino ang darating sa Huwebes, ika 5 ng Enero? **Exercise 5** 1. magluto 2. maglaba 3. maglaro **Exercise 6** 1. Maglaro tayo 2. Naglinis na ako ng kotse 3. Naghuhugas ng pinggan si Maria 4. Magdasal tayo 5. Magluluto sina Lina. **Exercise 7** 1. Mga sampung oras 2. Hindi 3. Tarlac 4. Lima

Exercise 8 1. Alas 7.45 ang dating ng bus galing sa Baguio. 2. Umalis ito sa Baguio kaninang alas 9.00 ng umaga. 3. Hihinto ito sa Ilocos, Pangasinan, Tarlac, Pampanga at Bulacan Exercise 9 1. 81 pesos 2. Mali. Ang numero ng tiket ay: anim, dalawa, dalawa, tatlo, talo, anim 3. wala. 4. 10–60 5. Hindi. 6. Hindi Exercise 10 1. maligo 2. nakikinig 3. naupo 4. mahiga 5. natulog Exercise 11 1. Anong oras hihinto ang bus sa Pampanga? 2. Saan pa kayo hihinto? 3. Mayroon bang kubeta doon? 4. Gusto kong pumunta sa kubeta Exercise 12 1. Magandang umaga 2. Oo. Pero hindi ko sigurado kung anong oras ito babalik sa Maynila 3. Bukas nang hapon ang balik naming 4. Alas tres. Okay lang 5. Isang biyahe lang. Para sa tatlong adults 6. Heto ang bayad namin 7. Maraming salamat din. Exercise 13 1. nakapaglalaro 2. makakaalis 3. makakabili 4. makakapagluto 5. nakatulog

---

Unit 14

Exercise 1 1. Kasi maganda ang panahon 2. Mamamasyal muna 3. Mga mangingisda 4. Oo. Sa palagay ko, mura ang pag-arkila ng bangka 5. Hindi. Pagbalik na nila. Exercise 2 1. Mamimitas ako ng prutas bukas 2. Mangingisda sila sa Miyerkoles 3. Maraming mandurukot sa palengke 4. Mamamasiyal ako mamayang gabi 5. Mamili tayo! Exercise 3 1. mamimitas 2. mangisda 3. namimili 4. nandurukot 5. nanahi Exercise 4 1.a 2.a 3.a Exercise 5 1. Malapit na ang pasko 2. Hindi pa ako nakakakain 3. Sa Sabado na ba ang binyag ng anak mo? 4. Alam mo ba ang sagot sa tanong? 5. Kumakain pa ba sila? Exercise 6 1. Si Bill 2. Malalaking isda 3. Nakakapangisda sila 4. Oo. Nasiyahan sila 5. Lumangoy sila. Exercise 7 1. Namamangka ang pamilya Cook. 2. Lumalangoy ang pamilya Cook. Exercise 8 1. nakabili 2. nakakapaglaro 3. nakahiram 4. nakakaalis 5. makabalik. Exercise 9 1. Makakapangisda 2. Makakabili 3. nakakain 4. nakabisita 5. Nakakain Exercise 10 1. Salamat. Nakapamahinga kami. Nakapangisda rin kami 2. Oo. Nakapangisda kami ng tulingan at dalawang Lapulapu 3. Oo! Sana makabalik kami sa susunod na taon at makahuli nang maraming isda 4. Heto ang bayad namin sa bangka 5. Maraming salamat din.

332

Unit 15

Exercise 1 1. Tinanong nila si Roy kung ibig niyang maging ninong. 2. Apat 3. Sa kapilya sa bukid 4. Oo 5. si Jobert. **Exercise 2** 1. Bukas ba ninyo bibilhin ang bagong stereo? 2. Ginagawa niya ang bulaklak na papel 3. Tinatahi mo ba ito? 4. Tinutugtog niya ang kundiman sa piyano 5. Nililinis ko pa ang kuwarto ko 6. Piliin mo ang sariwang gulay. **Exercise 3** 1. Maaari bang kunan kita ng retrato? 2. Maaari bang kunan mo ako ng retrato? 3. Gusto ko ang damit mo, maganda ito/Ang ganda ng damit mo! 4. sumama ka sa amin. **Exercise 4** 1. iibigin, iniibig, inibig 2. kakainin, kinakain, kinain 3. lilinisin, nililinis, nilinis 4. susulatin, sinusulat, sinulat 5. tatapusin, tinatapos, tinapos **Exercise 5** 1. hinuhuli 2. kinain 3. tatahiin 4. sasabihin 5. nilinis **Exercise 6** 1. kinukuha, binili 2. nililinis, kinukuskos 3. niluluto, sinasaing **Exercise 7** 1. Ninong ka rin ba? 2. Ilan kayong ninong? 3. Narito ba ang mga magulang mo? 4. Pupunta ka ba sa salu-salo? **Exercise 8** 1.4 2.2 3.1 4.3 **Exercise 9** 1. pala 2. nga 3. kaya 4. yata 5. ba

Unit 16

Exercise 1 1. Maaari bang ipakihulog mo ang mga sulat ko? 2. Labindalawa 3. Sapagka't walang selyo si Louise 4. sa Post Office. **Exercise 2** 1. ibinibigay 2. itinatapon 3. isinusukat **Exercise 3** 1. ibibigay 2. isasama 3. ipinirito 4. isinulat 5. iniluluto 6. inihulog 7. itatapon 8. inilagay **Exercise 4** 1. Kasi maraming naitulong si Jobert sa pamilya Cook 2. Dahil sa malaki ang itinulong ng pamilya kay Jobert sa London 3. Dinala nila si Jobert sa iba't ibang lugar, ibinili nila sa Jobert ng kailangan niya 4. Aba, oo. **Exercise 5** 1. Maraming bumibili ng libro dito araw-araw 2. May kumakatok yata sa pinto 3. May kinuha ako kahapon sa kaniya 4. Walang sumama sa akin sa ospital noong Linggo 5. May naglalaro na naman ng tennis sa kabila. **Exercise 6** 1. Tumayo ka! 2. Maupo po kayo. 3. Matulog na tayo. 4. Maari po bang huwag kayong manigarilyo? 5. Mamasiyal tayo. **Exercise 7** 1. Magandang umaga 2. May semento ba kayo 3. Puwede bang ipagreserba mo ako ng sampung sako? 4. May Marine plywood ba kayo? 5. Aluminum roofing sheets, mayroon ba kayo? 6. Mabuti. Puwede bang ipagreserba mo ako ng labindalawang sheets? 7. Oo. Dalawang kilo nga 8. Wala na. Iyan lang. Pupunta ako riyan nang mga tanghali 9. Paalam.

Unit 17

Exercise 1 1. Mali 2. Tama 3. Mali 4. Tama. Exercise 2 ninong, simbahan, pulot-gata, ninang, retratista, singsing, pagkain Exercise 3 1. Kakainan ko ng pansit ang plato 2. Tinutulungan ko siya 3. Lalagyan namin ng rosas ang halaman dito 4. Gusto kong bigyan si Larry nito 5. Lalagyan ba natin nito doon? 6. Huwag mong aalisan ng libro ang mesa Exercise 4 1. tutulungan 2. nilakihan 3. sinuklian 4. sasamahan 5. binigyan 6. hinalikan 7. sarapan 8. palitan Exercise 5 1. Paglabas. . . 2. Maraming kumuha. . . . 3. Maraming sasakyan. . . 4. Dumating ang bagong. . . . 5. Inihanda ng mga tagapagluto. . . . 6. Maraming pagkain 7. Ang mga nagluluto 8. Tumulong sa paghahain 9. Habang kumakain 10. May tugtugin. . . 11. Isa sa mga tugtugin 12. Inanyayahan ng mga panauhin 13. Tuwang-tuwa 14. Napagod sa pagsayaw 15. Sa dulang, nagbigay ng. . . 16. Nagbigay din 17. Isa-isang nagpaalam Exercise 7 1. Nasusulatan mo na ba si Sophie? 2. Maitatapon ni Harry ang basura lagi 3. May binubuksan siyang kabinet ngayon 4. Hindi masasamahan ni Caroline si Phil sa bayan mamayang gabi 5. Sino ang naisakay mo sa kotse kagabi? Exercise 8 1. Ang paghalik sa kamay ng mga lolo at lola. 2. Ang lola 3. Upang maging puhunan 4. Ang unang makarating sa bahay ang boss Exercise 9 1. siya mismo 2. Mismong kami 3. nila mismo 4. ikaw, mismo 5. Mismong sina Fred Exercise 10 1. natutulog 2. nakikipag-usap sa kaibigan 3. naliligo 4. naglalaba 5. namamasiyal 6. umiinom

Unit 18

Exercise 1 1. pista 2.mamayang gabi 3. mga damit at mga laruan 4. dapat mayaman siya 5. pag-akyat sa kawayan, pagsungkit ng laso, pagsakay sa kalabaw 6. upang ilibot sa bayan 7. ang

tenyente **Exercise 2** 1. kapalaran 2. katamaran 3. kawalan
4. kayamanan 5. kabahayan 6. kamalian **Exercise 3** karunungan
2. kasinungalingan 3. kalalakihan, kababaihan 4. karapatan
5. kakayahan **Exercise 5** 1. False (gusto) 2. False (upang maghanda
3. False. (ginagastos kaagad) 4. False. (Hindi mabuti) 5. False.
(Hindi mabuti para sa lahat). **Exercise 6** 1. Oo, pupunta kami sa
pista 2. Mahilig akong sumayaw 3. Saan makakabili ng pagkain at
inumin? 4. Salamat, sumama ka sa amin. 5. O sige, hahanapin ka
namin mamaya 6. Paalam. **Exercise 7** 1. Makikikain si Auntie Marge
sa kanila mamaya. 2. Kanino ka nakiupo? 3. Makikipamili ka ba
kina auntie dot? 4. Nakikipag-away na naman si Jose 5. Nakikipag-
usap pa ako kay Janet. **Exercise 8** 1. Maaari bang makipag-usap
kami kay Ginoong Reyes? 2. Puwede bang makitulog ako sa kanila?
3. Huwag sana kayong makipag-away sa mga bata 4. Maaari bang
makisakay kami kina Baby? 5. Puwede bang makipagluto ang mga
bisita dito? **Exercise 9** 1. Nag-aaral siyang humawak ng kalabaw
2. Medyo kausapin ang kalabaw 3. Oo. Maaari siyang sumakay
sa kalabaw 4. Nagtrabaho siya sa isang sabsaban ng kabayo sa
Inglaterra. **Exercise 10** 1. Ganoon kabait si ginoong Cruz sa amin
2. Ganito ba ang paggawa ng silyang rattan? 3. Paano ang pagsara
ng kahong ito? 4. Hindi ba ganito ang pagluto ng adobo? 5. Sabihin
mo sa akin ang pagtugtog ng himig na ito. **Exercise 11** 1. ganito
2. ganiyan 3. ganiyan 4. ganito 5. ganoon 6. ganito 7. ganiyan
8. ganoon 9. ganito 10. ganiyan 11. ganoon 12. ganito

Unit 19

Exercise 1 1. mga punong-kahoy 2. rosal, sampaguita, rosas, camia
3. Gumawa siya ng palaisdaan 4. Nagpaluto ng kakanin si Kiko
5. Maganda ang buhay sa bukid: may mga punong-kahoy, masarap
ang pagkain, may mga bulaklak etc. **Exercise 2** 1. Nagpapakuha ako
ng libro sa kanila 2. Magpapalabas ba tayo ng silya? 3. Nagpapasok
ba si Henry ng mga maleta kanina? 4. Saan ka nagpapabibili ng
gulay at prutas? 5. Nagpabasa siya ng aklat sa klase. **Exercise 3** 1)
Seven 2) a) Medyo huli na ako OR Alas_____ ako nakarating. b)
Oo, natrapik ako. c) Nasa kusina ang Nanay ko. d) Hindi lahat.
Nagpaluto ako ng ibang putahe. e) Oo. f) May kilala akong

masarap magluto. Chef siya. **Exercise 4** 1. Gusto niyang magpakain ng mga baboy 2. Si Kiko 3. Mga manok 4. Kasi pinagluto na ni Kiko ang Misis niya ng almusal. **Exercise 5** 1. pasusulatin 2. pinaglinis ng kotse 3. pagtatahiin ng bestida 4. nagpapagupit 5. nagpapaganda **Exercise 6** 1. Nagpapaligo si Mang Kiko ng kalabaw sa ilog 2. Nagpapakain ng manok si Roy 3. Nagsasampay ng damit ang asawa ni Mang Kiko 4. Pinaaalis ng batang babae ang mga ibon 5. Nagpapalipad ng saringgola ang batang lalaki. **Exercise 7** 3. Pinagbuti ni Elvie ang kaniyang trabaho kagabi 1. Pasasamahin ko si Michael kay Jim sa bayan sa isang linggo 2. Pinamili namin si Lisa kahapon 1. Pinapag-aral ni Lina si Georgina kanina. 2. Pinasulat daw ni Patricia si Larry noong isang buwan. **Exercise 8** 1. damo 2. si Roy 3. hinog na ang guyabano 4. para inumin ng mga hayop 5. sa loob ng murang niyog. **Exercise 9** 1. pinatutulog 2. pinatatakbo 3. pinaglilinis **Exercise 10** 1. ipalalagay 2. ipasok 3. ipamimigay 4. ipinaayos 5. papintahan

---

Unit 20

Exercise 1 1. Isang kalabaw na inukit sa kahoy 2. magdaramdam si Kiko 3. mga pagkain lang 4. Malaking abala ang ibinigay nila kay Kiko **Exercise 2** 1. Kasimbait ni Remy si Bing. (Remy is as kind as Bing) 2. Kasimputi ng camia ang rosal. (Camia is as white as rosal) 3. Kasintaas ng St. Paul's Cathedral ang BT Tower (The BT Tower is as tall as St. Paul's Cathedral) 4. Kasinluwang ng pantalon ko ang pantalon mo (My trousers are as wide as your trousers) 5. Kasingkipot nito iyan. (This is as tight as that) 6. Hindi kasingganda ang hardin ko ng hardin mo (My garden is not as pretty as yours) 7. Magkasimbuti ang gulay at prutas (Vegetables and fruits are equally good) **Exercise 3** 1. Kailangan niyang bumili ng pampasalubong 2. sa Priscilla's Gift Shop 3. para kay Viv at Tim 4. nilalang handbag 5. sa pamamagitan ng credit card 6. mag-iimpake pa sila. **Exercise 4** 1. panlakad 2. pambayad 3. pangkain **Exercise 5** 1. pangkamot 2. pamputol 3. panlaba 4. panulat 5. pamasyal **Exercise 6** 1. Pangkamot ng likod ang patpat 2. Pamputol ng kahoy ang itak 3. Panlaba ang sabon 4. Panulat ang lapis 5. Pamasyal ang gomang sapatos. **Exercise 7** 1. Aba, huwag kayong mag-alaala 2. Mas tahimik sa Inglaterra 3. Magandang kuwadro para sa kaniyang pamilya 4. sumulat lagi si roy o kaya'y tumawag. **Exercise 9** 1. Mas matangkad si Tom kaysa kay Benny 2. Higit na masipag si Benny kaysa kay Tom. 3. Mas mataba si Benny kaysa kay Tom. 4. Mas masaya si Benny kaysa kay Tom **Exercise 10** Self-assessment (Ask your Filipino friends to help)

Verb list

Stem	Meaning	-um-	mag+	mang+	+in	i+	+an
abang	to wait for	x	x	mang-abang	x	x	abangan
abay	to accompany	umabay	x	x	x	x	abayan
abot	to arrive, reach	umabot	x	x	abutin	x	abutan
ako	to claim	umako	x	mang-ako	akuin	x	x
aksaya	to waste (time)	umaksaya	mag-aksaya	x	aksayahin	x	x
akyat	to climb	umakyat	x	x	akyatin	x	akyatan
alaala	to remember	umalaala	x	x	alalahanin	x	x
alam	to know	x	x	x	alamin	x	x
alay	to offer/dedicate	x	mag-alay	mang-alay	x	ialay	alayan
alibadbad	to be nauseous	x	x	x	alibadbarin	x	alibadbaran
alis	to leave	umalis	x	x	x	x	x
alis	to remove	x	mag-alis	x	alisin	x	alisan
alsa	to raise/rise/strike	umalsa	mag-alsa	x	x	x	x
ambag	to contribute	umambag	mag-ambag	x	x	iambag	ambagan
anak	to treat as one's own child	x	mag-anak	x	anakin	x	x
anak	to have a baby	x	x	manganak	x	x	x
aral	to study	x	mag-aral	x	x	x	x
araw-araw	to do something daily	x	x	x	araw-arawin	x	x
awit	to sing	umawit	x	x	awitin	x	awitan
ayos	to tidy up	umayos	mag-ayos	x	ayusin	x	ayusan

Root	Meaning	-um-	mag-	mang-	-in	i-	-an
baba	to descend/go down	bumaba	x	x	babain	x	babaan
bago	to change	bumago	x	x	baguhin	x	x
bagsak	to drop/fall	bumagsak	magbagsak	x	x	ibagsak	bagsakan
bagyo	to be hit by typhoon	bumagyo	x	x	bagyuhin	x	x
bahin	to sneeze	bumahin	x	x	x	x	bahinan
balik	to come back	bumalik	x	x	x	x	x
balik	to return something	x	magbalik	x	x	ibalik	x
bangon	to get up (from lying down)	bumangon	magbangon	x	x	ibangon	x
bantay	to guard	x	magbantay	x	x	x	bantayan
baon	to bring provision	x	magbaon	x	baunin	x	x
baon	to bury	bumaon	magbaon	x	x	ibaon	x
basa	to read	bumasa	magbasa	x	basahin	x	basahan
basa	to wet	x	magbasa	mambasa	basain	x	x
basag	to break (as in glass)	bumasag	magbasag	mambasag	basagin	x	x
bastos	to be bad mannered/rude	bumastos	x	mambastos	bastusin	x	x
bata	to become young	bumata	x	x	x	x	x
bata	to suffer	x	magbata	x	batahin	x	x
batid	to know	x	x	x	batirin	x	x
bili	to buy	bumili	x	mamili	bilhin	ibili	bilhan
bili	to sell	x	magbili	x	x	x	x
bola	to fool someone	x	x	mambola	bolahin	x	x
bubo	to spill	x	magbubo	x	x	ibubo	bubuan
bukas	to open	by itself	bumukas	x	x	x	x x
bukas	to open something	x	magbukas	x	x	ibukas	buksan

bukid	*to farm*	x	magbukid	mambukid	bukirin	x	x
buhay	*to give life*	bumuhay	magbuhay	x	buhayin	x	x
buhay	*to live*	x	x	mamuhay	x	x	x
bunga	*to bear fruit*	bumunga	magbunga	x	x	ibunga	x
busog	*to make full (appetite)*	bumusog	x	x	busugin	x	x
buwis	*to pay tax*	x	magbuwis	x	x	x	buwisan
kaibigan	*to befriend*	kumaibigan	x	x	kaibiganin	x	x
kailangan	*to need*	kumailangan	x	mangailangan	kailanganin	x	x
kain	*to eat*	kumain	magkain	mangain	kainin	ikain	kainan
kagat	*to bite*	kumagat	x	mangagat	kagatin	ikagat	kagatan
kaliwa	*to turn left*	kumaliwa	x	mangaliwa	kaliwain	x	x
kamay	*to use the hand*	x	magkamay	x	kamayin	x	x
kanta	*to sing*	kumanta	x	x	kantahin	x	kantahan
kapit-bahay	*to visit neighbours*	x	x	mangapit-bahay	x	x	x
kilala	*to know*	kumilala	x	mangilala	kilalanin	x	x
kilos	*to move*	kumilos	x	x	x	ikilos	x
kita	*to earn*	kumita	x	x	kitain	x	x
kita	*to meet up*	x	magkita	x	kitain	x	x
kuha	*to get/take*	kumuha	x	manguha	kunin	ikuha	kunan
kulang	*to lack*	x	magkulang	x	kulangin	x	x
kulay	*to colour*	x	magkulay	x	x	ikulay	kulayan
dala	*to carry*	x	magdala	x	dalhin	x	x
dala	*to bring to someone*	x	x	x	x	x	dalhan
dala	*to catch fish with a net*	x	magdala	mandala	dalahin	x	x

Root	Meaning						
dalangin	*to pray*	dumalangin	x	manalangin	dalanginin	idalangan	dalanginan
dalaw	*to visit*	dumalaw	x	x	dalawin	idalaw	dalian
dali	*to make quick*	x	x	x	dalin	x	x
dama	*to feel*	dumama	magdama	x	damahin	x	
damihan	*to make many*						
damit	*to wear clothes*	x	magdamit	manamit	damitin	idamit	damitan
dapat	*to be a must/ought to*	x	x	x	x	x	x
dumi	*to dirty*	dumumi	magdumi	x	x	x	dumihan
dusa	*to suffer*	x	magdusa	x	x	x	x
eskandalo	*to create a scandal*	x	mageskandalo	x	eskandaluhin	x	x
eskoba	*to brush clothes*	x	mageskoba	x	eskubahin	x	eskubahan
gabi	*to be overtaken by night*	gumabi	x	x	gabihin	x	x
galing	*to come from*	x	x	manggaling	x	x	x
galing	*to become well*	gumaling	x	x	x	x	x
galit	*to be angry*	x	x	manggalit	galitin	x	x
gamit	*to use*	gumamit	x	x	gamitin	x	gamitan
gamot	*to treat/cure*	gumamot	x	manggamot	gamutin	x	x
gana	*to have appetite*	x	x	x	x	x	ganahan
ganda	*to make beautiful*	gumanda	x	x	x	x	gandahan
gata	*to cook in coconut milk*	x	maggata	x	x	igata	gataan
gawi	*to turn towards*	gumawi	x	x	x	igawi	gawian
gibik	*to shout for help*	gumibik	x	x	x	x	gibikan.

giling	to grind	gumiling	x	x	gilingin	x	x
gising	to wake up	gumising	x	manggising	gisingin	x	x
gusto	to like	gumusto	x	x	gustuhin	x	x
gutom	to feel hungry	gumutom	x	manggutom	gutumin	x	x
hakot	to load baggage	humakot	maghakot	x	hakutin	x	hakutan
hagilap	to search for/look for	humagilap	maghagilap	manghagilap	hagilapin	ihagilap	x
hagis	to throw	humagis	maghagis	manghagis	x	ihagis	hagisan
hangin	to blow (as in wind)	humangin	x	x	x	x	hanginan
hapo	to suffer from tiredness	x	x	x	hapuin	x	x
hasik	to plant seed	x	maghasik	x	x	ihasik	hasikan
hayag	to reveal	x	maghayag	x	x	ihayag	x
higa	to lie down (a **ma** verb)	mahiga	x	x	x	ihiga	higaan
hila	to pull	humila	maghila	manghila	hilahin	x	x
hindi	to say no/turn down	humindi	x	x	x	x	hindian
hintay	to wait	x	maghintay	x	hintayin	x	x
hinto	to stop	huminto	x	x	x	ihinto	hintuan
hipo	to touch	humipo	x	manghipo	hipuin	x	hipuan
hiram	to borrow	humiram	x	manghiram	hiramin	ihiram	hiraman
hithit	to smoke (i.e. cigarette etc.)	humithit	x	x	hithitin	x	x
hiyaw	to shout	humiyaw	x	x	x	ihiyaw	hiyawan
hubad	to undress	x	maghubad	x	hubarin	x	hubaran
hugas	to wash	x	maghugas	x	x	x	hugasan
hulog	to drop	x	maghulog	x	x	ihulog	hulugan

root	meaning	um-	mag-	mang-	-in	i-	-an
iba	*to change*	x	mag-iba	x	ibahin	x	x
ibig	*to love/like*	umibig	x	mangibig	ibigin	x	x
idlip	*to have a short nap*	umidlip	x	x	x	x	x
igib	*to fetch water*	umigib	x	x	x	x	x
imik	*to talk/speak*	umimik	x	x	x	x	imikan
isip	*to think*	umisip	mag-isip	x	isipin	x	x
init	*to become hot*	uminit	mag-init	x	initin	x	x
inom	*to drink*	uminom	x	x	inumin	x	inuman
isda	*to go fishing*	x	x	mangisda	x	x	x
itim	*to become dark*	umitim	x	mangitim	x	x	x
laba	*to wash clothes*	x	maglaba	x	x	x	labhan
labas	*to go outside*	lumabas	x	x	labasin	x	labasan
lakad	*to walk*	lumakad	maglakad	x	lakarin	ilakad	lakaran
lagay	*to place/put*	lumagay	maglagay	x	x	ilagay	lagyan
laglag	*to fail/fall*	lumaglag	maglaglag	maglaglag	x	ilaglag	laglagan
lala	*to become seriously ill*	lumala	x	x	x	x	x
lamok	*to be infested with mosquitoes*	x	x	x	lamukin	x	x
lapit	*to come close/near*	lumapit	x	x	x	ilapit	lapitan
laro	*to play*	x	maglaro	x	laruin	x	x
lasap	*to taste/experience*	lumasap	x	x	lasapin	x	x
lasing	*to get drunk*	lumasing	maglasing	x	lasingin	x	x
lawig	*to take a long time*	lumawig	maglawig	x	x	ilawig	lawigan
layag	*to sail*	lumayag	maglayag	x	x	x	x
layo	*to distance oneself*	lumayo	x	x	ilayo	ilayo	layuan

libak	to mock, humiliate	lumibak	x	manglibak	libakin	x	x
libing	to bury	x	maglibing	x	x	ilibing	x
ligo	to take a bath (a **ma** verb)	maligo	x	x	x	x	liguan
ligpit	to keep/tidy up	x	x	x	x	x	x
limos	to give alms	x	maglimos	x	x	ilimos	limusan
limot	to forget	lumimot	x	x	limutin	x	x
lindol	to have an earthquake	lumindol	x	x	x	x	x
linis	to clean	x	maglinis	x	linisin	x	linisan
lingkod	to serve	x	maglingkod	x	x	x	x
lipad	to fly	lumipad	x	x	liparin	ilipad	x
litaw	to appear	lumitaw	x	x	x	iltraw	litawan
liwanag	to become brighter	lumiwanag	magliwanag	x	liwanagin	x	liwanagan
loko	to fool	lumuko	magloko	manloko	lokohin	x	x
lukso	to jump	lumukso	x	x	luksuhin	x	luksuhan
lugas	to fall off	lumugas	x	x	lugasin	x	x
lulon	to swallow	lumulon	x	x	lulunin	x	x
may-ari	to own/claim	x	magmay-ari	x	x	x	x
meryenda	to have a snack	x	magmeryenda	x	meryendahin	x	x
mahal	to make dear/expensive	x	magmahal	x	x	x	mahalan
mahal	to love	x	x	x	mahalin	x	x
minindal	to have a snack	x	magminindal	x	minindalin	x	x
miting	to have a meeting	x	magmiting	x	x	x	x
mukha	to be similar to/look like	x	magmukha	x	x	x	x
mungkahi	to suggest	x	magmungkahi	x	x	imungkahi	x
mura	to become cheaper	x	magmura	x	x	x	murahan

nakaw	to steal	x	magnakaw	x	nakawin	x	nakawan
nais	to desire/wish	x	magnais	x	naisin	x	x
ningas	to have flame	x	magningas	x	x	x	x
ngiti	to smile	ngumiti	x	x	x	x	ngitian
nguya	to chew	ngumuya	magnguya	x	nguyain	inguya	x
obserba	to observe	x	mag-obserba	x	obserbahin	x	obserbahan
opera	to operate	umopera	mag-opera	x	uperahin	x	uperahan
oo	to say yes	umoo	x	x	x	x	uuhan
oras	to measure the time of	x	mag-oras	x	orasin	x	orasan
paa	to be barefooted	x	magpaa	x	paahin	x	x
paalam	to bid goodbye	x	magpaalam	x	x	x	
pakli	to reply/answer	pumakli	x	x	x	ipakli	x
paksiw	to cook this native dish	x	magpaksiw	x	paksiwin	ipaksiw	x
pakumbaba	to be humble	x	magpakumbaba	x	x	x	pakumbabaan
pakundangan	to have respect	x	magpakundangan	x	x	x	pakundanganan
pagitan	to be a go-between	pumagitan	x	mamagitan	x	ipagitan	pagitanan
pahimakas	to say farewell	x	magpahimakas	x	x	ipahimakas	pahimakasan
pahintulot	to give permission	x	magpahintulot	x	x	ipahintulot	pahintulutan
pahinga	to take a rest	x	magpahinga	mamahinga	x	x	pahingahan
pait	to become bitter	pumait	x	x	x	x	x
palamuti	to decorate	x	magpalamuti	x	x	ipalamuti	palamutihan
palayaw	to nickname	x	magpalayaw	x	x	ipalayaw	palayawan
palengke	to go to the market	x	x	mamalengke	x	x	x

panaginip	to dream	x	x	managinip	panaginipin	x	panaginipan
panalangin	to pray	x	x	manalangin	x	ipanalangin	panalanginan
pangako	to promise	x	magpangako	mangako	x	ipangako	pangakuan
paniwala	to believe	x	x	maniwala	x	x	paniwalaan
pangamba	to worry	x	x	mangamba	x	x	pangambahan
pasok	to enter	pumasok	x	x	pasukin	x	pasukan
para	to stop a bus/jeepney	pumara	magpara	x	parahin	ipara	parahan
pasko	to spend Christmas	x	magpasko	x	x	x	x
pasiya	to decide	x	magpasiya	x	x	ipasiya	pasuyahan
pasyal	to take a stroll	x	magpasyal	mamasyal	x	x	x
patay	to die	x	x	mamatay	x	x	x
patay	to kill	pumatay	magpatay	x	patayin	x	x
patnubay	to guide	pumatnubay	magpatnubay	mamatnubay	x	ipatnubay	patnubayan
patnugot	to direct	pumatnugot	x	mamatnugot	x	x	patnugutan
patubig	to irrigate	x	magpatubig	x	x	x	patubigan
patuloy	to continue	x	magpatuloy	x	x	x	x
pawis	to sweat	x	magpawis	mamawis	pawisin	x	pawisan
pikit	to close eyes	pumikit	magpikit	x	x	ipikit	pikitan
pihit	to turn	pumihit	magpihit	x	pihitin	x	x
pila	to queue up	pumila	x	x	x	ipila	pilahan
pili	to select/choose	pumila	magpili	mamili	piliin	ipili	pilian
pilipit	to twist	pumilipit	magpilipit	mamilipit	pilipitin	ipilipit	x
pilit	to insist	x	magpilit	mamilit	x	x	x
pirma	to sign	pumirma	x	x	x	ipirma	pirmahan
pisan	to put together/to join	pumisan	magpisan	x	x	ipisan	x
pista	to attend fiesta	x	magpista	mamista	x	x	x
pito	to whistle	pumito	x	x	x	x	pituhan

radyo	*to have the radio on*	x	mag-radyo	x	x	x	x
rikisa	*to search*	x	magrikisa	mangrikisa	rikisahin	x	rikisahan
regalo	*to offer a gift*	x	magregalo	x	x	iregalo	regaluhan
relos	*to wear a watch*	x	magrelos	x	x	x	relosan
repeke	*to peal (as in bells)*	rumepeke	magrepeke	x	repekehin	irepeke	x
rosaryo	*to recite the rosary*	x	magrosaryo	x	x	x	x
reseta	*to prescribe*	x	magreseta	x	x	ireseta	resetahan
resibo	*to issue/give a receipt*	x	magresibo	x	x	iresibo	resibuhan
sabi	*to say*	x	magsabi	x	sabihin	x	sabihan
sakal	*to choke*	magsakal	manakal	sakalin	x	x	x
sakay	*to ride*	sumakay	magsakay	x	x	isakay	sakyan
sakdal	*to charge or accuse in court*	x	magpasakdal	x	isakdal	x	x
sakmal	*to snatch*	sumakmal	x	manakmal	x	x	x
sakit	*to hurt*	sumakit	x	manakit	x	x	x
sagana	*to be abundant*	x	magsagana	managana	x	x	x
saglit	*to visit someone for a short time*	sumaglit	magsaglit	managlit	saglitin	isaglit	saglitan
sagot	*to answer*	sumagot	x	x	sagutin	isagot	sagutan
sagot	*to be answerable to one's actions*	x	x	managot	x	x	x
salat	*to feel*	x	x	manalat	salatin	x	x
salita	*to speak/talk/say*	x	magsalita	manalita	salitain	x	x
saliw	*to accompany (instrument)*	sumaliw	magsaliw	x	x	isaliw	saliwan

Root	Gloss						
sanay	to practice	x	magsanay	x	sanayin	x	x
sangguni	to consult	sumangguni	magsangguni	manangguni	x	isangguni	sanggunian
saplot	to wear clothes	x	magsaplot	x	saplutin	isaplot	saplutan
sarap	to make delicious	x	x	x	x	x	sarapan
sarili	to live on one's own	x	magsarili	manarili	x	x	x
sayaw	to dance	sumayaw	magsayaw	x	sayawin	isayaw	x
saysay	to narrate	x	magsaysay	x	x	isaysay	saysayan
sigaw	to shout	sumigaw	x	manigaw	x	isigaw	sigawan
sulat	to write	sumulat	magsulat	x	sulatin	isulat	sulatan
simula	to start/begin	x	magsimula	x	x	x	simulan
subo	to put some food into mouth	x	magsubo	x	x	isubo	subuan
suka	to vomit	sumuka	magsuka	x	x	isuka	sukahan
sulak	to boil	sumulak	magsulak	x	x	x	x
sumpa	to swear an oath	sumumpa	x	manumpa	sumpain	isumpa	x
sunod	to follow	sumunod	x	x	sunurin	isunod	sundan
sunog	to burn	sumunog	magsunog	manunog	sunugin	isunog	x
suot	to wear	x	magsuot	x	suutin	isuot	x
suweldo	to receive salary	sumuweldo	x	x	x	x	x
taas	to grow/to rise	tumaas	x	x	x	x	x
taas	to raise	x	magtaas	x	x	itaas	taasan
taba	to become fatter	tumaba	x	manaba	x	x	x
tabi	to be at one side	tumabi	x	x	x	x	tabihan
takbo	to run	tumakbo	x	x	takbuhin	x	takbuhan
takal	to measure	tumakal	magtakal	x	takalin	itakal	takalan

taklob	to cover	x	magtaklob	x	x	itaklob	takluban
tadtad	to chop into pieces	tumadtad	magtadtad	x	tadtarin	tadtad	x
tadyak	to kick	tumadyak	x	manadyak	x	x	tadyakan
tago	to hide	x	magtago	x	x	itago	x
tagumpay	to succeed	x	magtagumpay	managumpay	x	x	x
tahi	to sew	tumahi	magtahi	manahi	tahiin	itahi	x
talon	to jump	tumalon	x	x	talunin	x	x
talumpati	to make a speech	x	magtalumpati	manalumpati	x	italumpati	talumpatian
tama	to tally/to agree	x	magtama	x	x	itama	x
tanim	to plant	x	magtanim	x	x	itanim	tamnan
tanod	to keep guard	x	magtanod	x	x	x	tanuran
tanong	to ask	x	magtanong	x	tanungin	itanong	x
tanggap	to accept/receive	tumanggap	magtanggap	x	tanggapin	x	x
tapon	to throw	x	magtapon	x	x	itapon	tapunan
tapos	to finish	tumapos	magtapos	x	tapusin	x	x
tawa	to laugh	tumawa	magtawa	x	x	x	tawanan
tawag	to call	x	magtawag	x	tawagin	x	x
tawag	to call on the telephone	tumawag	x	x	x	x	tawagan
tayo	to stand up	tumayo	x	x	x	x	tayuan
tayo	to erect (a building etc.)	x	magtayo	x	x	itayo	x
tikim	to taste	tumikim	x	x	x	x	tikman
tamasa	to enjoy	x	magtamasa	x	tamasahin	x	x
tinda	to sell	x	magtinda	x	x	itinda	x
tira	to live (in a place)	tumira	x	manira	x	x	tirahan

tiyaga	to be patient	x	magtiyaga	x	x	x	x
tubo	to grow	tumubo	x	x	x	x	x
tugon	to reply/answer	tumugon	x	x	x	x	x
tugtog	to play an instrument	tumugtog	magtugtog	x	tugtugin	irugtog	tugtugan
tulala	to ignore	x	magtulala	x	x	x	tulalaan
tulay	to cross a bridge	tumulay	x	manulay	tulayin	x	tulayan
tulog	to sleep (ma verb)	matulog	x	x	x	irulog	tulugan
tuloy	to enter	tumuloy	magtuloy	x	x	x	x
tuloy	to continue	x	x	x	x	iruloy	x
tumba	to tumble down	tumumba	x	x	tumbahin	itumba	x
tunaw	to melt	tumunaw	magtunaw	x	tunawin	x	x
tupad	to fulfil	tumupad	x	x	tuparin	x	x
tupok	to be burned	x	x	x	tupukin	x	x
turo	to teach	x	magturo	x	x	ituro	turuan
turo	to point	tumuro	x	x	x	ituro	x
tuwang	to help	tumuwang	magtuwang	x	x	x	x
ubo	to cough	umubo	x	x	ubuhin	x	x
ubos	to consume/exhaust	umubos	x	x	ubusin	x	ubusan
ulinig	to listen to	x	x	x	ulinigin	x	ulinigan
ulit	to repeat	umulit	x	x	ulitin	x	x
umaga	to be caught by the dawn	x	mag-umaga	x	umagahin	x	x
ulan	to rain	umulan	x	x	ulanin	x	ulanan
untag	to remind	umuntag	x	x	untagin	x	x
uwi	to go home	umuwi	x	x	x	x	uwian

una	to go ahead first	umuna	mag-una	manguna	unahin	x	x
unawa	to understand	umunawa	x	x	unawain	x	x
upo	to sit down (**ma** verb)	maupo	x	x	x	x	upuan
usap	to converse	x	mag-usap	x	x	x	x
wakas	to end	x	magwakas	x	x	x	wakasan
wala	to lose	x	x	x	x	iwala	x
walang-hiya	to be shameless	x	magwalanghiya	x	x	x	x
yabong	to grow	yumabong	magyabong	x	x	x	x
yamot	to annoy	x	x	x	yamutin	x	x
yapak	to step on	yumapak	x	x	x	iyapak	yapakan

Tagalog–English glossary

Trying to pronounce unfamiliar words in a new language is often something of an uphill struggle. It can be frustrating to discover that words are not always pronounced as they appear on the page. With this in mind, we have provided three small symbols or 'accents' to help you find the correct stress or sound for each word in the Tagalog–English Glossary. The accents are as follows:

´ This accent serves to lengthen the sound of the vowel. For example, the Tagalog word **láta** (or 'tin' in English) would be pronounced *'lah-tah'*, with the stress on the first syllable. The first 'a' sound is long, something akin to the long 'a' in the English words 'bar' or 'car'. (In the unit dialogues this stress is shown by making the stressed syllable **bold**.)

` This accent is only ever found on the last vowel of a word. It informs you that the vowel sound is shorter than the vowel with the ´ accent. For example, the Tagalog word **kasápì** (*to be a member of*) would be pronounced *'ka-sah-pee'*, with a long 'ah' sound and a short 'ee' sound.

^ This accent is found on a number of words ending with a vowel. It indicates a glottal stop – a short, abrupt sound, almost as though the pronunciation of the vowel has been interrupted, like a tape recorder being switched off. For example, the Tagalog words **basâ** (*wet*) and **bása** (*to read*) are distinguished from one another by their very different accents. (Glottal stops are shown in the unit dialogues by *italics*.)

áalis   *will leave*
áal musalin   *what someone's having for breakfast*
abá   *oh!/hey!/well!*
abála   *disturbance*
abá oó/aba oo naman   *of course*
ábay   *consort*
abá ópò   *certainly, sir*

(mga) ábay sa kasál   *wedding assistant(s)*
adóbong pusít   *squid adobo*
áking ináanak   *my godchild*
aklát (libro)   *book*
akó rin   *me too*
alám   *know*
alam mo bá   *do you know*

alas dós nang hápon   2.00 p.m.
alas dóse   12.00
alas nuwébe y médya   9.30
alas saís y médya   6.30
alín   which one
alís   departure
almusál   breakfast
Amérika   America
áming   our
áming anák/anak namin   our
   child
ámpalaya   bitter melon
anák   son/daughter/child
ang   the
ang bahálà   will look after
ang datíng   the arrival
ang gágawâ   will do
ang mga itó   these
ang mga iyán   those
ang bill ngà námin   our bill,
   please
ang kailángan ninyó   what you
   need
ang kaínin mo   what you have
   to eat
ang kináin mo   what you ate
ang gusto ninyó(ng)   what you
   like
ang íbig ninyo   what you want
ang maiklíng gupít   short cut
ang nakáin mo   what you have
   eaten
ang paboríto ko(ng)   my
   favourite
ang pangálan ko   my name
ang púnta   the destination/
   going to
ang súkat   the size
ang súkat ko   my measurement

anó(ng)   what
anó ang mga óras ng   what are
   the times of
anó namán itó?   and what is
   this?
ano pá   what else
ano pò ang maipaglílingkod ko
   what (service) can I do
ano pong gupít   what (kind of)
   haircut
anóng edád   how old
anóng óras   what time
anóng pangálan ninyó   what's
   your name? (formal)
anu-anó   what (plural)
apó   grandchild
apritáda   a kind of dish
áraw   day/sun
araw-áraw   every day
asáwa   husband/wife
asáwa niyáng   his/her spouse
asín   salt
at   and
ate   older sister
at sakâ   and also
áyaw ko/ayoko   I don't like

bábahâ   will flood
babáe   female/woman
babágay pò sa inyó   it will suit
   you
babágyo   there will be a
   typhoon
bakâ   might/cow
baká hindî   might not
bakánte   vacancy
bakasyón ka bá   are you on
   vacation?
bákit   why

bákit hindî *why not*
bágay *thing*
bágay ba sa ákin *does it suit me*
bágo *new*
bágo(ng) binyag *newly baptized*
bágo(ng) kasal *newly wed*
bahálà na *come what may*
báhay *house*
baldé *bucket*
bále wala *means nothing*
bandá *band*
bangkâ *boat (canoe)*
bandéra/bandila *flag*
bangâ *earthen pot*
bangús *milkfish*
barkó *ship*
báryo *barrio/village*
báso *drinking glass*
bátà *child*
bátok *nape*
basúra *rubbish*
báwa't óras *each hour*
bayábas *guavas*
báyad ko *my payment*
bayáw *brother-in-law*
bíbigyan kitá *I'll give you*
bíbili *will buy*
bíbili akó ng *I'll buy/I'm going to buy*
biglá(ng) *suddenly*
bigyán mo akó *give me*
bibíg mo *your mouth*
bíbilhin *will buy*
bíbili akó *I will buy*
bibingká *a local delicacy*
bili ná *come and buy*
bilobiló *a local delicacy in coconut milk*

binátà *bachelor*
binigyán *was given*
binyág *baptism*
binyágan(g) ito *this baptism*
bintánà *window*
bisíta *guest/visitor*
biyáhe *travel*
blusá *blouse*
bólpen *pen*
bubúti *will become better*
búkas *tomorrow*
búkas nang gabí *tomorrow night*
búkas nang hápon *tomorrow afternoon*
búkas nang tanghálì *tomorrow midday*
búkas nang umága *tomorrow morning*
búhat sa *from*
búhay *life*
buhók ninyo (*also* inyong buhok) *your hair*
bulaklák *flower*
bumabâ ka *you alight/you get off*
bumalík *return*
bumílang *counted*
bumilí *to buy*
bumíbilí *buying/buy*
bumúbulong *whispering*
buntál *a kind of Philippine fibre*
buóng lugár *whole place*
burdádo(ng) *embroidered*

ka *you* (singular)
kaagád *immediately*
kaakit-ákit *attractive*

kabayánan *town*
kabáyo *horse*
kadálasan *often*
kailán *when*
kakáin *will eat*
kakánin *rice cakes*
kakláse *classmate*
kagabí *last night*
kagulúhan *chaos*
kahápon *yesterday*
kahápon nang hápon
  yesterday afternoon
káhit *even though*
káhit saán *anywhere*
kahón *box*
káhoy *wooden*
kaibígan *friend*
kailán *when*
kailángan ko (ng) *I need*
kailángan po námin *we need*
  (formal)
kalabása *squash/pumpkin*
kalabáw *water buffalo*
kalimútan *forget*
kaliwâ *left*
kalsáda/kalye *street*
kálye *road/street*
káma *bed*
kamáy *arm*
kamátis *tomatoes*
kámera/kodak *camera*
kamí *we*
kánin *boiled rice*
kanína *a while ago*
kaníno *whose*
kaníno pa *whose else*
kaniyá(ng) *her*
kánto *corner*
kaopisína ko *my officemates*

kapág *if/when*
kapaligirán *environment*
kapatíd *sister/brother*
karamíhan *many of*
kapitán *captain*
karósa *cart*
kasabáy *at the same time*
kasabihán *saying/adage*
kasál/kasálan *wedding*
kasáma *companion/together*
  with/with/including
kasáma ba *is it included?*
kasáma ko *I'm with*
kasáma nilá *accompanied by*
  them
kasí *because*
katabí kó *next to me*
katahimíkan *peace*
(ng) katawán *(of the) body*
katóliko *Catholic*
katúlad ng *like*
kaugalián *custom*
kaunting masáhe *a little*
  massage
kausápin *talk to*
kawáyan *bamboo*
kay [+ name] *for [+ name]*
kay/ke mahál ngà *in fact it's*
  expensive
kay gandá *how beautiful*
kayâ múna tayo *why don't we*
  first
kayâ *that's why*
kaya palá *no wonder*
kayó *you (plural informal/*
  formal singular)
kayo namán *oh! please!*
káysa *than*
kinákabitán *being attached*

ko *my*
kótse *car*
kubéta *toilet*
kukúnan *will take (a photograph)*
kukúnin *will get/fetch*
kúlay *colour*
kumáin *eat*
kumakáin *eating*
kumánan *turn right*
kumaliwâ *turn left*
kumbidádo *invited*
kumúha *took*
kumústa kayó *how are you (formal singular/informal plural)*
kúnan *to take*
kundî *instead*
kung *if*
kung áyaw ninyó *if you don't like*
kung bákit *why*
kung ganoón /gayon *if that's the case*
kung gústo mo(ng) *if you want*
kung hindî *if not/had not been*
kung maaárì *if possible*
kung mínsan *sometimes*
kung puwéde sána *if possible*
kung saán *where*
kung támà *if right*
kurtína *curtain*
kutsílyo *knife*
kutsintâ *a delicacy*
kuwárta *money*
kuwádro *frame*
kuwárto *room/quarter/one fourth*
kúya *older brother*

daán *road/way*
dágat *sea*
dáhil sa *because*
dáhil lang sa *just because of*
dalandán/dalanghítà *oranges*
dalawá *two*
dalawandaáng píso *200 pesos*
dalawampúng ányos *20 years old*
dalawáng reséta *two prescriptions*
daliín *be quick*
damít-pangkasál *wedding dress*
damó *grass*
dápat *must/should*
dárating *will arrive*
datíng *arrival*
dekorasyón(g) *decoration*
dilà-dílà *a delicacy*
díla mo *your tongue*
diláw *yellow*
direksiyón *direction*
dirétso *straight*
'di sa ákin *of course it's mine*
disiótso pésos *18 pesos*
díto/ríto *here*
díto lang po sa ibaba *just here below*
díto múna *just here*
doón *there*
doséna *dozen*
dos singkuwénta *2.50 pesos*
dúlang *table*
dumárating *arriving*
dumídilim *becoming dark*
dumirétso *to walk straight ahead*

estudyánte *student*
éto (see heto) *here is*
éto lang *just this*
éto po *here you are madam/sir*

gaáno kalakí *how big*
gabí *night*
gáling sa *from*
gamót *medicine*
ganito pô *like this, sir*
ganito(ng) úrì *this kind*
ganiyán *like that*
ganoón *like that*
ganoón bá *is that so/oh, my!*
ganoón láng *just like that*
ganoón ngà *really like that*
gáganapín *will be held*
gágastusin *will be spent*
ganiyán *like that*
gasolína *petrol*
gátas *milk*
gawín *be made*
gawin kó *I'd do*
ginágawâ *be made*
gínang *Mrs*
ginisáng gúlay *sauteed vegetables*
gúlay *vegetables*
gumabí *to become night*
gumandá *to become fine/ beautiful*
gumawâ *to make*
gúrò *teacher*
gustó *like/want*
gústo kó(ng) *I like/I want/I love*
gústo ninyó *you like*
gústo kong *I'd like*
gústo ko rín *I also like*

gústo pa namín ng *we want some more*
gústo po ba ninyó *do you like/ would you like*
guyabáno *guyabano fruit (large, soft white)*

halíkayo *come on everyone*
hábang *while*
haláman *plants*
handâ *food preparation*
handaán *reception*
hanggáng *until*
hanggáng itaás *reaching the top*
hanggáng sa *until*
hápon *afternoon*
hapúnan *supper*
harapán *front*
hátinggabi *midnight*
hawákan *hold*
háyop *animal*
héto/heto po *here you are/ here, sir*
héto ang bayad *here's the payment*
héto na *here comes*
higít *more*
hípon *prawns*
híhintò *will stop*
hindî *no*
hindí ba *isn't it?*
hindi ba mahál *not expensive (I hope)*
hinding-hindi *never*
hindí ko gustó *I don't like*
hindi na bále *never mind*
hindi namán *not quite/not so*
hindi na pô *not anymore*

hindi pa   *not yet*
hindí pò   *no, sir*
hindi sa ákin   *not mine*
hinóg   *ripe*
hintayín mo akó   *you wait for me*
hípag   *sister-in-law*
huhugásan ko lang   *I'll just wash*
humánap   *to find*
humángin   *was windy*
humíhingî   *asking*
humíhiram   *borrowing*
huwág   *don't*

ibáng kúlay rin   *other colours, too*
iba't ibáng   *different kinds*
íbig námin   *we want/like/ would like*
ibigáy   *to give*
ibíbigay   *will be given*
íbig n'yo ná   *would you like now*
íbig po ba ninyó ng   *do you want/like a*
ibilí   *to buy for*
ibinigáy   *handed/gave*
ibinuká   *opened*
ikalimáng gusálì   *fifth building*
ikatatló   *third*
ikáw ba talagá   *is it really you?*
ikinagágalak ko kayóng makilála   *I'm pleased to meet you*
ikinasál   *got married*
idéya   *idea*
iláng béses   *how many times*
ihúlog   *to post* (literally, *to drop*)

ihuhúlog   *will post*
íinom   *will drink*
íinumin   *will be drunk*
ilabás   *show/bring out*
ilán(g)   *how many/a few*
ilangílang   *ylangylang (flower)*
ililígid   *will be driven around*
inahín   *hen*
inanyayáhan   *invited*
inasikáso   *dealt with/attended to*
ináyos   *fixed/arranged*
iniabót   *handed over*
inihandâ   *prepared*
inihatíd   *took to*
iníhaw   *grilled*
inípon   *the savings*
inyong buhók   *your hair*
Inglatérra   *England*
inumín   *drinks*
inúkit   *carved*
ipakihúlog mo   *could you post*
ipalálagay   *will cause to put*
ipambáyad   *to pay with*
ipatápon   *will cause to throw*
ipapípitas   *will have something picked*
isá   *one*
isa ká sa mga   *you're one of the*
isáma   *to include*
isáng kahón   *one box*
isáng doséna(ng)   *one dozen*
isáng gabí   *per night*
isáng pláto(ng)   *a plate of*
isáng taón   *one year*
isdâ   *fish*
isináma   *accompanied*

358

isinúkat   *tried it on*
isúkat ninyó   *you try*
itátanong   *will ask*
itím   *black*
itó   *this*
itong itím   *this black (one)*
itutúrò   *will show/point*
iwásan lang   *please avoid*
iyán   *that*
iyan láng   *that's all (just those)*
iyón(g)   *that*

labánan   *contest*
labíndalawá   *twelve*
labinlimá   *fifteen*
lági   *always*
lahát   *everybody*
lahat-lahát   *all in all/altogether*
laláki   *man/male*
lakárin   *to walk (it)*
lálò na   *especially*
lamán   *contents*
lang   *only/just*
lángit   *sky*
lanzónes   *lanzones (fruit similar to lychee)*
láot   *sea*
lápis   *pencil*
laráwan   *photograph/picture*
laruán(g)   *toy*
likurán   *behind/at the back*
lima(ng) píso   *five pesos*
limandaán(g)   *500*
Linggó   *Sunday*
línggo-linggó   *every week*
litsón   *suckling pig*
lóla   *grandmother*
lólo   *grandfather*
lúbusan   *earnestly*

lugár   *place*
lumákad   *to walk/move*
lumangóy   *to swim*

maaárì   *can*
maaári ba(ng)   *is it possible/ (see puwede bang)*
maaábot   *be able to reach*
mabáhò   *smelly*
mabaít   *kind*
mabangó   *fragrant*
mabilís   *fast*
mabúti   *good*
mabúti kung ganoón   *that's good*
mabúti rin namán   *I'm fine, too*
mabúti po namán   *I'm fine, too (formal)*
makapág-almusál   *can have breakfast*
makapágbánat   *to be able to stretch*
makapághandâ   *be able to prepare*
makapál   *thick*
makatáwag   *to be able to call*
makatutúlong   *will be able to help*
makúlay   *colourful*
madádalâ   *be turned off*
madalî(ng)   *easily*
madalí lang   *just easy*
magalíng   *good at/clever*
mag-áatubili   *hesitate*
mag-alalá   *worry*
mag-almusál   *to have breakfast*
magandá   *beautiful*

magandáng umága *good morning*

magandáng gabi pô *good evening (**formal**)*

magandáng hápon *good afternoon*

mag-aáral *will study*

magbábakasyon *will go on vacation*

magbábasa *will read*

magbabáyad *will pay*

magbiyáhe *to travel*

magkáno *how much*

magkáno namán *how much is it?*

magkakáno *how much each*

magdádagdag *will add*

magdáramdam *will feel bad*

mag-enjoy *to enjoy*

maghandâ *to prepare*

mag-íimpake *will get packing*

mag-isíp *to worry/think deeply*

magpalamíg muna *have some refreshment first*

magpápakain *will feed*

magpápagod *to become tired*

magpápalit *to change (money)*

magpagupít *have a haircut*

magpasénsiya *to accept our shortcomings*

magsúkat pa *try some more*

magtanóng *enquire*

magúlang *parents*

magustuhán sana ninyo *I hope you'd like it*

mahábà *long*

mahírap *difficult/poor*

mahiyâ ka namán *are you without shame*

mahúsay *fine/very good at*

maiklî *short (e.g. pencil)*

maiklíng buhók *short hair*

maínit *hot*

malaki *big*

malakí-lakí *quite big*

malamíg *cold*

malápit *near*

maláyò *far*

maléta *suitcase*

maligáya(ng) *happy*

maligáyang pagdatíng *welcome*

malínis *clean*

maliít *small*

maliít sa ákin *small for me*

malulúgi *I'll lose*

maluwáng *loose*

mámayâ *later*

mamangkâ *to go boating*

mamasyál *to take a stroll*

mámayang gabí *tonight*

manggá *mango*

mangingisdâ *fisherman*

manók *chicken*

manoód *watch*

mantikílya *margarine*

mápa *map*

mapagpípilian *to choose from*

marámi *many/plenty*

maráming salámat *thank you very much*

marumí *dirty*

marúnong *know*

masakít *hurting/painful*

masaráp *delicious/great/nice/good*

masayá *happy*

mas bágay *suits better*

mas lálò *more*

mas maága *earlier*

mas malakí *bigger*

mag-aalalá *more bothered/be worried*

masúsunod *will be followed*

masyádo(ng) *very/too/quite/extremely*

mataás *high*

matabáng *bland/flat in taste*

mata mó *your eyes*

matatandâ *the old ones*

matatápos na gawáin *jobs will be finished*

matúto *will learn*

matutúlog *will sleep*

mawáwalâ *will disappear*

may *has/have, there is/there are*

mayáman *rich*

mayáman namán kayó *anyway, you are rich*

máy binili akó(ng) *I bought*

may kilála akó *I know someone*

may mésa ba kayó *do you have a table*

may makakaínan bang *is there any place to eat*

may nakalimútan *forgot something*

may napílì *has selected/chosen*

mayroón/meron *has/have there is/there are*

médyo *sort of/somewhat*

médyo maliít *slightly small*

médyo masikíp *slightly small*

médyo nagúlat *somewhat surprised*

mésa *table*

mésa ninyó *your table*

mechádo *pork/beef with tomato sauce, pepper and potatoes*

minsánan *in one go*

mga *pluralizer, similar to the English 's'*

mga alás siyéte medya *about 7.30*

mga limá *about five*

modistá *dressmaker*

mukhá(ng) *looks/appears/seems*

mukháng malínis *looks quite clean*

mulî *again/once more*

múna *first, for the time being*

muntí(ng) regálo *small gift*

múra *cheap*

múra na pò *it's already cheap, ma'am*

múra ang halagá *the price is cheap/right*

múrang niyóg *young coconut*

múrang-múra *very cheap*

na *now/already*

naáyos *managed to arrange*

na namán *again*

na binilí ko dito *that I bought here*

naka-arkilá *was able to hire*

nakákahiyâ *embarrassing*

nakákapangisdâ *are able/manage to catch fish*

nakakitá *happened to see/was able to see*
nakaháwak *managed to handle*
nakaháwak *holding on to*
nakahigâ *lying down*
nakatayô *standing*
nakapamasyál *managed to take a stroll*
nakatirá *living*
nakíta ba ninyó *did you see?*
nakikíta mo *you see*
nág-abalá *bothered*
nagawâ *what's been done*
náiintindihán *understand*
naiísip *able to think about*
náis po ba ninyó *do you want*
nag-aáral *studying/study*
nagbigáy *gave*
nag-enjóy *enjoyed*
naghandâ *prepared food*
nagkoronasyón *crowned*
nag-iípon ng péra *saving money*
nag-íisa *alone*
naglulútò *cooking*
nagmamáno *kissing the hand*
nag-paálam *said goodbye*
nágpagupit *had a haircut*
nagpalútò *caused someone to cook*
nagpápa-akyát *ask someone to climb*
nagpápabango *making (something) fragrant*
nagpapakáin *give them food*
nagpápaganda *making (something) pretty*

nagpápalaki *making (something) grow*
nagpápalit din ba kayó *do you also change?*
nágpasalamat *gave thanks*
nagpuntá *went*
nagséseremonya *officiating*
nagtátaka *wondering*
nagtátae akó *I've got diarrhoea*
nagtítinda ba kayó *do you sell*
nagtrabáho *worked*
nagustuhán *I liked*
nag-úunahan *beating each other* (in a race)
nahíhiyâ *embarrassed*
namámangkâ *boating*
nakabálot *wrapped*
nakabilí *was able to buy*
nakapamangkâ *was able to go boating*
nakatúlog *managed to sleep*
namán *too/on the other hand*
námin *our*
nanálo *won*
nánay *mother*
nanggabí *at night*
nang hápon *in the afternoon*
nang ibigáy *when (it) was given*
nangingísdâ *fishing*
nang maága *early*
nang mabúti *soundly/well/better*
nang maluwág *loosely*
nang umága *in the morning*
nangungútang *borrow money*
nápakagandá *very pretty*
napakarámi(ng) *so many*

napágod   *got tired*
nápansin   *noticed*
nárito ná   *here now/here comes*
nása (prefix)   *at/on/in/at the/on the/in the*
násaan   *where*
nása parke   *at the park*
nasiyáhan   *was pleased*
naúbos   *finished/consumed*
naupô   *sat down*
ngayón   *now/today*
ngayón láng   *just now*
ngayóng linggó   *this week*
ngumitî   *smiled*
nilála(ng)   *woven*
nínang   *godmother*
nínong   *godfather*
ninyó   *your*
nitó   *this,* (in the **ng** form) *of this*
niyá   *his/her*
niyáng   *of that*
ng   *of/of the*
ng bandána   *a scarf*
ng ibá   *other ones*
ngâ   *please/indeed/it's true*
ngayón   *now/today*
ngayóng alas dós   *today at 2 o'clock*
ngayóng hápon   *this afternoon*
ngayóng umága   *this morning*
ng mga anák   *of the children*
ng size ninyó   *your size*
noón   *then/before*
noóng   *when/during*
noóng isáng linggó   *last week*
número   *number*

o kayá'y   *or/otherwise*
okey láng   *just all right*

o, síge   *all right*
oo, mabúti   *yes, good*
oo ngà   *I agree*
oo nga palá   *by the way*
ópò   *yes (**formal**)*
óras   *time*
pa   *still*
paálam   *goodbye*
paarkiláhan   *a place to hire*
pakaínin   *to serve/feed*
pakéte   *parcel*
pakiabót sa akin   *please pass to me/hand to me*
pakilagáy   *please put/place*
pakipára mo   *please stop at*
pakiúlit mo ngâ   *please repeat*
págbabakasyón   *vacationing*
pagbalík   *when you return*
pagháwak   *how to hold*
pagkáin   *food/eating*
pagkatápos   *afterwards/then*
pagháwak   *handling/holding*
paglabás ninyó   *once you've come out*
pagtanggáp   *reception*
págtataním   *planting*
paikliín   *be shortened*
palagyán   *will ask to be put*
palarô   *games*
palawít   *bunting*
palígid   *around*
pálda   *skirt*
pangálan   *name*
pangalawáng order   *second order*
pang-shopping   *for shopping*
pag-akyát   *climbing*
pág-alalá   *concern*

pagkatápos *afterwards*
pagkukúlang *shortcomings*
paghaháin *offering*
paglabás *upon leaving*
páglalakbáy *trip*
pagód *tired*
pagsakáy *riding*
pagsayáw *dancing*
págsisilbi *serving*
pagsungkít *hooking with a pole*
pagtakbó *running*
págtatae *diarrhoea*
pala' *so!*
pála *spade*
palaisdaán *fishpond*
palarúan *playground*
paláyan *rice field*
paléngke *market*
páliguan *bathroom*
(ang) palít *exchange*
pálipáran *airport*
pamangkín *niece/nephew*
pamasáhe *fare*
pamaypáy *fan*
pambálot *wrapping paper*
pamigáy *to give around*
pamilyá *family*
pamimilí *shopping*
pamímilihin *things to buy*
pamintá *pepper*
pámpalamig *refreshment*
pampasalúbong *gifts*
panahón *weather/time*
panaúhin *guests*
pandalawáhan *double*
pangálan *name*
pang-aabála *disturbance*

pang-isáhan *single*
pang-okasyón *for certain occasions*
pansít *noodles (cooked the Filipino way)*
panyolíto *handkerchiefs*
papalitán namin iyan *we will replace it*
papáya *pawpaw*
papuntá sa *going to*
paputók *fireworks*
pára *so that/in order to*
paráda *parade*
párang *seems/ like/as if*
pára kaníno *for whom*
pára sa *for*
pára sa akín *for me*
pára sa ámin/atin *for us*
pára sa anák ko(ng) *for my son*
pára sa áraw ng kasal ko *for my wedding day*
pára sa inyó *for you*
pára sa sakít ng tiyán *for stomach ache*
párke *park*
párì *priest*
pasalúbong *gift*
pasahéro *passenger*
pasapórte *passport*
pasénsiya na *accept our apologies*
páyong *umbrella*
pechay *pak choi*
péra/pera ko *money/my money*
péro *but*
pinakabunsó *youngest*

364

pinakakáin *give food/feed*
pinakamalápit *nearest*
pinagamásan *had it cleaned*
pinaglútò *asked to cook/ cooked for*
pinapágod ka *tiring you*
pinggán/plato *plate*
pínya *pineapple*
pirmahán lang *(just) please sign*
pisára *blackboard*
pistá(ng) *feast day*
pistá(ng) bayan *town fiesta*
pitákà *wallet*
platíto *saucer*
pósporo *a box of matches*
probléma *problem*
prútas *fruit*
puhúnan *capital*
pulá(ng) handbag *red handbag*
pumíli pa *choose some more*
pulútan *finger food to go with drinks*
pulót-gatâ *honeymoon*
pumíli po kayó *please choose*
pumunta ká *you go/you visit/ stop by*
púnong-káhoy *fruit trees*
púpunta *will go*
puwéde *can*
puwéde akó *I'm available*
puwéde ba(ng) *is it possible/ could you*
puwéde na *will suffice/that will do*
puwéde na pò bá *is it all right, sir/ma'am?*
puwésto *stalls*

raw/daw *apparently*
resíbo ninyó *your receipt*
rekomendádo *recommended*
regálo *gift*
regálong ito *this gift*
rénda *reins*
repólyo *cabbage*
reséta ng doktor *doctor's prescription*
retratísta *photographer*
retráto *picture*
réyna *queen*
rin/din *also/too/as well*
rosál *gardenia*

sa (preposition) *to/in/at/on/at the/in the/on the*
saán *where* (direction)
saán akó pípirma *where do I sign*
(ang) sa ákin *(what is) mine*
sa áraw *during the day*
sabáy na *do it together/at the same time*
Sábado *Saturday*
sa báryo *at the barrio*
sa báhay *at my place/at my home*
sabáw *thin soup/stock*
sabíhin *tell/say*
sábong *cockfight*
sabsában *stable*
sabungán *cockpit*
sa kaniyá *to him/her*
sáko *sack*
sa kápitbáhay natin *our neighbours'*
ságing *banana*
sa halíp na *instead of*

sa inyó   *to you (singular formal/informal plural)*
sa inyóng lahát   *to you all*
sa isáng   *to one/against one*
sa isáng áraw   *the day after tomorrow*
sa isang linggó   *next week*
sa loób ng   *in(side)*
sa (loób ng) isang araw   *in one day*
salámat   *thank you*
sa lahát nang oras   *at any time*
sa lugár na ito   *here in this place*
salu-sálo   *party*
sa may   *near*
sampagúita   *the national flower*
sána   *I hope*
sandalì láng   *wait a minute*
sang-áyon   *agree*
sang-áyon sa   *according to*
sanggól   *baby*
sa palagay kó   *in my opinion*
sarisári(ng)   *assorted*
saríwa(ng)   *fresh*
saríwang lumpiâ   *fresh spring rolls*
sársa   *sauce/dressing*
sasabíhin   *will tell*
sasakyán   *vehicle*
sa súsunod   *next time*
sa tabí   *next/beside*
sa timbángan   *on the scales*
sa trabáho   *at work*
sa tuktók   *at the top*
sa umága   *in the morning*
sa únang béses   *for the first time*

sélyo   *stamp*
siksíkan   *crowded*
síge   *all right/OK/so long*
síge lang   *OK*
sigúro   *perhaps*
síli   *pepper (chilli or bell pepper)*
silíd-tulugán   *bedroom*
sílya   *chair*
simbáhan(g)   *church*
sinabúgan   *sprinkled with/ showered with*
sinasábi lang   *just say*
sinigáng na bangús   *stewed milkfish (with vinegar or tamarind and garlic)*
síno   *who*
sóbra siguro   *perhaps too much*
sóbre   *envelope*
sombréro   *hat*
sópas manók   *chicken soup*
sorbétes   *ice cream*
subáli't   *but*
súlat   *letter*
sumakáy   *ride*
sumáma   *to come/go with*
sumasáma (from *masama*, adj.)   *becoming worse*
sumayáw   *danced*
sumisíkat   *shining*
sumúlat   *write*
sumunód po kayó sa ákin   *please follow me*
sungáyin   *charge with his horn*
susúlat   *will write*
street guide   *street guide*

táksi   *taxi*
tagá   *from (place of origin)*

tagapagdalá ng singsíng *ring bearer*

tagapaglútò *cook*

tahánan *home*

tahímik *quiet*

talagá *really*

talóng *eggplant/aubergine*

tálì *string*

támà *right/correct*

tandáng *rooster*

tanghálì *midday*

tanghalían *lunch*

táo pò *anyone at home*

tápa *sliced fried beef*

tapós *afterwards/then*

tatlóng béses isáng áraw *three times a day*

tátay *father*

tátayô *will stand*

téka *just a moment/wait a minute*

telépono *telephone*

tenyénte *captain*

téna *let's go*

térnong sáya *a lady's long gown (of Spanish origin)*

tíket *ticket*

tíket ninyó *your ticket*

tig/tiga *each*

tigatlóng píso *three pesos each*

timbángan *scales*

tinanggáp *received*

tinanóng *was asked*

tinápay *bread*

tinatáwag *calling*

tindáhan *store*

tindáhan ng laruán *toy store*

tindá(ng) damít *clothes for sale*

tindéra/tindéro *vendor/sales assistant*

tingnán *look*

tingnan ko ngâ *let me see/examine*

tingnan ninyó/mo *you have a look*

tinulúngan *helped*

títingnan ko *let me see*

tiráhan *residence/address*

tíya *aunt*

tiyán ko *my stomach*

totoó *true*

tíyo *uncle*

tóyo *soy sauce*

tradisyón(g) *tradition*

tsá *tea*

tséke *cheque*

tsubíbo *ferris wheel*

tsupér *(boat) driver*

túbig *water*

tugtúgin *music*

tulóy *as a result/as well*

tumátakbo *running*

tumáwag *call*

tumawíd ka *you cross*

tumígil *stopped*

tumingín *look*

tumugtóg *played*

tumúlong *helped*

tumútunóg *making a sound*

tungkól sa *about*

tutulúngan *will help*

tuwáng-tuwâ *happy*

tuwíng Linggó *every Sunday*

ubos ná *ran out/consumed/finished*

ulán *rain*

úlo niyá   *his/her head*
umakyát   *climb up*
umága   *morning*
umalís   *departed*
umarkilá ng bangkâ   *to hire a boat*
uminóm   *to drink*
umiklî   *to become short*
umórder   *to order*
umórder pa táyo   *let's order some more*
umulán   *rained*
úna   *first*
úpang   *in order to/so that*

útang na loób   *debt of gratitude*
uulítin   *will repeat*

walâ   *no/none*
waláng asáwa   *not married/ unmarried*
wala báng táwad   *any chance of a discount?*
wala póng anumán   *you're welcome*

yárì sa   *made of*
yátà   *I think*
yelo   *ice*

English–Tagalog glossary

All verbs in this glossary are in the root form unless otherwise indicated.

about   *tungkol sa*
accompanied   *isinama*
according to   *sang-ayon sa*
add   *magdagdag*
afternoon   *hapon*
afterwards/then   *pagkatapos/
tapos*
again/once more   *muli*
agree   *sang-ayon*
agree, I   *oo nga*
airport   *paliparan*
alight/get off   *baba*
all in all/altogether   *lahat-lahat*
all right/OK/so long   *o, sige*
alone   *nag-iisa*
already   *na*
also   *saka; rin/din*
always   *lagi*
America   *America*
and   *at*
animal   *hayop*
anywhere   *kahit saan*
apparently   *daw/raw*
apritada   *apritada (a kind of
main dish, fried)*
arm   *bisig*
around   *paligid*
arrive   *dating*
arrival   *dating*
as a result/as well   *tuloy*
ask (for something)   *hingi*

ask (a question)   *tanong*
assorted   *sarisari(ng)*
at   *nasa (**prefix**)*
at   *sa*
attractive   *kaakit-akit*
attach   *kabit*
aunt   *tiya*
(I'm) available   *puwede ako*

(newborn) baby   *sanggol*
bachelor   *binata*
bamboo   *kawayan*
banana   *saging*
band   *banda*
baptism   *binyagan*
barrio   *baryo*
bathroom   *paliguan/banyo*
beautiful   *maganda*
because   *kasi/dahil sa/sapagka't*
bed   *kama*
bedroom   *silid-tulugan*
behind/at the back   *likuran*
big   *malaki*
(quite) big   *malaki-laki*
bigger   *mas malaki*
bitter melon   *ampalaya*
black   *itim*
blackboard   *pisara*
bland/flat in taste   *matabang*
blouse   *blusa*
boat (canoe)   *bangka*

(to go) boating *mamangka*
body *katawan*
boiled rice *kanin*
book *aklat*
borrow *hiram*
borrow money *nangungutang*
bother *abala*
(I) bought *may binili ako(ng)*
box *kahon*
bread *tinapay*
breakfast *almusal*
(to have) breakfast *mag-almusal*
brother *kapatid*
brother (older) *kuya*
brother-in-law *bayaw*
bucket *balde*
buntal (Philippine fibre) *buntal*
bunting *palawit*
but *pero/subali't*
buy *bili*
(to) buy for *ibili*

cabbage *repolyo*
call *tawag*
camera *kamera*
can/possible *maaari/puwede*
capital *puhunan*
captain *kapitan/tenyente*
car *kotse*
cart *karosa*
carved *inukit*
Catholic *katoliko*
chair *silya*
chaos *kaguluhan*
(to) change *magpalit*
cheap *mura*
cheque *tseke*

chicken *manok*
chicken soup *sopas manok*
child *bata/anak*
choose *pili*
(to) choose from *mapagpipilian*
church *simbahan*
classmates *kaklase*
clean *malinis*
clever/good at *magaling/marunong*
climb *akyat*
climb up *umakyat*
clothes *damit*
cockfight *sabong*
cockpit *sabungan*
coconut, young *murang niyog*
cold *malamig*
colour *kulay*
colourful *makulay*
come on *halikayo*
(to) come with/go with *sumama*
companion *kasama*
concern *pag-alaala*
consort *abay*
consume *ubos*
contest *labanan/paligsahan*
cook *luto*
cook (noun) *tagapagluto*
corner *kanto*
count *bilang*
cross *tawid*
crowded *siksikan*
crown *korona*
curtain *kurtina*
custom *kaugalian*

dance *sayaw*
dancing *pagsayaw*
darken *dumidilim*
daughter *anak*
day/sun *araw*
decoration *dekorasyon*
(a) delicacy *kutsinta/dila-dila*
delicious *masarap*
depart *alis*
departure *alis*
destination *punta*
diarrhoea *pagtatae*
difficult/poor *mahirap*
dirty *marumi*
disturbance *pang-aabala/abala*
disappear *mawala*
do *gawa*
don't *huwag*
double *pandalawahan*
dozen *dosena*
dressmaker *modista*
(to) drink *uminom*
drinking glass *baso*
drinks *inumin*
drive *ligid*
(boat) driver *tsuper*
during *noon*

each *tig/tiga*
early *nang maaga*
earnestly *lubusan(g)*
easily *madali(ng)*
eat *kain*
eggplant/aubergine *talong*
embarrassed *nahihiya*
embarrassing *nakakahiya*
embroidered *burdado(ng)*
England *Inglaterra*
(to) enjoy *mag-enjoy*

enquire *magtanong*
envelope *sobre*
environment *kapaligiran*
everybody *lahat*
every day *araw-araw*
exchange *(ang) palit*
expensive *mahal*
eyes *mata*

family *pamilya*
fan *pamaypay*
far *malayo*
fare *pamasahe*
fast *mabilis*
father *tatay/ama/itay*
favourite *paborito*
feast day *pista(ng)*
feed *pinakakain*
female/woman *babae*
ferris wheel *tsubibo*
fiesta *pista*
fifteen *labinlima*
(to) find *humanap*
fine/pretty *maganda*
(I'm) fine *mabuti rin naman*
finger food to go with
    drinks *pulutan*
finished/consumed *naubos*
fireworks *paputok*
first *una*
fish *isda*
fisherman *mangingisda*
fishing *nangingisda*
fish pond *palaisdaan*
fixed/arranged *inayos*
flag *bandera/bandila*
flood *baha*
flower *bulaklak*
food/eating *pagkain*

food preparation *handa*
follow *sunod*
for *para sa*
forget *kalimutan*
fragrant *mabango*
frame *kuwadro*
fresh *sariwa(ng)*
friend *kaibigan*
from *buhat sa/galing sa*
from (origin) *taga*
fruit *prutas*
fruit trees *punong kahoy*

games *palaro*
gardenia *rosal*
gifts *pasalubong/regalo*
(to) be given *ibigay*
get/fetch *kuha*
give *bigay*
(to) give around *pamigay*
go *punta*
godchild *inaanak*
godfather *ninong*
godmother *ninang*
going to *papunta sa*
good *mabuti*
good afternoon *magandang hapon*
goodbye *paalam*
good evening (formal) *magandang gabi po*
good morning *magandang umaga*
gore *suwagin*
grandchild *apo*
grandfather *lolo*
grandmother *lola*
grass *damo*
grilled *inihaw*

guava *bayabas*
guest/visitor *bisita/panauhin*
guyabano (soursap) *guyabano*

haircut *gupit*
(to have a) haircut *magpagupit*
hair *buhok*
hand *kamay*
hand over *abot*
handkerchiefs *panyolito*
happy *maligaya(ng)/masaya tuwang-tuwa*
has/have *may/mayroon*
help *tulong*
hat *sombrero*
hen *inahin*
her *kaniya(ng)*
here *dito*
here is *heto*
hesitate *mag-aatubili*
high *mataas*
hire *arkila*
(to) hire a boat *umarkila ng bangka*
his/her *niya*
hold *hawak*
home *bahay*
honeymoon *pulot-gata*
hook with a pole *sungkit*
(I) hope *sana*
horse *kabayo*
hot *mainit*
hour *oras*
house *bahay*
how are you (formal singular) *kumusta kayo*
how many/a few *ilan(g)*
how much *magkano*

how much is it? *magkano naman* (informal plural)
(to) hurry *daliin*
hurting/painful *masakit*
husband *asawa*

ice cream *sorbetes*
idea *ideya*
if/when *kapag/kung*
ilangilang *ilangilang flower*
immediately *kaagad*
improve *bumuti*
in *nasa/sa*
(to) include *isama*
including *kasama*
in order to/so that *upang*
isn't it? *hindi ba*
inside *sa loob (ng)*
instead of *sa halip na*
instead *kundi*
invited *imbitado/kumbidado*

job *gawain*

kind *mabait*
kinds *uri*
kissing the hand *nagmamano*
knife *kutsilyo*
know *alam*

lanzones (fruit similar to lychees) *lansones*
last night *kagabi*
last week *noong isang linggo*
later *mamaya*
learn *matuto*
leave *alis*
left *kaliwa*
letter *sulat*
life *buhay*

(I) like *gusto ko*
like (comparison) *katulad ng*
like that *ganiyan/ganoon*
living/residence *nakatira*
long *mahaba*
look after *bahala*
look *tingnan/tumingin*
looks/appears/seems *mukhang*
loose *maluwag/maluwang*
loosely *nang maluwag*
lose *malulugi*
love *gusto*
lunch *tanghalian*
lying down *nakahiga*

made of *yari sa*
(to) make *gumawa*
man/male *lalaki*
mango *mangga*
many/plenty *marami(ng)*
many of *karamihan*
map *mapa*
margarine *mantikilya*
market *palengke*
married *ikinasal*
massage *masahe*
matches *posporo*
measurement *sukat*
medicine *gamot*
midday *tanghali*
might/cow *baka*
milk *gatas*
milkfish *bangus*
money *pera/kuwarta*
more *higit/mas lalo*
morning *umaga*
mother *nanay/inay/ina*
mouth *bibig*
Mrs *ginang*

music *tugtugin*
must/should *dapat*
my *ko*

name *pangalan*
nape *batok*
near *malapit, sa may*
nearest *pinakamalapit*
need *kailangan*
neighbours *kapitbahay*
nephew *pamangkin*
never *hinding-hindi*
new *bago*
next/beside *sa tabi*
next time *sa susunod*
next week *sa isang linggo*
nice *masarap*
niece *pamangkin*
night *gabi*
no *hindi*
no/none *wala*
noodles cooked in the Filipino
    way *pansit*
noticed *napansin*
now *na/ngayon*
number *numero*

of/of the *ng*
of course *aba oo/aba oo
    naman*
offering *paghahain/pag-aalay*
officemates *kaopisina*
officiating *nagseseremonya*
often *kadalasan*
on *nasa/sa*
one *isa*
only/just *lang*
opened *ibinuka*
opinion *palagay*
or *o kaya'y*

oranges *dalanghita*
(to) order *umorder*
other *iba*
our *namin*

pak choi *pechay*
parade *parada*
parcel *pakete*
parents *magulang*
park *parke*
party *salu-salo*
pass *abot*
passenger *pasahero*
passport *pasaporte*
pawpaw *papaya*
payment *bayad*
(to) pay with *ipambayad*
peace *katahimikan*
pen *bolpen*
pencil *lapis*
pepper *paminta/sili*
perhaps *siguro*
petrol *gasolina*
photograph/picture *larawan*
photographer *retratista*
picture *retrato*
pineapple *pinya*
place *lugar*
planting *pagtanim*
plants *halaman*
(a) plate of *isang plato (ng)*
plate *plato/pinggan*
play *laro*
playground *palaruan*
pleased to meet you
    (formal) *ikinagagalak ko
    kayong makilala*
pleased *nasiyahan*
(to) post *ihulog*

prawns *hipon*
prepare *handa*
prepared food *naghanda*
prescriptions *reseta*
pretty *maganda*
price *halaga*
priest *pari*
problem *problema*
put *lagay*

queen *reyna*
quiet *tahimik*

rain *ulan*
reach *abot*
read *basa*
really *talaga*
reception *handaan*
receipt *resibo*
receive *tanggap*
recommend *rekomenda*
refreshment *pampalamig*
reins *renda*
repeat *ulit*
replace *palitan*
residence/address *tirahan*
return *balik*
rice cakes *kakanin*
rice field *palayan*
rich *mayaman*
rid *sakay*
ride *sumakay*
right (direction) *kanan*
right/correct *tama*
ring bearer *tagapagdala
 ng singsing*
ripe *hinog*
road/way/path *daan*
room *kuwarto/quarter/one
 fourth*

rooster *tandang*
rubbish *basura*
run *takbo*

sack *sako*
salt *asin*
Saturday *Sabado*
sauce/dressing *sarsa*
saucer *platito*
sauteed vegetable *ginisang
 gulay*
(the) savings *inimpok/inipon*
saving money *nag-iipon ng
 pera*
say *sabi*
scales *timbangan*
(a) scarf *ng bandana*
sea *dagat*
see *kita*
seems like/as if *parang*
sell *tinda*
(to) serve/feed *pakainin*
serving *pagsisilbi*
shame *mahiya /hiya*
shine *sikat*
ship *barko*
shopping *pamimili*
short *maikli*
shortcomings *pagkukulang*
(to) shorten *paikliin/umikli*
single *pang-isahan*
sister (older) *ate*
sister *kapatid*
sister-in-law *hipag*
sit down *upo*
size *sukat*
skirt *palda*
sky *langit/himpapawid*
sleep *tulog*

slightly *medyo*
small *maliit*
smelly *mabaho*
smile *ngiti*
so *pala*
sometimes *kung minsan*
son *anak*
so that/in order to *para*
soy sauce *toyo*
spade *pala*
spend *gastos*
spouse *asawa*
spring rolls *lumpia*
sprinkle with *sabog*
squash *kalabasa*
squid adobo *adobong pusit*
stable *sabsaban*
stalls *puwesto*
stamp *selyo*
stand *tayo*
standing *nakatayo*
stewed milkfish (with vinegar or tamarind and garlic) *sinigang na bangus*
still *pa*
stomach *tiyan*
stomach ache *sakit ng tiyan*
stop *para/tigil/hinto*
store *tindahan*
straight *diretso/tuwid*
street *kalye/kalsada/road*
street guide *street guide*
stretch *banat*
string *tali*
(to take a) stroll *mamasyal*
student *estudyante*
study *nag-aaral*
suckling pig *litson*

suddenly *bigla*
suffice/that will do *puwede na*
suit *bagay*
suitcase *maleta*
Sunday *Linggo*
surprised *nagulat*
swallow *inom/lunok*
(to) swim *lumangoy*

table *mesa*
take *kuha*
(to) take from *kunan*
talk to *kausapin*
taxi *taksi*
tea *tsaa*
teacher *guro*
telephone *telepono*
tell *sabi*
terno (a long gown of Spanish origin) *ternong saya*
than *kaysa/kaysa sa*
thank you *salamat*
thank you very much *maraming salamat*
that *iyan*
that (over there) *iyon*
that's all (just those) *iyan lang*
that's why *kaya*
the *ang*
then/before *noon*
there *doon*
there is/there are *may/mayroon*
throw *tapon*
these *ang mga ito*
thick *makapal*
thing *bagay*
think *mag-isip*
(I) think *yata*

this *ito/nito*
those *ang mga iyan*
ticket *tiket*
time *oras*
tired *pagod*
tire oneself, to *magpagod*
to *sa*
today *ngayong*
toilet *kubeta*
tomatoes *kamatis*
tomorrow *bukas*
tongue *dila*
tonight *mamayang gabi*
town *kabayanan*
toy *laruan(g)*
toy store *tindahan ng laruan*
tradition *tradisyon(g)*
travel *biyahe*
trip *paglalakbay*
true *totoo*
try *isukat*
two *dalawa*
typhoon *bagyo*

umbrella *payong*
uncle *tiyo*
understand *naiintindihan*
unmarried *walang asawa*
until *hanggang sa*

vacancy *bakante*
vacation *bakasyon*
vegetables *gulay*
vehicle *sasakyan*
vendor/sales assistant *tindera/ tindero*
very/too/quite/extremely *masyado(ng)*
village *baryo*

visit/stop by *punta*

walk/move, to *lumakad*
(to) walk straight ahead *dumiretso*
wallet *pitaka*
want *gusto/nais*
wash *hugas*
(to) watch *manood*
water *tubig*
water/liquid *sabaw*
water buffalo *kalabaw*
we *tayo/kami*
weather *panahon*
wedding *kasal/kasalan*
wedding assistant(s) *(mga) abay sa kasal*
wedding dress *damit pangkasal*
week *linggo*
welcome *maligayang pagdating*
(you're) welcome *wala pong anuman/ano(ng)*
what *ano (ng), anu-ano (formal)*
what time *anong oras*
when *kailan*
when/during *noong*
where (location) *nasaan*
where (direction) *saan*
which *alin*
while *habang*
whispering *bumubulong*
who *sino*
whole *buo*
whose *kanino*
why *bakit/kung bakit*
wife *asawa*
window *bintana*

windy *humangin*
with *kasama*
wooden *kahoy*
(to) win *manalo*
wonder *taka*
work *trabaho*
(to) worry *mag-alala/mag-isip*
worsen *sumasama*
woven *nilala(ng)*
wrapped *nakabalot*
wrapping paper *pambalot*
write *sulat*

year *taon*
yellow *dilaw*
yes (formal) *opo*
yesterday *kahapon*
yet *pa*
you (singular) *ka*
you (plural informal/formal singular) *kayo*
youngest *pinakabunso*
your *ninyo/inyong*